D0928063

The
Critique
of Pure
Modernity

WITHDRAWN
ALEXANDER MACK LIBRARY
BRIDGEWATER COLLEGE
BRIDGEWATER, VA 22812

The Critique of Pure Modernity

Hegel,

Heidegger

and After

David Kolb

THE UNIVERSITY OF CHICAGO PRESS
Chicago and London

DAVID A. KOLB is professor and chairman of the
Department of Philosophy at Bates College in
Lewiston, Maine.

The University of Chicago Press, Chicago 60637
The University of Chicago Press, Ltd., London

© 1986 by The University of Chicago
All rights reserved. Published 1986
Printed in the United States of America

95 94 93 92 91 90 89 88 87 86   54321

Library of Congress Cataloging-in-Publication Data

Kolb, David.
   The critique of pure modernity.

   Bibliography: p.
   Includes index.
   1. Hegel, George Wilhelm Friedrich, 1770–1831.
2. Heidegger, Martin, 1889–1976.   3. Civilization,
Modern.   I. Title.   II. Title: Modernity.
B2948.K598 1986   190   86-11224
ISBN 0-226-45031-7

193
H462YKol
1986

FOR ANNE,

Haru no iro

Contents

Preface

This study has grown out of the conviction that much of the debate about the good or bad points of "the modern world" starts from presuppositions that need to be questioned. I have long been fascinated by the differences between our contemporary world and more traditional societies, as well as the novelty of modern ideas and institutions compared with their Greek ancestors or with those of other cultures. What accounts for those differences? Is there some root from which they spring? While the positive benefits of modern liberation are obvious, so too are the terrors and evils of our world. Must we keep to the modern way lest we fall back into a traditional life that would lose our freedom and the benefits of progress? Are the terrors the price we pay for freedom, or just obstacles to be removed on the way to a more perfect freedom? Might they come from the same source as modern liberation? Must we choose between modern freedom and traditional meaning? From vague questions such as these the present study was born, and as it grew, I came to doubt many of the presuppositions behind the questions I had started with.

The chapters that follow center on one strategy for thinking about modernity: the refusal to take as final the categories of modernity's standard self-description. Modernity needs to be put in its place within the larger context that makes it possible and that cannot be described in standard modern terms. To help in exploring this strategy I use as guides two German philosophers, Hegel and Heidegger.

Each reacted to the modern world as he saw it, and each refused to think in the categories we find normal.

I do not hold a brief for either of the two Germans. I much enjoy the complexities of the Hegelian system; he is the greater constructive thinker, as Heidegger would readily admit. But it is not clear that we need more great systems just now. If I had to choose, I would pick Heidegger's deconstructive living over Hegel's justified life, but for looking at situations in detail it is more helpful to mine the fragments of Hegel's system.

The thought of each of the two Germans is fascinating in its own right, but I treat them together for a special reason. Although they share the same overall strategy in approaching modernity, they come to quite different results. By examining those results and viewing each thinker from the perspective of the other, we can learn better the possibilities and pitfalls of that approach to modernity.

I try to use the thought of Hegel and Heidegger to further our own thinking about the modern world. I am not just expounding the two Germans, although given the difficulty of their texts the amount of exposition is considerable. I offer no knockdown arguments for my own conclusions, but the goal is to persuade as well as inform. My aim is to open possibilities for thought and suggest descriptions in which we can recognize ourselves, and so undermine other conclusions whose plausibility depends on working from a more limited set of initial alternatives. This book is an elaborate set of reminders for a purpose: dispelling a theoretical and practical illusion about the uniqueness and the unified character of the modern world.

General Plan

For a description of the standard presuppositions about modern selves and institutions, I look to some common clichés and to the sociological analyses of Peter Berger and Max Weber. The specific aspect of modernity that concerns me is the notion of the distanced self formally defined in terms of its power to choose. This notion lies behind the feeling that one becomes modern when one sheds the substantive limitations imposed by traditional values and ways of life. Substantive values limit one's access to a wider field of possibilities; the widest field of possibilities is correlated to an "empty" self, defined by its formal role of maximizing chosen satisfactions or attaining its goals with greatest efficiency.

Hegel and Heidegger could both accept this prima facie description of the worlds they called modern, but each would say that something deeper was going on. Neither thinker would accept the dilemma, common in liberal versus conservative debates in the United States, that we must either return to substantive tradition or affirm the deracinated modern individual. Both would reject Weberian methodological individualism and would argue that what it is to be an individual changes throughout history. Modern individualism is not the transhistorical essence of what it is to be a person.

Both Hegel and Heidegger would put modernity in its place. They would locate modern subjectivity within the context that makes it possible, a context that cannot be presented in the familiar terms of the usual modern self-description. There is something beyond the subject-object relation typical of modern selfhood. We must let that something more happen as it does, accepting modern selfhood as already made possible within some deeper context. When we acknowledge that context as what it is, we find ourselves accepting limitations and no longer facing the indefinitely open possibilities characteristic of modernity.

The two Germans go about this critique very differently. In Hegel we find a critique of romantic subjectivity and a critique of the modern economic community he calls "civil society," together with the proposal for a rational community he calls the "state." Behind this stands the criticism of the basic categories of modernity carried out in the *Science of Logic*, where Hegel works over the categories of form and content, universal and particular, and finds the "absolute form" of spirit's movement, which is the motion of our having a meaningful world at all. These mediations are applied in the transition from civil society to state and show how the typical modern dichotomies can be overcome in a form of life that is to blend the best of ancient substantive community and modern freedom.

As Charles Taylor points out, Hegel criticizes the atomistic individualism of modernity's standard self-image without falling into the easy romantic counterposition. He also escapes the standard liberal or conservative labels we like to apply to those who think about modernity. (Taylor 1979, 72, 130; Taylor 1975, 424f, 449f).

In stressing the importance of Hegel's *Logic* I mean to disagree with Taylor and others who see in Hegel an acute analyst of politics and culture who had an unfortunate metaphysical remedy in mind. I do not think that Hegel's criticisms can be fully understood unless seen with their logical grounding. This will make it clear that Hegel's proposal is far more sophisticated than proposing we meld ourselves with some Absolute to escape modern separations.

Heidegger treats modernity in his discussions of subjectivity, technology, and universal imposition (*das Gestell*), and the propriative event (*das Ereignis*). These put modern selfhood in its place. We must dwell where we are, but as we understand how we are involved with the granting of the fields of possibility within which we move, our life will be more than the activity of manipulated manipulators, which our age assigns us to be. We will have a new way of living within the modern world, and a hope for its eventual change. Although the effect of Heidegger's thought is neither clear nor unambiguous, I argue that he is not proposing a rustic retreat to the Black Forest nor an eschatological rejection of the modern world.

After discussing the two thinkers separately, I draw out the parallels and differences between them and construct a critique of each from the standpoint of the other. This offers us suggestions while showing us the pitfalls we must avoid if we want to use the general strategy of locating modern dichotomies and dilemmas within a wider context that cannot be described in modern terms.

The descriptions of modernity in Heidegger parallel to a large extent Hegel's discussions in the *Philosophy of Right*. Heidegger's account of the history of being leading to our age of universal imposition has many parallels to Hegel's account of history. Both thinkers use the Greeks in analogous ways as contrast and as ancestors. For Hegel, however, there is a final definitive account provided by the pure logical sequence of categories. It is tempting to view Heidegger's discussion of the propriative event as parallel to Hegel's logical account. Strategically they do play similar roles, but the differences between the two thinkers are at their most extreme where they might seem most similar, although I will insist on important parallels even here.[1]

Heidegger sees Hegel as remaining within the principles of modernity because he keeps the concentration on subjectivity and the drive to total presence characteristic of that metaphysics leading inevitably to the technological world. I agree with Heidegger's description of Hegel as "metaphysical" in the special sense used, but I disagree with his charge that Hegel remains within the bounds of the metaphysics of subjectivity. (To put the point in Heidegger's technical jargon, I agree with his characterization of Hegel in terms of *Subjektität* but not his characterization in terms of *Subjektivität*).

Heidegger's method of reading does not work well with a thinker such as Hegel, and Heidegger's own presuppositions get in the way of understanding what Hegel is about at crucial points.

If Hegel could read Heidegger, he would criticize him as failing to overcome modernity, because Heidegger remains tied to certain classic distinctions in the Kantian tradition of transcendental philosophy: form and content, essential and inessential, plus the phenomenological stance that understands better than the "natural" consciousness it describes. The result is too much unity in Heidegger's characterization of the conditions making modernity possible, and this continues some basic modern dilemmas.

In the final part I offer some suggestions for taking advantage of the strategy shared by Hegel and Heidegger without falling into the traps that their mutual criticism illuminates. There is no synthesis to be made of the two thinkers, but we can learn from both. Stressing the refusal of self-coincidence on any level, I urge that we think ourselves as "thrown projects" with a greater multiplicity than Heidegger would allow, a multiplicity that can, without Hegel's emphasis on closure, make use of many of Hegel's analyses.

We find ourselves always already in motion within an encompassing but multiple context that lacks totality and has no foothold for the transcendental move shared in different ways by Hegel and Heidegger. When we look at ourselves as modern people, we find that in this light we are neither the formally defined members of civil society nor the manipulated manipulators in the world of universal imposition. Hegel and Heidegger both think they know the essence of the modern world. If we accept a deeper multiplicity, there is no saying which is the essential aspect of modernity, because there is no one story to be told. So we cannot dismiss other less "modern" aspects as peripheral survivals. Nor can we expect a unitary "postmodern" age, though current discussions of postmodernity may be quite useful in describing our world. As part of the enterprise of questioning the ultimacy of the basic dichotomies that structure the modern view of the world, we come to question the very distinction between modern and traditional society. When we put modernity in its place, we may find we are neither so free nor so restricted as we had thought.

Matters of Style

I have tried to avoid carrying over into English the German use of capital letters. This resolve denies me the convenience of distinguishing by purely orthographic means Hegel's Concept from his concepts, or Heidegger's Being from beings. It is good to be forced to think out the differences rather than to fall back on the easy recourse of capitalization. I have used *concept* when Hegel's *Begriff* is meant in its technical sense, and *notion* or other words when talking of concepts in the looser ordinary sense. This inverts the usage of some Hegel translations but keeps the needed etymological relation between *con-cept* and *be-greifen*. I have used the verb *conceive*, and other locutions, to render the German use of *think* (*denken*) as a transitive verb, but in some places I have echoed the German usage in my English. For Heidegger's *Sein* I have used *being* without a capital letter; the standard capitalization too much increases the temptation to view *Sein* as a source or cause. For *Seienden* I have used a variety of words: *entities*, *beings* (in contexts where there was no confusion possible), and often the general English word *things*. This last has the advantage of being ordinary and not suggesting some metaphysical construct; it has the disadvantage of possible confusion with Heidegger's use of *Ding* in a special sense in his later thought. On the few occasions where that confusion threatens I have explicitly noted it. There is also the danger that *thing* will suggest that all entities are to be thought on the model of the simple presence of objects (*Vorhandensein*) discussed in *Being and Time*, but that connotation is a learned one and is not ordinarily associated with the English word. As to my translations of *Gestell* and *Ereignis* as *universal imposition* and *propriative event*, respectively, these are discussed when they are first introduced.[2]

Most references in the text (for example, Taylor 1979) refer to the general bibliography at the end of the book. Works of Hegel and Heidegger are referred to in the text by abbreviations (for example, Encyclopedia #539) and are listed in separate bibliographies. I have used standard translations but modified them when it seemed appropriate to do so.

A Word in Gratitude

I express my thankfulness to many who have helped me find my way amid the dark Germanic forests. I thank those who helped me study Hegel: Quentin Lauer, Kenley Dove, and John Findlay, and those who introduced me to Heidegger: William Richardson and Karsten Harries. They all may feel I have strayed far from the truth. Stephan Körner's advice and ideas are present in less obvious ways.

I thank too the members of the Hegel Society of America and the Heidegger Conference, who have helped me in many formal and informal conversations, and the members of the Collegium Phenomenologicum in Perugia, where the idea for this book was born. I owe a special debt for talks with Paul Ricoeur, Tom Sheehan, David Krell, and Robert Bernasconi. For much encouragement and criticism, and for the patience to read all or portions of earlier versions, I thank my collegues Kenneth Shapiro and Mark Okrent. I hold all these persons partly responsible—but you should not hold them guilty—for what is said in this book.

The writing of this book was made possible by a timely grant from the National Endowment for the Humanities, whose efficient support and advice I acknowledge gladly. Because the chance to treat Heidegger's ideas on technology while writing on a word processor was too enticing, I have no typist to thank, but Julie Bourisk and Clare Schmoll have helped with many drafts of the articles which led to this book. And, first of all, I thank my wife, Anne, for her companionship in many worlds.

The Modern World

We have many different beliefs about ourselves and our modern age. Among them is the belief that modern man is becoming cut off from traditional values and ways of life. Those who feel that liberation from tradition is a good thing rejoice at this change, while those who fear the results lament the loss of roots. We can see the signs of this change in the mobile consumer society around us; we can read the signs in recent literature and antiliterature; we can walk through buildings that symbolize the change with the strictures of the international style or the eclecticism of postmodern architecture.

Beginning our study of two philosophers' reactions to the modern world, this first chapter moves through a series of concentric circles that gradually focus the issues of concern. I will start by collecting some commonplaces about our age as different from traditional society. Though these are one-sided clichés they reveal issues that trouble us. Then I will look at social science discussions of the modern age that treat those issues in a useful way. Finally I will discuss the basic categories and distinctions behind standard beliefs and attitudes about the modern world. It is these categories and distinctions that Hegel and Heidegger question.

The term *modern* derives from a Latin word meaning "in this time." The English word quickly developed two uses, one meaning "contemporary, present day" and the other adding the connotation that in modern times the world had changed from the classic and medieval world. As used today the word retains both meanings, but several more historical periods have been added to the list with which the present age is contrasted. In social science and to some extent in popular use a more precise contrast has developed between modern and traditional ways of life. Many ages may have felt that they were different, but we tend to feel that our uniqueness goes beyond the usual differences; we are developing something new in history.

One of our self-images is that we live at a distance from what was taken for granted by earlier ages or may still be taken for granted in some other societies in the world. We do not follow traditions as if they were the one natural way to be. We do not define ourselves by the social givens as closely as we think our ancestors did. We refuse to take as unchanging either our place within the social framework of classes, values, roles, and institutions or that framework itself. Even when we live within these social arrangements, we do not feel as identified with them as we imagine the medieval peasant or the Roman soldier must have felt. Nor as we might imagine the Spanish or the Japanese feeling today. We have more choices, more possibilities.

Along with distance comes control. We try for a degree of power over the physical world that earlier societies did not possess. We have the taste for this control. Descartes said in his *Discourse on Method* that we would become "masters and possessors of the earth." Even when we decide to let an area remain forever wild, we have cast our will and control over it by the very act of abstaining from developing it.

Our control over social givens is notoriously less effective than our control over many aspects of physical nature, but we try to be planners and manipulators in society too. Advertising, economic intervention, education and reeducation, social science advising: all this is intended to be similar to our control of nature. It *is* the control of nature in another of its manifestations.

We identify everything around us, including ourselves, as possible objects for planning and control. This is a sign of the new distance, and it provokes a revolt against the mentality of control. We are told we are going too far; we will wake or build the monsters that will destroy us. There are limits to our knowledge of nature and our ability to predict the outcome of our interventions in the ecosystem or the economy. Such objections, however, only challenge the mentality of control to become more effective.

Another common reaction to our distance emphasizes our enclosure within the web of life. We are not separate; we remain intimately within a larger whole whose rhythms and laws we must respect and from which we can draw support. Such images of nearness and connection testify to our feelings of distance and separation. This sense of separation and distance has been traced to many things: the book of Genesis, Christianity, capitalism, science, patriarchy.

It is not very clear exactly what the separation and distance are that these signs point to, but there is always a contrast with a past or future state of greater connectedness within society and between us and nature.

Our relations to ourselves are also affected by distance. We are told that we are free, that we should choose a rewarding life-style. We are told we have the chance to construct a happy life by working to maximize whatever satisfactions we choose to pursue. We make such choices based on what is around us and on our inner desires and values. But those desires and values are themselves not fixed. We are told how to instill the correct desires and values into our children, and self-help books suggest how to go about changing them in ourselves. We regard even our inner desires as manipulable. Nothing about us seems to have the solidity we imagine the people of old possessed, yet our selves have become the unifying point of our lives.

We are doing self-development. That process itself seems more important than the particular direction it may take. Fashion or whim or advertising may change the goal of our work on ourselves, but we can still talk about developing ourselves. That process can be defined independently of any particular content it possesses. We are striving to unify our selves, for freedom, development, new possibilities, individuality—notice that all these goals can be talked about without mentioning any concrete content for our choices. The process of self-development itself becomes a goal. We see this in society, when progress is often defined as an endless process of change without any goal to be reached. (See Bellah et al. 1985, 126–27, 139.)

Traditional versus Modern Identity

We are modern individuals and we want our society to reflect that fact. There is an ambiguity here, however. Should we consider being modern individuals as a particular way of being persons, just another kind of traditional identity? We are individualists; we are told the

Japanese prefer to put the group first; in Bali they undoubtedly have a different arrangement. Is our individualism just one particular set of values, one particular traditional identity among others? Or is being a modern individual somehow different from having a traditional identity? Is being an American individual a particular ethnic identity? Or is it what you become when you take away all ethnic identity?

We are inconsistent about this. We often compare ourselves to others as if we moderns were members of a group with its own traditional ways, but when we think about the superiority of modern individualist ways, we tend to think that we are what one becomes when one sheds traditional ways. We are the modern people who can judge and accept or reject. We are not bound by tradition—of course, there are those who argue that we should be so bound, but that only testifies to the widespread feeling that we are not. Our modern individualism is a purer "human" identity that has something to do with being an "individual" *before* one is Italian or Swedish or Japanese. One is free to choose, free from the restraints of traditional fixed values.

This way of thinking about modern (or American) individualism sees traditional ethnic ways as restrictions. There is a wider field of possibilities open to one who has escaped the bonds of allegiance to unquestioned traditional values. The widest field of possibilities would be correlated to a self defined only as a choosing individual, with no particular values or content of choice defined in advance, able to make of himself or herself whatever he or she chooses. Such a self-definition would involve a feeling of distance from any natural or social givens. This conception of modern individuality explains some of the distance spoken about earlier.

Similarly, our public institutions can be thought of either as embodying a particular set of individualist virtues and traditional values or as being neutral, value-free, procedural institutions for brokering and facilitating the choices of pure individuals.

A similar ambiguity runs through our attitudes toward the process of change affecting other societies. Sometimes we call that process "development," which suggests that the other nations have within them something as yet undeveloped, something that will grow into its fullness and become a modern version of their particular traditions. Sometimes we call that process "Westernization," which suggests that a foreign set of values is being imposed on a traditional society. Sometimes we call that process "modernization," which suggests a change from a traditional society to something else, a detraditionalized society full of modern individuals rather than people who define themselves primarily by some traditional identity.

There is merit in the "modernity" of a society, apart from any other virtues it may have. Being modern is being "advanced" and being advanced means being rich, free of the encumbrances of familial authority, religious authority, and deferentiality. It means being rational and being "rationalized." . . . If such rationalization were achieved, all traditions except the traditions of secularity, scientism, and hedonism would be overpowered. (Shils 1981, 288, 290)

This last image suggests that in the future all societies will be the same, an unattractive picture. But just as we imagine that modern individuals will make different choices based in part on what they choose to keep from their childhood, so we can imagine that different societies will keep aspects of their traditional identities, though they will relate to them in a new planned and distant way. Different societies might become the communal equivalent of different individual life styles, something like clubs one is free to join or leave, with rules agreed on out of convenience and a certain respect for past practices.

One common understanding of progress and development urges the creation or liberation of something like a pure personal individuality and a pure human society. At the same time we also feel it is important to have roots that can give us more than modern distance seems able to provide. Throughout the world there are reassertions of tradition and reactions against modernization. Of course there are groups, such as the Amish, that have always resisted assuming the modern identity. There are also groups that maintain a traditional identity as a salable product for tourism. But recently we have seen aggressive groups that deny the universalistic modern identity. I am not thinking just of such strongly antimodern movements as those in the Islamic world. More puzzling perhaps are the ethnic movements such as those among the Welsh, the Basques, the Scots, the Bretons, and other regional groupings in Europe. Even in America the melting pot image has gone out of favor, and the age of the hyphenated-American has arrived. The world seems full of groups that want to define their own life and language, but not on the model of the voluntary club. If the Basques were to set up a semi-independent region, one would not be able to join it as one might join a tennis club or move to a more swinging suburb. Not all ethnic or minority identities have been successfully turned into commodities.

The upsurge of such movements is a puzzle for modern consciousness. Is there a flight from modern society back to tradition? Or is it a predictable extension of the modern right to choose, now turned against the large nation state? Or is it something our standard categories do not well describe?[1]

The commonplaces I have been collecting suggest that many people think being modern involves a new ideal of personal and social identity, a new way of relating to values. The self as unified and unifying becomes the center of reference. This does not necessarily mean a selfish "me first" attitude; altruism is also a value one can choose. The point is that one chooses. If one decides to live within some traditional values and ways, they are something unified in terms of the self, a chosen self-definition rather than something taken for granted and defining the self. The modern individual is stripped down to a unified core, a perceiving, choosing being potentially free to maximize whatever is desired. One chooses among the widest possible field of possibilities, without any of the possibilities being taken as defining what one is. New roles are to be created to meet new needs or to overcome old oppressions. The community in which one lives is to respect choices and act in a largely procedural way to keep possibilities open.

By collecting these commonplaces about modernity I do not mean to claim that there are not other conflicting commonplaces, for example, those concerning more activist versions of the state. Nor am I claiming that these commonplaces are fully accurate. I will argue later that they express an impossible ideal. But it is an important feature of our world that people believe they are different from earlier ages in the distance and separation that gives them increased freedom.

The modern ideal can be presented either as liberation from the dead weight of tradition or as a particularly streamlined tradition, pared down to the essentials of what it means to be a human person. In either case, what is striking is what is not said. Human identity is defined without reference to history, set values, or God; let alone race, creed, or national origin. A person is defined in a way that separates the process of choice from the content chosen.

Descriptions of Modernity

To obtain a clearer way of talking about modernity than the commonplaces collected so far, we can recall some typical sociological descriptions of our situation. We are familiar with the words used to describe the negative effects of modern distance: *alienation, disenchantment, fragmentation, anomie.* In the tradition stemming from Max Weber we can find concepts to help define more carefully how all this relates to modern freedom and individuality. This will let us make our discussion of Hegel and Heidegger more pointed.[2]

Consider, for example, Peter Berger's characterization of the modern age: "The conception of the naked self, beyond institutions and roles, as the *ens realissimum* of human being, is the very heart of modernity" (Berger, Berger, and Kellner 1974, 213). Berger discusses how the concept of self has changed by replacement of the notion of the honor appropriate to a person's office or status with the notion of an equal human dignity shared by all persons.

The concept of honor implies that identity is essentially, or at least importantly, linked to institutional roles. The modern concept of dignity, by contrast, implies that identity is essentially independent of institutional roles. . . . In a world of honor the individual is the social symbols emblazoned on his escutcheon. The true self of the knight is revealed as he rides out to do battle in the full regalia of his role; by comparison, the naked man in bed with a woman represents a lesser reality of the self. In a world of dignity, in the modern sense, the social symbolism governing the interaction of men is a disguise. The escutcheons hide the true self. It is precisely the naked man, and even more specifically the naked man expressing his sexuality, who represents himself more truthfully. Consequently, the understanding of self-discovery and self-mystification is reversed as between these two worlds. In a world of honor the individual discovers his true identity in his roles, and to turn away from the roles is to turn away from himself—in "false consciousness," one is tempted to add. In a world of dignity, the individual can only discover his true identity by emancipating himself from his socially imposed roles—the latter are only masks, entangling him in illusion, "alienation," and "bad faith." It follows that the two worlds have a different relation to history. It is through the performance of institutional roles that the individual participates in history, not only the history of the particular institution but that of his society as a whole. It is precisely for this reason that modern consciousness, in its conception of the self, tends toward a curious ahistoricity. In a world of honor, identity is firmly linked to the past through the reiterated performance of prototypical acts. In a world of dignity, history is the succession of mystifications from which the individual must free himself to attain "authenticity." (Berger, Berger, and Kellner 1974, 90–91)

Berger is at best a cautious partisan of modern dignity. He feels we are forced to make our way preserving its good achievements and trying to ameliorate its bad effects. We face dilemmas because the good achievements and the bad effects are brought about by the very same causes. Berger discusses the dilemmas produced by the influences that spread modern consciousness. Technological production, bureaucratic administration, and other modernizing factors bring about an economy that is efficient but also encourages the spread of an atomizing and calculating style into other areas of our lives. Attitudes toward time inherent in modern production encourage a planning and engineering attitude toward the future, in personal relations as well as in business and administration. We have trouble keeping our personal life rich and concrete when our working relations tend toward abstraction and role specialization. Modern society tends to push medium-sized social structures aside so that the deeply individualized self faces depersonalized mega-structures. But trying to create mediating structures risks losing the good effects of individualism and its moral sensitivity to human dignity and needs. The modern expectation is that everything can be changed, that things could and probably should be different from what they have been. It is difficult to preserve wholeness in a world that disallows contentment and demands that we constantly seek improvement.[3]

Berger notes that the chief modern method for dealing with these dilemmas has been to divide life into public and private spheres and apportion the tension-creating oppositions accordingly. Private life can be rich while working life is narrow; public time is future-oriented while private time is present-oriented; and so on. But pressures for modernization tend to infect the private sphere as well. In any case, such a split seems to reinforce the dilemmas involving distance and separation within the self.

Finally, as Berger points out, the way we are asking these questions about our society is itself modern. We are presuming that we can study and control the social environment. We are asking what changes can be made, what trends can be directed or controlled. We want to moderate the effects of technology and protect our social values from the bad aspects of modernity. Such goals embody just that modern mentality of distance and control and planning that caused the dilemmas in the first place. Yet there seems no way out of this reaffirmation of modernity. Are there other ways to understand our possibilities and escape the circle of planning and control?

Max Weber

By turning to Berger's predecessor, Max Weber, we can look more closely at the nature of modern selfhood. It is too easy to equate modernity with bureaucratization or with technology; bureaucracy has existed in many cultures, and we cannot be sure that advanced technology can exist only in our kind of society. Weber tries to describe a more basic contrast between modern and traditional society. Though the details of his analyses are not accepted by all, his general notions are widespread even among those who disagree with such details as his treatment of bureaucracy or the causal importance he assigns to religion.

Weber's theory is itself typically modern. He postulates that the creator of all meaning is the individual self. The self's beliefs and attitudes unify experience and create values. The social world with its meanings and roles is the result of shared construction of meaning by individuals. Of course individuals are constrained by natural phenomena and are influenced by inherited constructions. Furthermore, meaning creations do not always have the results intended, and they often have quite unexpected side effects. Still, Weber says that the basis of meaning and social possibility is the individual. "The transcendental presupposition of every cultural science lies . . . in the fact that we are cultural beings, endowed with the capacity and the will to take a deliberate attitude towards the world and to lend it significance" (Roth and Schluchter 1979, 73n). The Kantian echo is deliberate in this quote, but in opposition to Kant the making of meaning has become an act of deliberate choice on the part of the individual. Given this presupposition, which has been called "methodological individualism," it follows that the modern view that explicitly recognizes the individual's beliefs and attitudes as the basis of social constructions is closer to the truth about human selfhood than was the traditional belief that there was some pattern in the nature of things that society and individuals should follow. In Weber's eyes, modernity is an explicit recognition of what the self and society have been all along. Modern identity is not just another in a sequence of historic constructions; it is the unveiling of what has been at the root of those constructions.

This is a common modern theme, that we have at last achieved self-consciousness, either to our happiness or to our loss. We assure ourselves that our self-understanding is final because it is formal. We have discovered the process within which all historical constructions have been taking place. That process can be described in quite formal terms, devoid of this or that historical content. There may still be some unmasking to perform, some hidden biases to uproot, but in principle we have achieved a self-understanding that cannot be gone behind, because it makes the self empty and free. Beliefs of this type account for the American conviction that American-style individualism is the natural goal of every other culture's history. Self-confident moderns seldom ask whether that formal and empty self could be itself a mask over something deeper.

For Weber, the transition to modernity takes place largely through increasing rationalization. Rationality denotes following a rule as opposed to acting on impulse or at random. Rationality means consistency in linking our thoughts or statements, creating the logical order of premise to conclusion. It also means consistency in linking our actions, creating the efficient order of means to end.

Weber meant by rationalization the coherent ordering of beliefs and actions in accordance with a unifying central criterion. The systematization of belief is the elimination of logical inconsistencies, the disarming of demons and local deities, the denial of magical technology, the increased comprehensiveness or generality of a theory, and the reduction of all individual instances, whatever their diversity, to the status of general classes. Rationalization of belief is the elimination of particular judgments which cannot be subsumed under a more general judgment. The rationalization of action is the elimination of decisions which cannot be justified in accordance with their anticipated consequences, themselves rationally assessed by more generally defined ends and rendered predictable by generally valid empirical laws. Rationalization is the organization of actions aimed at the attainment of an optimal combination of ends— whether the actions be those of a single individual planning his own course of action or whether they be those of a large number of individuals. Rationalization is the systematization of belief; it is the systematization of action. (Shils 1981, 291)

Roth and Schluchter distinguish three areas where Weber thought rationalization could increase: the control of the world through

calculation, the systematization of meaning and value into an overall
consistent ethical view, and the methodical living of daily life according to rules (1979, 14–15; cf. Gerth and Mills 1975, 55). Weber
was particularly interested in how the advance of rationalization in
one area affected the other areas. The modern world as we know
it is the result of interconnected changes in all these areas.

Formal Rationality

One particular change can be noted in all the areas of modern life:
the prominence of formal rationality over substantive rationality. In
Weber's mind the guiding contrast seems to be between the image
of a tribal member or a religious believer living according to values
that he takes as the only natural way to live and a modern person
who makes decisions in a pragmatic way to maximize self-chosen
values.[4]

In the case of substantive rationality there are values that are
accepted as simply true and that fit with a picture of the world so
accepted. Modernity is not just a weakening of such a tradition but
a reversal. No longer will calculations of efficiency and consistency
be limited by a given substantive set of values and ways of life. Rather
the norms themselves will be judged in terms of their efficiency and
consistency in achieving chosen goals and meanings. Those chosen
goals and meanings have no further legitimation; they are simply
chosen.

The self judges and chooses among the possibilities open before
it. A system of substantive rationality restricts those possibilities by
accepting norms that cannot themselves be judged for consistency
and efficiency. While all rationality connotes consistency and efficiency, formal rationality makes these the only norms, untrammeled
by substantive restrictions. It therefore faces the widest possible field
of possibilities. True to his methodology, Weber regards this as a
difference of attitude on the part of individuals. In a substantively
rational institution, individuals take meanings or goals as grounded
in the structure of the world, providing the measure for all decisions.
Thus, for Weber, a theological system erected with great logical
acumen upon a set of unquestioned beliefs would be substantively
rational. In the social sphere, the Indian caste system would be a
substantively rational organization of society. A bureaucratic state
like ancient China would be substantively rational because it still
possessed in the emperor and his family a point of authority simply

given and accepted in terms of belief in the structure of the world. A bureaucratic society like the modern United States approaches formal rationality to the degree that it acts more like a procedural state whose power is legitimated in terms of efficiency and abstract rules of procedure.

Obviously there are degrees between the two pure forms of rationality. It is indeed questionable whether the distinction is valid in the way Weber uses it. Historical examples of pure substantive rationality tend to evaporate when looked at closely. Theological systems, for example, usually involve a much more nuanced attitude toward traditional belief formulations than Weber allows, and the Indian caste system and its associated beliefs could be looked at functionally as a masterpiece of efficient social planning when considered in their historical and anthropological context. Many writers have discussed the kinds of revisions that would be needed to make Weber's distinction more serviceable in analyzing concrete situations.[5]

My own purpose here is not to defend or to attack Weber's distinction but to use it to express more accurately some beliefs that modern society holds about itself.

Weber thought that with growing liberation from the restraints of substantive rationality man might exercise increased freedom. Modernity might finally dispel the great illusion that there existed some one harmonious scheme of values. There are many gods to follow and no high god or supreme value to arbitrate among them. We choose our values, come in contact with one another, and work out the consequences. This free culture had the potential for a more varied and exciting world than any in history. But Weber was pessimistic. Modernity was more likely to become a gloomy bureaucratic state where administered uniformity severely limited freedom. People were likely to flee the modern necessity of choosing meaning and value, running back into the arms of religious or political monotheisms that provide a secure, naturally meaningful world. The growing bureaucracy would encourage uniformity because it made administration more efficient. There were no new continents to expand into, and life would be dominated by the great continental empires, not the variegated small nations. The future would belong to benevolent feudalism and welfare bureaucracies. The best we could hope for was "tarrying for loving companionship and the experience of art as a this-worldly escape from institutional routines" (in Gerth and Mills 1975, 74). It would be interesting to relate Weber and G. E. Moore in their attitudes about what made life valuable in the modern age; does Weber perhaps belong in Bloomsbury?

If there was an escape from this "iron cage" of bureaucracy and formal rationality, it lay in the will, not in reason.

The question is: how are freedom and democracy in the long run possible at all under the domination of highly developed capitalism? Freedom and democracy are only possible where the resolute will of a nation not to allow itself to be ruled like sheep is permanently alive. We are "individualists" and partisans of "democratic" institutions "against the stream" of material constellations. . . . The rational construction of institutional life, doubtless after having destroyed innumerable "values," today, at least in principle, has done its work. In the wake of the standardization of production, it has made the external way of life uniform. Under present conditions of business, the impact of such standardization is universal. (Gerth and Mills 1975, 71)

The will not to be ruled like sheep could be mobilized in true democratic institutions, but Weber had little hope of these continuing to be vital. The most likely political course would be a stifling bureaucracy disturbed from time to time by charismatic politicians who could put their personal passion into new values and awaken the will of the people. Then their charisma would pass, be routinized, and end by giving the bureaucrats more legitimacy. The system could be disturbed only from the outside by such irruptions of passion, but they would not prevent the iron cage from closing again.

It is important to recall Weber's pessimism, because it expresses fears widely shared today. Weber believed we could not go back to a traditional society. Magic cannot be put back into nature. Fixed meanings cannot be reestablished. Individuals may try to do so in their own lives, but the overall structure will remain bureaucratic and formally rational. Modern rationality will make for inhumane living, because it was substantive rationality that gave charm and interest to life. Everything will be a matter of efficiency and consistency. Against this Weber offers only the resolute will, which he fears is doomed to failure in its struggle against rigidifying structure.[6]

The simple opposition Weber makes between rigid structure and the force of will should give us pause for thought. The relation of structure and force need not be taken as a relation of the purely static versus the purely dynamic. In some currents of Freudian thought, in poststructuralist writings, in some areas of process thought today, there are attempts to think about the relation of structure to desire and will in new ways. These connect to the effort we will see later in Hegel and Heidegger to think about determinateness without thinking in terms of limitation, or to think about desire and will without thinking in terms of the Platonic *eros*.

Weber sees few options for modern man. It may be, however, that his vision is limited by the oppositions he uses to structure his thought. We have just seen one of those: structure versus will. That in turn implies another dichotomy Weber uses, the opposition between a formal process and and its content.

Formal rationality describes the form of the process of being rational. Substantive rationality adds fixed content restricting that process. Modern society removes the fixed content and leaves a process of living that can be described in terms of its form alone.

There could be different degrees of formal process. A clearly substantive arrangement might be a governmental and economic system working under the Islamic law or the Hindu law of Manu. In such a society the formally describable economic processes would be blocked at times by prohibitions stemming from religiously based substantive laws. The government might seek goals that were not those of the citizens but were enjoined in the laws.

A more formal process would efficiently and consistently work to realize goals that were not considered as grounded in any law of nature but were known to be the result of pure decisions on the part of some installed but not "natural" authority (such as a dictator or an oligarchy). This has been called the decisionist model of rationality.

Another more formal process might be an administrative system charged with judging and revising its own goals as experience dictates. Goals were not specified from the outside but were evolved historically. This has been called the pragmatic model of rationality.

A third yet more formal process could be imagined with no particular policy goals at all except to operate its own machinery efficiently and facilitate the various inputs it receives. This has been called the technocratic model of rationality. There has been considerable discussion of which of these last models Weber meant, or should have meant, in his discussions of formal rationality.

For our purposes it is interesting that all these models depend in differing degrees on the separation of a formally described process from its content. Earlier we noted that moderns might describe themselves as free choosers without having to specify any content for those choices. Now we are hearing about possible social systems that could be described as devices for maximizing whatever content is put into them by the choices of those modern selves. The social system by itself would offer no content to the individuals, only a form for their mutual interaction.

There is a second distinction at work in Weber's thought, that of universal from particular. I am not referring directly to the onto-logical controversy about "abstract entities" but to the social sphere. There has always been a difference between the universal rule and the particular case to which it is applied. In traditional societies when a person was born in a certain class, son of a shoemaker, his overall purposes were decided by those facts and the universal rules that assigned him his place. In such a society the universal rules specified a great deal of particular content. Correspondingly, the particular values and goals of any one person could be perceived as part of the harmonious whole articulated in the network of places, duties, and obligations. In a sense the shoemaker's son had the universal good of society as part of his purpose, insofar as he knew how his place in society fit harmoniously into the picture of the whole.

What is distinctive about the modern situation is that the uni-versal rules have become quite formal and do not specify any content to the particular case, but only some restrictions imposed by the formal process for entering into the general interaction. In such a society the universal rules specify no particular content and the individuals are told to seek only their own good and let the invisible hand care for the universal good. The separation of universal from particular has become institutionalized.

Modernity in Weber's version is structured by the coming together of these two distinctions: formal process versus content and universal versus particular. Both are institutionalized in the free market and minimal state. The modern self discussed earlier in terms of distance and separation can also be described in terms of these distinctions. Distance and manipulation occur as the social institutions and their associated attitudes and beliefs allow the self to relate to itself and to others as a pure chooser, with no necessary substantive content.

It is no accident that economics provides the best and almost the only examples of such formal institutions. Modernity is marked by the distinction of economics from politics. The economic system can be imagined as directed not to any substantive goal but to consistent and efficient dealing with the multitude of individual goals that are its inputs. The free market and its associated minimal state are supposed to be such institutions. The system has no goal other than facilitation and protection of the individual purposes presented to it. Of course the market and the state do present restraints to the individuals entering, but those restraints are thought to come from natural facts (such as scarcities), from the purposes of other individuals, or from the need for formal equality, not from some substantive values embedded in the system as such.

It is also possible to imagine an individual treating life in a manner embodying an analogous split of formal process from its content. Such a person might devote his or her efforts to maximizing the intensity and satisfaction of whatever perceptions and desires come along, without any overall goal or demand for long-term consistency. Such a person is a recognizable modern character, similar to Kierkegaard's aesthetic personality, who possesses an overall "life-plan" with no content but an empty process waiting for adventitious input.

Modern society, as Weber envisions it, is a process waiting for content to come from the choices of its citizens. Weber fears, though, that the efficient operation of the process will itself push individual choices into dull uniformity with only occasional charismatic interruptions. There seems no way out other than a return to traditional society, which is impossible. Weber is caught, because for him the separation of formal process from its content has become complete. In the earlier stages of history there were complex interactions between the forms of social process and the substantive content they served. Now all that is over, the separation has been institutionalized, and we are caught in the aftermath.

When modernity is discussed in these terms, there seems no option but to continue modern separations or to return to traditional society.[7]

There is no obvious way to put the pieces back together. If we could return to tradition, we would have meaning and humane living but at the price of freedom and (for Weber) truthfulness. Modernity promises freedom and rationality but may give us deadening routine. It also forces us to choose, without any grounds for our choice, what values we will hold. Many current debates in the United States are cast in terms implicitly structured along the lines suggested by Weber.

Can we avoid the dilemma of rootless freedom versus oppressive tradition? If there were some way to question the ultimacy of the distinction between formal process and its content, there might be a way to envision other alternatives for modern man.

In later chapters we will see how Hegel and Heidegger look for a way to think about modernity that does not accept our standard picture of ourselves. They deny the distinctions that structure modernity's image of itself. Though they do not agree, they share a common strategy, and if we think about that strategy and the different ways they attempt it, we may find new space for our own thought.

Other Signs of Modernity

The accent has been mainly sociological so far, but the patterns and distinctions we have been discussing can be found in many spheres of life. Philosophy in our time has been increasingly occupied either with the separations we have been discussing or with critiques directed against them. One could trace the beginnings of those separations back to the Greeks. Hegel and Heidegger do so, but for now it is enough to point out that with Descartes's canonization of the isolated ego and with the social contract theories of Hobbes and Locke the relation of the individual to accepted social content, to values and meanings, began to be thought about in a new way. With Kant the modern individual is explicitly discussed in purely formal terms. Our cognitive and volitional lives are analyzed into a process that works for unification, consistency, and universality. What content they receive is a contingent matter; the process itself can be known in purely formal terms. The categories and associated rules, the categorical imperative and its corollaries—these represent a definition of the self without reference to any particular substantive content. In Kant's opinion it was exactly the formal purity of his system that made it scientific and necessary knowledge. [8]

In our day the Kantian project has been reworked in terms of the formal analysis of language. The logical positivists and their successors took their stand on the very separations we have been discussing. The goal of philosophy was defined as the study of the pure universal form of language distinct from its particular empirical content. Quine, Wittgenstein, and the newer philosophers of science all attacked the logical positivists by blurring or collapsing the crucial distinctions. The distinctions, however, often in their positivist versions, remain well entrenched in much psychological and social scientific theory.

On the European side a similar movement occurred with the neo-Kantians (and, in a different way, Husserl) championing a view of the self as a formal process, while Scheler, Heidegger, and others attacked the ultimacy of the distinctions involved. Structuralism and the reactions to it might provide another version of the same story.

In ethics this century has seen debates between theories offering substantive ethical norms and those offering formal guidelines for conduct. The first debates were between the substantive ethics of the intuitionists and the natural law theorists, on the one hand, and the formal ethics of the Kantians, the utilitarians, and the rational egoists, on the other. Now most debate centers on rival formal approaches. Kant hoped to derive moral norms from the pure formal necessities of the act of rational choice. Utilitarians and rational egoists both describe moral life as a process of maximization of whatever content the self chooses. A formal process is applied to whatever "utilities" are chosen. Such a pattern fits well with Weber's basic picture.

Present-day critics of formalism in ethics try to reconceptualize the self and its action to avoid describing judgment as the application of a formal criterion. Such trends often lead in the direction of a historically minded Aristotelianism such as might be found variously in the writings of Alasdair MacIntyre or Hilary Putnam. But the question is open whether these avoid appeal to the separation of form and content.[9]

Thus we can find in recent philosophy the same emphasis on the distinctions of formal process from content and universal from particular that we saw in Weber's theory and in the modern commonplaces about the self. It is striking, though, how loud and insistent the criticism of these distinctions has become in philosophy, while in the social sciences they are taken more for granted. One might praise the philosophers for being more radical or praise the social scientists for realizing how difficult it is to criticize modernity without losing its benefits.

Another place where the separation of formal process from content, and the new relation of universal rules to particular persons, has been noticed, forwarded, praised, and cursed is in the arts. There have been many schools of art and criticism devoted to purely formal goals, and modern art has achieved a reflexive preoccupation with the process of its own creation. Art in our century has displayed a modernist tendency toward constant revolution and the invention of new forms. It has been important to break the former rules and create new modes of art. Even the realistic and other reactions against the modernist impulse usually reinforce the typically modern selfhood of the artist who chooses his styles and defines himself over against the fixity of some tradition, in this case the tradition of modernism itself.

The modernist movement in art is an ambiguous phenomenon; it shows a kind of empty subjectivity at work in its refusal to be settled within any set of rules or forms, and in its frequent plays of self-reference. Yet it refuses what in many other areas of life is a typically modern desire for unity and system, for *the* pure form. Is it then modern or does it lead to a new postmodern art? The term *postmodern* has recently been in vogue with little clear meaning, but it suggests an important problem area.

Jean-François Lyotard has characterized our modern world in terms of the Enlightenment drive to seize and systematize the world and to liberate human possibilities by mastering the conditions of life (Lyotard, 1984). This description touches only one of the ways in which empty modern subjectivity can face the world; there have been as well romantic, ironic, and despairing modes of modern life. But Lyotard touches a central theme in modernity. He then offers a description of a new postmodern age; his characterization of this age is closely related to the continual creation of new forms by the modernist tradition in the arts. In the concluding chapter of this study I will essay a few remarks on ways in which postmodernity might be understood, especially in relation to the claims made by Lyotard, and by Charles Jencks.

We turn now to the alternative descriptions Hegel and Heidegger offer to replace the standard modern self-description. Their proposals are in one sense anti-modern in the sense that neither the modern age nor its overcoming are taken as matters for our individual choice and control. But the two thinkers will not urge us to return to substantive tradition. Neither Hegel nor Heidegger accepts the common alternatives in which our own discussions tend to get mired. We can learn from them as we try to deal with the modern age which we can neither do without nor totally abide.

2

Hegel's Criticisms of Civil Society

It may seem strange to speak of Hegel as a critic of the modern age. His philosophy is meant to crown and perfect modernity rather than to reject it. For Hegel, however, to perfect something is to remove the onesidedness and abstraction with which it first appeared. Modernity is no exception.

Perhaps what misleads us is Hegel's tone. He is not an alienated critic, and we tend to think the great critics must be alienated from their society. Hegel approved what he saw as the general direction of his culture and society. He enthusiastically supported what he took to be the key development of the modern age. "The right of the subject's particularity, his right to be satisfied, or in other words the right of subjective freedom, is the pivot and center of the difference between antiquity and modern times" (Philosophy of Right #124z). For Hegel the cluster of revolutionary changes that brings on the modern age frees individual subjects from subjection to society and tradition. The individual is made a genuine force in the community; the single individual can relate with God directly and not through a priesthood; the sensible world of particular things assumes a role in science that makes man's activity powerful against the forces of nature. These revolutions mark the most dramatic step forward in the task of liberating man's subjective freedom from immersion in substantive community or in the brute givenness of nature.

On the other hand, the results of these revolutions are still stated in terms of oppositions: individual versus community, man versus nature, inner versus outer world. This indicates to Hegel that they cannot be quite the last word; there must be a further step so that unity as well as opposition can be expressed.

Hegel was an adolescent during the French Revolution. Watching these new events from what he and his friends perceived as a static Germany cut up into outmoded states with irrational constitutions, Hegel saw in France a decisive turn in history. The principle of subjectivity and individuality had been made the operative principle for the political sphere. Hegel and his friends planted a liberty tree for the revolution, and even in his later "conservative" years he praised the "immortal deed" of Luther and the "banner of free spirit" introduced at the Reformation (see Ritter 1982, 52). Hegel every year drank a toast on the anniversary of the storming of the Bastille, and he asserted that "every present and future legal and political order must presuppose and proceed from the Revolution's universal principle of freedom" (Ritter 1982, 182).

It is important to realize how enthusiastic Hegel remained about the political and intellectual changes that brought the modern age, and how decisive he saw them to be. Otherwise his attempts to criticize and mediate them may seem a kind of metaphysical disinfectant. The picture of Hegel as the father of the totalitarian state still persists, though it has been refuted.[1]

Hegel criticized as he approved. Hegel is never simply for or against anything except in a very few cases, such as his sarcastic opposition to the restoration political theories of von Haller, a thinker whose views are similar to those attributed to Hegel by his twentieth-century critic, Sir Karl Popper.

For all his enthusiasm about modernity, Hegel has his worries. The principle of modern subjectivity is realized at first in an abstract and formal manner. Many institutions remain at that level, and many theorists have seized upon formal and abstract individuality instead of advancing to that final stage whose outline Hegel thinks he can discern in current events and current philosophy. So Hegel sets himself to criticize many of the achievements and formulations of modernity in the name of a yet further stage of modern individuality that will confirm and in some ways limit the pretensions of modern subjectivity.

Hegel's remarks about current events and figures are often difficult to disentangle from his abstract prose, or they are tucked away in footnotes and prefaces. We could develop Hegel's general picture of modernity from remarks in his *Lectures on the Philosophy of Art* or *Lectures on the Philosophy of Religion*. In the *Phenomenology of Spirit*, chapter 6 contains a sharp critique of many aspects of the early modern age. It is more difficult to get an adequate view of Hegel's intentions from the *Lectures on the Philosophy of History*, which are all of Hegel that many people read. I will concentrate on the *Philosophy of Right* and its discussion and critique of civil society. I will turn to the logical works to examine the background for Hegel's criticism, then return to the *Philosophy of Right* to see how the criticism is worked out in his theory of the state.

Civil Society

It is not surprising that it should be in his course on "right," that is, on ethics, politics, and law, that Hegel most clearly confronts modern subjectivity. In a sense, all the revolutions of the modern age converge upon the creation of a mode of communal living based on free individuality and formally universal institutions, especially the free market in goods and labor. Ritter is only exaggerating a little when he says that "it dawns on [Hegel] that the historical essence of the Revolution and of the entire age and all its problems is the emergence of the modern industrial civil society of labor" (Ritter 1982, 68).[2]

The modern age has its many births in events such as the Protestant Reformation, the French Revolution, the new science, the Industrial Revolution, Cartesian and Kantian philosophy, and what Hegel calls "romantic" or late Christian art. All of these free individual subjectivity from previous restrictions, but it is in what Hegel calls "civil society" that individual freedom finds itself taken into account in social institutions and politics. Hegel's term in German is *bürgerliche Gesellschaft*, the society of burghers or city folk, the society of people involved in the market. This is not the same for Hegel as the Latin term, *societas civilis*, from which the English translation is taken. In Roman law that term designated the public as opposed to the familial realm. It is in this sense that the term *civil society* was used by Locke and other English writers. Hegel takes over many points from the discussions of civil society in Locke and the English economists. But his use of the term is not identical to theirs. For them it designates the form of interaction and the governmental institutions appropriate to a liberal free market economy—what today might be called the minimal or procedural state.

For Hegel it designates that too, though he does not conceive the governmental institutions quite as minimally. But where the English term stands in opposition to the familial or private sphere, Hegel's concept stands in a double opposition: to the familial sphere as something civil society transcends, and to the state, a nonminimal political sphere transcending civil society.

It is this additional sphere surrounding civil society that has helped earn Hegel his reputation as a totalitarian. Hegel's criticism of modern subjectivity consists in the development that demands some such additional sphere beyond the "liberal" minimal government. Hegel distinguishes a political from a civil sphere of activity, each with its corresponding notion of freedom (see Pelczynski 1984b, 4).

Civil society comprises an economic system where members can work and trade to satisfy their needs, plus the civil institutions needed to keep such a system going: markets, courts and an administration of justice, public works, minimal welfare and antimonopoly systems. Hegel's definition of civil society is as follows: "An association of members as self-sufficient individuals in a universality which because of their self-sufficiency is only formal. Their association is brought about by their needs, by the legal system—the means to security of person and property—and by an external organization for obtaining their particular and common interests" (Philosophy of Right #157). The following pages elucidate this definition from a number of complementary points of view.

Mutual Recognition

Civil society encourages certain motivations and attitudes on the part of the individuals concerned. But it is not constituted by those motivations and attitudes, in the fashion of Weber's methodological individualism. For Hegel all social institutions involve patterns and structures of mutual recognition through which a person achieves his own identity by recognizing others as persons who are recognizing him as a person. There is no prior self to which would be assigned beliefs and attitudes that in Weber's terms would be the basis of social institutions.

A human subject is a self-conscious being. Self-consciousness means I can be aware of myself, the identical knower and agent, as distinct from all objects I know. This is structurally different from the knowledge of objects, yet it includes knowledge of objects because the self knows itself as a different kind of being known in a

different way, and so defines its self-awareness over against the
knowledge of objects.

Hegel claims, however, that humans are not self-aware automatically and immediately from the start. Only in relation to other selves
can the complex maneuver of self-awareness be possible. It is
"learned" through the "interiorized" (both words are inadequate
here) experiences of desire, fear, and the production of one's life in
labor. Only in relating to another self can this happen; interactions
with objects alone cannot bring about the needed reflexive movement of self-awareness. In mutual recognition with another self,
peaceful or conflictual, this can happen. Hegel concludes that

self-consciousness exists in and for itself when and only by the fact that
it so exists for another; that is, it exists only in being acknowledged. (Phenomenology of Spirit 141/#178)

Each [self-consciousness] is the mediating term to the other, through
which each mediates and unites itself with itself. Each is to itself and to
the other as immediate self-existing reality, which at the same time exists
thus for itself through this mediation. They recognize themselves as mutually recognizing each other. (Phenomenology of Spirit 143/#184)

Even if one grants Hegel's conclusion, which is worked out in
the tortuous pages of the *Phenomenology of Spirit*, the argument seems
to indicate only that I discover my self in mutual relation, not that
it exists only in such a relation. Hegel argues, however, that a self
is a being conscious of its relation to itself. This active self-relation
is achieved only in mutual interaction with other selves. Hegel does
not deny, of course, that before interaction humans must be constituted so as to be capable of it, as a stone or a fish is not. In that
sense the individual is prior to interaction, but in that sense the
individual is not yet a fully human self.[3]

Self-conscious mutual recognition is not an abstraction; it demands some structure of interaction: a set of roles, moves to be
made, customs to be followed so that I may recognize you as recognizing me. The structure of interaction is not logically subsequent
to the achieved selfhood of the individuals involved. It is a way for
them to be selves at all. In this sense the self exists only in interaction.

What is at stake here is whether social patterns, values, and customs should be taken as structures for interaction logically prior to
the individuals enabled through them, or whether they should be
taken in Weberian fashion as correlated sets of beliefs in the heads

of individuals who are already selves before the interactions these beliefs help shape. Hegel would argue that one cannot be a property holder, a citizen, a father, or even an aware self just by having events we would call beliefs and attitudes in one's head. There needs to be mutual recognition from others within a field of appropriate roles and actions. It follows that for Hegel theories of politics and society that begin with atomized individuals (whether or not these are in a "state of nature") are radically mistaken.

Structures of mutual recognition are not vaguely general. They exist in particular forms or not at all. Hegel discusses the many kinds of mutual recognition that humans can develop. In the historical lectures he treats these chronologically, while in the *Philosophy of Right* and the *Phenomenology of Spirit* the treatment is more structural and conceptual, though reference to history is not lacking.

Modern freedom does not consist in disassociating individuals from mutual recognition. Modern society depends as much as any other on structures of mutual recognition that are prior to the achieved selfhood of the individuals involved. Individualism depends not on an absence of but rather a particular kind of mutual recognition. What is peculiar to modern society is that the form of interaction is unusually bare.

In a traditional society such as heroic Greece, persons recognize one another as human through recognizing themselves as belonging to some appropriate role or group. Each member is aware of himself as recognizing and recognized by the others according to particular roles fitting into a social whole that is immediately present in the acts of all.

The unity of being-for-another and being-for-oneself, this universal substance, speaks its universal language in the customs and laws of its nation. . . . The laws proclaim what each individual is and does; the individual knows them not only as his universal objective . . . but equally knows himself in them, and in each of his fellow citizens. . . . Just as this unity exists through me, so it exists through the others too. (Phenomenology of Spirit 257/#351)

The single individual consciousness . . . is a solid unshaken trust in which spirit has not, for the individual, resolved itself into its abstract moments, and therefore he is not aware of himself as being a pure individuality on his own account. But once he has arrived at this idea, as he must, then this immediate unity . . . his trust, is lost. (Phenomenology of Spirit 259/#355)

Achilles *is* a hero, not a person deciding to be a hero or someone persuaded to assume the role of hero. His anxieties concern meeting the demands of the role identified with his self; he has no existential anxiety over whether or on what basis he has chosen to be a hero.

This immediate identification breaks down in the course of the history of the West. The breakdown occurs through tensions inherent in the immediate identification of the particular role and the universal good. Carrying out one's particular roles, which have the sacred sanction of the social whole, one comes into conflicts with other equally sanctioned roles. The situation is portrayed in Hegel's interpretation of Sophocles' *Antigone*. It leads people to begin separating explicitly the particularity of the roles from the wholeness of the universal society. What had been fused together and provided the identity for the individual self falls apart. The individual self no longer has a clear definition on either side. Socrates stands as a sign of this split when he offers a way back to wholeness, but a way mediated though the investigating mind of the individual person.

Hegel traces this development through history to its culmination in modern times. Man is freed from identification with contingent social roles and values, whether particular or general. "A man counts as a man in virtue of his manhood alone, not because he is a Jew, Catholic, Protestant, German, Italian, etc." (Philosophy of Right #209z). The recognition of this principle begins with Socrates, and its institutionalization begins with Roman law, but only in civil society is it freed from all restrictions and made the basis of a social life based on a purely formal description of persons in terms of freedom and property. "The concept of liberty, as it exists as such, without further specification and development, is abstract subjectivity, as a person capable of property" (Encyclopedia #539). We will see later why the "concept" is said to "exist as such"; for now we want to investigate the modern notion of individuality functioning in civil society.

Civil society's definition of an individual as a free being, capable of property, connotes a whole framework of interaction and institutional roles that are quite formal in their nature. Being capable of property is not a quality which an individual can possess by himself. Individuals in civil society recognize one another as selves who recognize each other as people capable of putting their freedom into objects they own. My recognition of you as capable of owning property, which I respect as you respect mine—that structure of mutual recognition is carried by a whole system of contract and exchange. What is modern is that no limitations of privilege or status are required for you to be a person in this sense, and there are no substantive restrictions from the market on what we may contract about (though there are some procedural restrictions). Modern persons recognize one another as individuals who can make choices and have needs: first the need to exist and make choices and have a hold in the world through property, then the natural needs connected with self-maintenance, then socially developed needs. Even the natural needs exist as involved in a social structure of mutual recognition.

Through this structure, individuals come to define themselves in the modern fashion described in the first chapter. The purity and formality of the structures of mutual recognition in civil society define a purified and formal individuality, distinct from a person's social roles. All the substantive content of life such as natural gifts, talents, labor power, but also values and ways of thinking and living, become objects of individual choice by the now purified individual subject. The institutions of civil society presume that individuals will have definite goals and content to bring to their interactions, but the structure of mutual recognition does not depend on the content being this or that in particular. We have seen such a relation between formal universality and particular content in the last chapter.

There is then a double separation of formal process from particular content. First, civil society as a formally defined process of interaction does not care what particular content I bring to it. Second, my basic recognized and self-recognized identity as a modern citizen is as a free person. Mutual recognition, and hence self-identity, does not depend on any particular content. My identity as free is primary; what I choose is secondary. Even my needs and desires are a content with which I am not fully identical. I experience this when I must choose among them and order them with measure and rationality. I show I am not identical with my needs by searching for happiness, which is not merely a sum of satisfied needs but a unified whole involving thought and ordering of my needs. In making these choices and measures I cannot fall back on any guaranteed traditional content or role. I must choose the measure, and this gives me experience of my identity defined as a formal and empty chooser.

The self-sufficiency mentioned in Hegel's definition of civil society is not isolation. There is no Robinson Crusoe ideal. In civil society people are dependent upon one another for the fulfillment of their needs. The self-sufficiency in question is the independence with which each individual gives his life content. All are free to construct goals and follow chosen desires and needs. They need not care about the whole. Civil society is the product of self-centered motives, not of political wisdom and virtuous action such as the ancient state demanded. Civil society's members should feel no pressure to care for the whole except the formal requirements of procedural justice and the external requirements of trade and exchange. Granted that these may be considerable pressures; still, in taking account of them the individual is in principle self-sufficient in determining the particular shape of his or her life. What is distinctive about civil society is not that it does away with structures of mutual recognition but that it renders those structures empty and formal.

Freedom and the Novelty of Civil Society

Hegel's account of modernity differs from Weber's because it does not presume methodological individualism. This difference has consequences for history. For Weber, substantive goals have always rested on individual choice and attitude, but individuals were pushed into their roles and attitudes without individual reflection and choice. Their basic freedom was concealed, but modernity has demystified man's situation. Hegel, however, does not admit that individualism has always been a hidden truth about the foundations of society and culture. The modern self is the achievement of a long process, and modern individualism as such is something new in history. Civil society is not the final recognition of a permanent condition; it is the creation of a new condition. This is true because the structures of mutual recognition, and the consequent selfhood of the individuals involved, change at different stages of history.

This may seem an improbable claim. Even though Hegel tells a good historical tale, surely men have always in some sense been free. Isn't civil society just the recognition of that freedom?

When Hegel discusses human freedom abstractly, in the early sections of the *Philosophy of Right*, he distinguishes two component moments. (The word *moment* is used by Hegel to refer to aspects distinguished and united in the dialectic. He probably took the word not from temporal instants but from something like "moment of inertia" or similar quantities which can be distinguished, measured, but not separated from one another.) Freedom implies first the ability to pull back from my desires and impulses into a unity with myself as ego so that I am not automatically determined by the dictates of my desires and impulses. "The will contains the element of pure indeterminacy or that pure reflection of the ego into itself which involves the dissipation of every restriction and every content either immediately presented by nature, by needs, desires, and impulses, or given and determined by any means whatever" (Philosophy of Right #5). Then freedom means the ability to move from that state of indetermination—to determine myself. The chosen content will be *mine* in a stronger sense than a desire or impulse I happen to have is mine. "At the same time, the ego is also the transition from undifferentiated indeterminacy to differentiation and determination, positing some determination as a content and object" (Philosophy of Right #6). Hegel does not assume that the self produces the content of its choices out of nothing. In our choices we freely take up content found either in nature or found within the logical development of spirit. "Now, further, this content may either be given by nature or engendered by the concept of spirit." This distinction will be relevant later when we ask how Hegel develops content for modern subjectivity.

In the *Philosophy of Right* Hegel more or less appeals to experience to verify this description, and he remarks that the real proof lies in the development of the concept of the self already accomplished in his logic (#4).

What is new about modernity is that this process of freedom as withdrawal and self-determination is institutionalized in a more complete way. In earlier societies there was no separation between a person's identity as a person and his or her definite social role. It is true that a person could have drawn such a separation in his or her own thought, but there was no institution in which one could live a life based on that separation. The separation was not recognized within the structures by which people confirmed one another's selfhood in society. There was no form of mutual recognition set up for "human person as such" and truly empty of contingent social content. There were always references to this tribe, this people, this nation, this role, these beliefs, these manners, to define what it was to be a human being as such. If someone tried to live a definition of his or her humanity in abstraction from all socially given content, the result was a powerless inner life in thought or withdrawal from society.

Throughout the history of the West the notion of human identity was gradually purified of contingent content. During the French Revolution people attempted a society and politics with structures of recognition that defined individuals as pure choosers. But this attempt defined the self only negatively, as not restricted by contingent content. The result was destructive of society.

[In the first aspect of freedom] it is only one side of the will which is described . . . my flight from every content as from a restriction. When the will's self-determination consists in this alone . . . we have negative freedom. This is the freedom of the void which rises to a passion and takes shape in the world; while still remaining theoretical, it takes shape in religion as the Hindu fanaticism of pure contemplation, but when it turns to actual practice, it takes shape in religion and politics alike as the fanaticism of destruction. . . . Only in destroying something does the negative will possess the feeling of itself as existent. Of course it imagines that it is willing some positive state of affairs, such as universal equality or universal religious life, but in fact it does not will that this shall be positively actualized, and for this reason: such actuality leads at once to some sort of order, to a particularization of organizations and individuals alike; yet it is precisely out of the annihilation of particularity and objective characterization that the self-consciousness of this negative freedom proceeds. (Philosophy of Right #5z)

Hegel analyzes the Terror during the revolution as a product of this negative freedom, which can never allow itself to be structured in institutions. Charles Taylor has drawn attention to many ways in which this analysis applies to movements and sentiments in our own recent history.[4]

Civil society involves institutions that allow men to live a life defined by their pure human freedom. It does this in structures of mutual recognition that distinguish the formal process of freedom from its content. When I recognize you as a free person capable of property and contract and labor, I recognize you in a way affirming both self-withdrawal and self-determination. One does not contract with an animal incapable of the self-control needed to keep a promise. In the mutuality of civil society I recognize you as recognizing me as a pure self not identified with any particular role or content of choice. As a result I can relate to myself in a new way. My own free individuality can become a focal aspect of my existence in a way it could not in earlier cultures, when it was not involved as such in the process of mutual recognition.

So, for Hegel, civil society is something radically new, and the kind of individuality it creates has not existed before, even in a hidden fashion. Civil society embodies both the negative and positive aspects of freedom, under the sign of the separation of formal process from content. In Hegel's jargon that distinction is now *posited* as such within the community and within the individual. Freedom is taken into account in a new and powerful way in the new mode of social relation and the new mode of self-related individuality.

It seems obvious that the description I have so far given of civil society is somewhat idealized. We often judge our societies deficient in regard to equality or procedural justice or other ideals implied in the notion of civil society. The fact that we do make such judgments indicates, however, that such ideals are active in a special way. An appeal to a purified notion of human identity and its consequences for procedural justice would have meant little to a slaveholding Greek or to a Han dynasty Chinese landowner. Also, the notion of endless progress so congenial to modern society implies that there are no substantive values whose achievement would define the goal of progress. If there were such substantive goals, progress would have a visible final stage when the substantive goals had been achieved, or at least there would be ways to measure the approach to such goals. Thus it seems the structure of mutual recognition in our society does contain reference to the formal purity Hegel described, even if the everyday reality of our society does not always live up to what it implies. This question is misleading in any case, since it presupposes that civil society could furnish the complete structure for human life, which Hegel will argue is impossible. Hegel will contend (as will I in a different fashion) that civil society in its purity does not exist and cannot exist as a social whole; hence, the lack of purity on the part of modern institutions is not surprising. The question then becomes, within what kind of larger context do the supposedly purely formal institutions really exist?

The Critique of Civil Society

Hegel celebrates the achievement of modern freedom, and worries about its effects. Civil society is based on a separation, but full freedom demands unity as well. "The will . . . is the self-determination of the ego, which means that at one and the same time the ego posits itself as its own negative, i.e. as restricted and determinate, and yet remains by itself, i.e. in its self-identity and universality. It determines itself and yet at the same time binds itself together with itself" (Philosophy of Right #7). The institutions of civil society embody self-determination, but they do not do so fully. The separation of formal process from content seems to allow full freedom, but in fact it causes problems leading on to a further stage. Hegel analyzes those problems in the *Phenomenology of Spirit*, chapter 6, and in his discussion of the transition from civil society to state in the *Philosophy of Right*.

My freedom is not linked to any particular content. "As *this* will it has no content of its own" (Philosophy of Right #137). That is not to say I have no content. I am amply provided with desires and needs and impulses and ideals both natural and socially encouraged. Too amply provided—I must choose among them. I must either passively accept the strongest impulses or find some criterion of choice. Civil society tells me only to respect others, be efficient, and choose goals that fit into the general circulation of needs and commodities. It tells me a great deal about means but nothing about ends. This leaves me free to choose my goals. The situation is familiar from Weber's description of the dominance of formal rationality. Hegel finds it unsatisfactory.

Many people would argue that civil society's version of freedom is the ideal. Hegel disagrees and argues against this individualistic point of view in four ways. First, he tries to show that civil society left to itself produces a whole catalogue of harms. Second, he argues that civil society leads to an inhumane culture. Third, he tries to show in the *Science of Logic* that the structural categories behind civil society presume a more encompassing context, that is, that a formally universal process can exist only as an aspect of a more concrete whole. Fourth, congruent with the logical analysis, he tries to show in the *Philosophy of Right* that within civil society there are self-transcending tendencies that lead to a deeper kind of mutual recognition in the more encompassing community he calls the state. I will examine the first two arguments in the remainder of this chapter; the third and fourth arguments will be in the following chapters.

Because of their empty formal quality, modern modes of mutual recognition imply no natural limits on society's activity. There are no substantial values or traditions limiting what kinds or quantities can be taken up into civil society's circulation of needs and goods. Hence, all aspects of civil society can expand without restriction from within. The accumulation of capital and the growth of markets are encouraged by the expansion of needs, for there is no way within civil society to say some needs are unnatural and should be shunned. As the system expands, the means of production grow more refined, which for Hegel meant more specialized. The workers come to lead a more machinelike life, while the rich can live a more opulent life, satisfying what may become quite trivial needs. More and more aspects of human life can come to be treated as commodities to be exchanged. Nothing is sacred.

There are, of course, always external restrictions such as scarcities of natural resources or limited population. When the expanding system of needs meets such obstacles, it will seek new resources and new markets, overleaping the oceans until it becomes a worldwide system. As Shlomo Avineri has shown, Hegel's discussions of poverty and alienation, crises of production, colonialism and international tension within civil society show depressingly accurate foresight.[5]

A catalog of economic harms, no matter how long, does not by itself show a need for the state as a sphere superordinate to civil society. In fact, Hegel himself accepted most of the economic bad effects of civil society as inevitable. The state could exercise ameliorative action but could not eradicate the harms rooted in the structure of civil society. Hegel confessed he saw no solution to growing inequities in the distribution of wealth and the creation of a rabble (*Pöbel*) not caught up in the attempt to mediate all social oppositions. Hegel presents these as problems for future action to lessen as much as possible. They are sad but necessary products of "the work of the negative" within history. There is a deep sense in which Hegel, with all his metaphysical optimism, was less optimistic historically and socially than Marx.

Hegel did not regard, however, the cultural dangers of civil society as inevitable. The freedom of civil society, because of its separation from all content, threatened to trivialize life and convert all human relations into commodity relations. "Individuals will exist for each other only by means of objects of the will and so 'only as owners' " (Philosophy of Right #40; Ritter 1982, 137; cf. Riedel 1970, 46). This could not be the last word about human life.

Likewise, because of its liberating separation of the act of choice from any particular content, civil society uproots individuals, depriving their lives of the weight given them by traditional roles and values. Human relations become matters of contract, and there is nothing to be respected for itself. Because of this, and because individuals define themselves as empty of any substantive content, it is caprice, accident and idiosyncrasy that will settle the direction of life. Individual freedom, given full play and no direction, trivializes human life.

In civil society each member is his own end, everything else is nothing to him. But except in contact with others he cannot attain the whole compass of his ends, and therefore these others are means to the end of the particular member. A particular end, however, assumes the form of universality through this relation to other people, and it is attained in the simultaneous attainment of the welfare of others. Since particularity is inevitably conditioned by universality, the whole sphere of civil society is the territory of mediation where there is free play for every idiosyncrasy, every talent, every accident of birth and fortune, and where waves of every passion gush forth, regulated only by reason glittering through them. Particularity, restricted by universality, is the only standard whereby each particular member promotes his welfare. (Philosophy of Right #182a)

Those who see in modern individualism the ultimate form of human association have a powerful argument against Hegel at this point. "You, Hegel, admit that the economic difficulties the free market system causes some people are necessary to its functioning and can only be alleviated, not removed completely. Why not say the same about the cultural effects of civil society? What you call harms are the price of freedom. We must face the possible emptiness of our lives in a realm of freedom, and then boldly choose to give ourselves worthwhile content for our lives." Answering this objection will bring us deeper into Hegel's critique of modernity.

Civil society is one realization of modern freedom. There are others as well, in religion, in art, in science, in philosophy. In chapter 6 of the *Phenomenology of Spirit*, Hegel discusses many areas in which the separations typical of modernity are embodied in the centuries from Luther to Goethe: for example, the Enlightenment mode of analysis into simple units; deism; the leveling effects of utilitarian ethics; the fight between cold clear demythologizing intellect and warm living appeals to the heart; Kant's formal analysis of human life; Jacobi's foundation of all knowledge on an act of faith; the romantic yearning for a beyond that cannot be given content on pain of destroying the yearning; the cult of the beautiful soul too pure to be sullied in action; morality conceived as an infinite task never to be reconciled with empirical conditions; and the glorifying of ironic distance as the only stable stance in art and life. Diverse and mutually at war as these trends might be, the space within which they and their disputes took place was shaped by the modern divisions of formal process from particular content and universal rule from particular self.

Many of these forms of life and thought exhibit a duplicity Hegel finds throughout the modern insistence on freedom. To demand freedom from all particular content is, in the end, to put yourself all the more thoroughly under the domination of contingent and arbitrary content. When no content is accepted as binding and authoritative, one does not get purity and transcendence; rather, one is controlled by changing whims and arbitrary impulses, which one mistakes for sovereign freedom. An individual who lives only by the rule that he will decide his own goals and values can reach

the culminating form of this subjectivity which conceives itself as the final court of appeal . . . subjectivity knowing itself as the arbiter and judge of truth, right, and duty. . . . As the master of law and thing alike, I simply play with them as with my caprice; my consciously ironical attitude lets the highest perish and I merely hug myself at the thought. This type of subjectivism not merely substitutes a void for the whole content of ethics, right, duties, and laws—and so is evil—but in addition its form is a subjective void, i.e. it knows itself as this contentless void and in this knowledge knows itself as absolute. (Philosophy of Right #140)

The dialectical twist remains that such an individual in such a posture really lives at the mercy of his impulses and whims, the most immediate and least thoughtful content for life.

The question remains whether this is not a price we must pay for freedom. Hegel argues that in trying to relate to ourselves and others as pure and free we are tied to contingent content all the more firmly. True self-determination has not been fully achieved. Civil society illustrates this dialectic but masks it by the efficient satisfaction of needs. Though in fact the member of civil society never identifies himself with any of his needs and impulses, his life is nonetheless ruled by them. He has nothing beyond them to give content to his life. The emptiness of his freedom and his domination by impulse are among the roots of the endless drive for *more* which infects every aspect of civil society.

It sounds as if Hegel is advocating a return to traditional society that will place restrictions and define goals. He does wish to find restrictions and goals, but not in the givenness of simple tradition. He is trying to find a third alternative. Today people may try to return to a traditional life (find a guru, return to the land, embrace a fundamentalist religious or political faith) or they can live a de-racinated and formal modern life. Many of our political and cultural debates are framed in these terms, whether the labels be conservative and liberal, or religious and humanistic, or others. Hegel wants a new kind of individuality, different both from the traditional self identified with its role and its values and from the modern self distanced from all content.

How is this to be done? The problem is to find a nonarbitrary and yet nonimposed criterion for deciding what goals to pursue and what desires to prefer over others. Civil society offers only formal rationality, but this does not select goals; it only tests means. Only a criterion with some content can suggest where civil society should be limited and guided and what aspects of life should be off limits to civil society's leveling effects.

Hegel says that the guides we need are customs, *Sitten*. We need customs that tell us what kind of person we should be. Customs are ways of life in a community, structures for mutual recognition. Looked at another way, they are sets of rights and duties.

But how are we to find these customs? Modernity has emerged from submission to traditional customs. We cannot just return to the solidity of traditional community. Free subjectivity cannot be un-discovered. We could only return ironically, our customs something chosen and at the disposal of the modern individual. Along that path lies either playacting or the self-deceiving that Sartre called "bad faith." Even if we could return, modernity would reassert itself since it results from tensions within the seeming solidity of traditional culture. There is no escape backwards.

Hegel saw Kant as providing the clue to a solution though Kant himself remained tied to separations of form from content, which Fichte and some romantics took even further. They appealed to a formal self that swallows up everything in its own self-relation, but leaves us in practical matters with the thoroughly untranscended empirical self and its contingent content.

Still, Kant had seen that objective content could be found by an analysis of the conditions of freedom. In Kant's theory of knowledge not just any sequence of perceptions will qualify as perceptions of an independent object; there are rules derived from an analysis of the nature of experience that allow one to distinguish objective content. What is "objective" in this sense is the nonarbitrary, not-up-to-me, even if it can only exist through me. In Kant's practical philosophy, not just any sequence of actions will qualify as a free decision. Rules derived from an analysis of the nature of freedom allow one to distinguish.

Hegel mixes Kantian and Aristotelian themes. The customs we need to give content to our lives resemble Aristotle's taken-for-granted social background and its virtues that describe what kind of persons we should be. But Hegel does not take the customs directly from any particular society. He tries to find a structure of customs implied by the concept of freedom itself. Kant tried something similar, but he remained bound to dualities that undermined his attempt. Hegel sets out to find a deeper structure within freedom, what he will call the "absolute form" of freedom as opposed to the "abstract form" of freedom—the structure found in Kant's analysis and embodied in civil society. The absolute form of freedom is more complex than the two stages of withdrawal and self-determination so far discussed. When the conditions for the existence of this fuller notion of freedom are studied, the structure of the state will appear. The state is the fuller community within which civil society has its concrete existence and is given rational limits.

Thus the task of finding customs that will give content to modern individuality without canceling its freedom turns out to be the process described in Hegel's third and fourth arguments against the ultimacy of civil society. These arguments trace the developments Hegel believes are inherent in the logical structures of formality and universality and in the concrete lived structures of civil society. The result will be a fuller context that contains and limits modernity while making it possible in the first place.

3

Hegel's Logic and Its Movements

Hegel wants to affirm the power and success of modern individuality and its institutions. They have achieved a new level of freedom and creativity. Yet left unchecked they turn into empty inhumanity. In order to overcome the excesses of modern subjectivity, Hegel wants to rethink what modern individuals are and what context they fit within. Though he disagrees with some crucial features of modernity, he is not fleeing from it in a way that leaves it unchanged. Nor is he accepting modernity as it describes itself and merely adding something to qualify it. He will criticize our categories for thinking about modern subjectivity, and propose new ones fitting modernity into a larger context.

Hegel takes on the task of bringing together the free individuality of modern citizens with the solid community of traditional society, though neither will remain unchanged in the new combination. Put in Hegel's technical terms, the problem is that the difference, but not the unity, of formally universal process and particular content has been posited in the institutions and selves of modern man. When the unity is posited as well as the difference, there will be deeper human identity and community.

In order to see why Hegel thinks civil society must exist within the deeper community he calls "the state," we need to spend some time looking at the abstract categories he develops for describing the unity of self and of society. This demands that we have a sense of how Hegel's logic works and what he thinks it can achieve. This and the next two chapters discuss Hegel's logic as it is relevant to modernity.

The Need for the Logic

Hegel believes that only by integrating modern subjectivity into a systematic context can the excesses of modernity be controlled. "System" means that particular content has been developed and linked to form a nonarbitrary whole. Not just any chosen content will fit into a system. Hegel wants a system not out of a passion for unity but because he can see no other way to heal the splits on which modern subjectivity bases itself. Only a system, and only one with the peculiar circular nature of Hegel's own, can encompass the power of modern subjectivity. Any system of thought or society that had a linear structure, moving from fixed starting points to conclusions, would fail to stop the power of modern individuals to question starting points and transcend given solutions. Modern subjects define themselves by the way they stand beyond whatever is before them for inspection, judging and manipulating as they choose. Hegel believes that only a system like his own, which incorporates the movement of subjectivity within a larger circular motion, can provide modern individuality with content intimate enough to permit nonarbitrary limits on and directions for the decisions and activities of such individuals.

In addition, Hegel feels that only a system of speculative logic can give the clarity needed to locate and limit modern subjectivity without violating the modern right to knowledge and self-determination. Clarity may seem a strange word to use in connection with Hegel, but perhaps this is because people today do not often read Hamann or Böhme or Schelling. Hegel feels that only the self-inclusion and self-transparency his logic provides could insert modern individuality into its proper context, and not risk appealing to inarticulate faith or vague intuitions of unity, which violate the modern right to know.

The logic is the core of Hegel's system. When he describes civil society as "an association of members as self-sufficient individuals in a universality which because of their self-sufficiency is only formal" (Philosophy of Right #157) the logical terminology of *universal*, *individual*, and *formal* is crucial. Hegel's use of these terms is revisionary. He rethinks most of the common ontological and logical categories. In reworking and reconnecting the categories involved in subjectivity and individuality he finds the "objective content" he seeks as a base for a mode of life richer than civil society.

Many who write about Hegel find his concrete analyses in the *Phenomenology of Spirit* and the *Philosophy of Right* insightful but the logical analysis devious and frustrating. Why embed perceptive social commentary in an outdated metaphysics we can no longer take seriously? Charles Taylor claims that "while Hegel's ontology is near incredible his philosophy is very relevant to our age" (1979, 135). Taylor is the most articulate spokesman for accepting Hegel's concrete diagnoses and rejecting the metaphysical cure. Anthony Quinton encourages the same attitude in a review of Hegel literature in the *New York Review of Books*: "Hegel's metaphysics is composed of all the dross in Kant, carefully purged of all his insight. . . . [People should] confine themselves to Hegel as a theorist of society and culture" (1975, 42). Taylor draws from Hegel's discussion of structures of mutual recognition an argument against the modern conception of subjectivity. While I am sympathetic to this argument, I think that his interpretation of Hegel as offering a similar point enlarged to cosmic proportions mistakes Hegel's mode of procedure in dealing with modernity.

Although I agree with Taylor that Hegel's solution is not workable, my overall interpretation is different. The more concrete discussions cannot easily be separated from Hegel's logical analysis. If the logic could be put aside, then Hegel's treatment of modern society would be based only on the discussion of the harms of civil society, which we looked at in the last chapter. A firm defender of modernity can dismiss those harms as problems to be worked at in the modern way or as the inevitable costs of freedom. Weber could agree with all Hegel's worries, then give a resigned sigh. Hegel wants a stronger argument, and he believes that the logical analysis provides it. I will try to make clear the nature of that argument and how it guides the concrete analysis.

What the Logic Is Doing

To understand why Hegel thinks his logic has something to say about modern life, we need to understand what Hegel is trying to do. This is a difficult matter about which there are many disputes. Hegel says that "philosophy may be said to do nothing but transform representations into thought" (Encyclopedia #20). Philosophy makes available to us the categorial structure of the thinking that turns images and sensations into knowledge of things in the world. It is in the determinations of thought and in the concept that anything is what it is. Hegel will study the categories through which we think of anything as real. The enterprise resembles Kant's transcendental deduction but does not share Kant's goal of finding conditions of possibility for thought within finite subjectivity.[1]

Hegel said that his logic was a metaphysics, but he was using the word as Kant did when he spoke of the "metaphysics of morals" or the "metaphysics of nature." For Kant these denote studies of the necessary structure of our knowing activity in the areas in question and, therefore, the necessary structure of all rational actions or knowable objects in those areas. Discovering such structure enables Kant to critique attempts to extend knowledge beyond the field opened and organized by the necessary categories and principles. Hegel's logic will be a metaphysics in this Kantian sense, a study of the necessary structure of thought. It is a transcendental analysis of the categories of thought rather than a precritical attempt to hypothesize or intuit the necessary structures of being.

While Hegel adopts Kant's transcendental analysis, he subverts Kant's attempt to locate the conditions for knowledge within a larger field that can be "thought" but not "known." As a result Hegel's critique will not be practiced by limiting knowledge to a part of what is thinkable but by showing that the view to be critiqued involves categories not fully developed.

Hegel wants Kant's crucial distinctions of subject from object and appearance from reality to be made within the sequence of categories in the logic and not, as he interprets Kant to say, within the nature of the finite subject. He does not use the subject-object distinction to tell a story about the status of the sequence of categories itself. There cannot be for Hegel two stories, one about the categories necessary for our thought to understand the world and another about the ontological location or basis of our thought. Still less can there be a story we can never know, about "things in themselves." In this sense Hegel is an idealist, but to say that the categories are therefore only "in" or "products of" a mind is to mistake his view. To say that the subject-object relation is within the system of categories of thought is not to say that it is within your act or my act of thinking, in Berkeleyan fashion. On the other hand, it is not the triviality that subjects and objects are one thing we think about.

Hegel is closer to Plato and Aristotle in their claim that the forms and categories of things are independent of subjective thought. Yet he wants to marry this approach with the modern insistence on the activity and primacy of the subject.

What the Logic Is Not Doing

While Hegel studies the categories of thought he does not claim that a large mind, spirit, or God makes the structures of thought and reality what they are. Hegel's claim is both more modest and more audacious. Nothing makes the categories of reality; they are, and they can be known in their self-contained, self-generating necessary interrelations and inclusions. The logic studies the genesis and interconnection of the categories. If the study is complete, thought should arrive at a fully adequate self-description not involving connections to anything other than itself. The logically developed sequence of categories will be self-sufficient, needing no reference to acts of will or choice or construction except insofar as these are already thought within the sequence.

The categories behind modern individualism and civil society will be criticized precisely for not being self-sufficient, for needing to be included within more complex thought structures if they are to be thought at all. Correspondingly, the institutions and modes of life which embody the categories of individualism and civil society cannot be final; they must be embedded within a richer set of institutions and practices making it possible for them to be at all. Modernity exists within a necessary context not describable in the usual modern terms. Our task is to stop pretending modernity is absolute and to act within the sustaining and limiting context.

Hegel himself does not use the words *transcendental* and *category* as I have in the above paragraphs. He tends to restrict the term *category* to the structures of thought in the first part of the logical sequence, and he uses *transcendental* mainly when referring to Kant. He prefers the term *speculative* to distinguish his own method. In current English *transcendental* is likely to have fewer misleading connotations than *speculative*, which usually designates elaborate metaphysical constructions beyond any evidence. But Hegel's logic is not a metaphysics in the usual sense.

When I say the logic is not a metaphysics, I want most of all to preclude the idea that Hegel provides a cosmology including the discovery of a wondrous new superentity, a cosmic self or a world soul or a supermind. In the English-speaking world, Charles Taylor and, more recently, Michael Inwood have offered influential interpretations of this sort.[2]

Hegel does not solve the problems of modernity by telling us that we are all parts of some large entity. Such interpretations of Hegel sin by taking for granted some category, usually "mind" or "subject," and then making it very large (and often complaining either that we get swallowed up or that our relation to the large entity is puzzling). Perhaps Hegel's system as a whole tells us in some sense what is real, but the logic is not a collection of metaphysical claims. It is a study of the categories that must be used in thinking. It makes no claim except that various structures of thought cannot really stand on their own but must be included as moments in other structures. Among the ways of thought rejected are those used in the cosmological or large entity interpretations of Hegel.[3]

Charles Taylor's reading in terms of expressive unity presents Hegel solving all dilemmas by advocating that we realize our involvement in the life of a cosmic subject with purposes that our finite subjectivity realizes and expresses. (See Taylor 1979, 55–6, 62, 79–80, and the analogous passages in Taylor 1975.) Hegel's distance from "expressive pantheism" is greater, however, than Taylor thinks (Taylor 1979, 139). Hegel's "teleology" is not a question of purpose, as if the cosmic subject chose among various possibilities this or that particular set, but a matter of discerning what it means for there to be possibilities at all for anything. Taylor's picture is too personalized. It is less true that there is a cosmic subject wanting to "know itself in the world" (Taylor 1979, 73) than that the system enforces self-coincidence, presence, transparency, on reality in general and as a whole. This is true not because there is a subject who wants to know itself but because this is what it means to be or to be thought at all. The reconciliation Hegel wants is to be discovered by studying the conditions for anything to exist. Any cosmic subject would be subject to such conditions; it would not itself be such a condition, as Taylor seems to suggest. It is better to speak in terms of total rationality. Hegel is more of a panlogist than a pantheist, if *logos* is properly understood as the gathering of all things into clarity and self-coincidence. Taylor is thinking in terms of metaphysical claims instead of in the self-enclosed circle of the logic and the system.

The question is not whether we find a cosmic subject incredible but whether that circle closes and encloses.

This does not mean the logic has no bearing on traditional metaphysical questions. Some questions, such as "what is the relation between body and soul?" are undermined and discarded as depending on inadequate categories. When the categories are straightened out, the question vanishes. Other questions, such as "is reality composed of a mass of discrete singular entities contingently related, as the atomists have said?" are answered ("on some levels, yes, but overall, no"). But even here the "answer" comes through a discovery that the rejected alternative depends on inadequate categorial structures. We will look at this question again when we examine the problem of "applying" the logic.

It may seem that I am trying to deemphasize the side of Hegel most familiar in history texts: the monistic absolute, the updated Spinoza, the revised metaphysics for Christianity. Hegel did want to join Kant and Spinoza and to provide a way to think through Christianity in the modern world. But I insist that Hegel's solution for modernity is not some resignation of the self into a large entity. Hegel's opinions about what exists and how it exists are expressed through the overarching unity of the system, not through metaphysical claims. He does not develop a set of categories and then offer them in hypotheses about what kinds of external entities do or do not exist.

Treating the logic as a study of categorial genesis and categorial relations tends to underplay the aspect of love, life, and existential pathos in Hegel. He is, however, trying to think such important experiences through the logical categories and so recast them. He is not using the logical categories as code words for already familiar ideas and experiences. Hegel wants to give the familiar words new dimensions by setting them in the basic context revealed in the categorial study.

We will see later that Heidegger criticizes Hegel for being too "metaphysical" (in yet another sense of that polyvalent word). One reason for my austere interpretation of the logic is to highlight the confrontation between these two thinkers. If we interpret Hegel as proposing some cosmology or large entity, then Heidegger's reproach strikes home too easily. In fact, Heidegger's objection applies even to the categorial interpretation of Hegel's system; this will make the crucial issues between the two thinkers all the more apparent.

Involuted Movements

As the logic moves, more complex differences and unities and in-clusions appear in the categories treated. The order is systematic and necessary, Hegel claims. The context that makes possible the simpler beginning categories is gradually made explicit within the richer ending categories. Finally there is a complete capturing of the context within the categories. (This last is a claim at which a long tradition of critiques of Hegel, including Heidegger's, takes aim.) The early categories are abstract versions of the fuller thought structures of the later categories, which include the earlier ones properly unified and put in their mutual relationships.

In general the chain of categories moves from less to more dif-ferentiated, but there are doublings and twists; there is no simple advance. In fact the image of a chain is not really appropriate at all, despite the lovely pullout chart in Stace ([1924] 1955) and the seductive linear table of contents in most editions.

Hegel's books do consist of a series of narrated transitions, but the movement is not a linear sum of a series of microtransitions. It is better to think of the movement as one large gesture consisting of itself repeated in ever smaller units until it is made fully at the end, which encompasses the beginning. The large motion consists of workings out of itself in the small, but it is not built up from little independent transitions.

None of the categories of the logic are empirical concepts. To-gether they form the framework making empirical sense and ref-erence possible. Presenting them is not a matter of analyzing their components but of showing their involvement in their ever more explicitly nuanced context. That context turns out to be the logical sequence and its motions. It is as though Hegel were presenting a series of kernels for ever more complexly thought-out ontologies—not more inclusive ontologies, as if there were some neutral reservoir of entities becoming more and more incorporated, but ontologies with ever fuller conceptions of what it means to be.

Hegel says that the logic moves because of contradictions. There has been long debate on what he meant by this and whether he carried out what he promised. The most common opinion (Findlay and Henrich) is that he was not careful enough about formal logical terms and used "contradiction" when he meant only contrary con-cepts or conceptual tensions of various types, which he did succeed in illustrating. Others claim that he did mean strict contradiction but he did not in fact succeed in showing this (Düsing). Others argue that Hegel both meant and achieved contradictions in the modern sense (Hartmann, Winfield). My own claim below, that there is no criterion for deciding among various versions of the logical progression, implies that whatever the "motor" of the logical movement it does not achieve the strict necessary outcome Hegel wanted.[4]

The logic starts with categories of reality as just there, immediate being. When explored immediate being eventually gives way to categories of reality as existing by containing inner tension and division (essence and existence, ground and grounded, things and qualities, laws and their expressions, forms and matter, and so on). The third stage involves categories of reality as comprehensive unity existing through inner differentiation. It is on this third level that the categories appropriate to thinking civil society will be found.

The large movement (immediate presence, inner division, comprehensive unity) is repeated on smaller levels. For example, the section dealing with formal universality such as we find in civil society stands as the moment of inner division ("the particular universal") within the immediate presentation ("the concept") of the immediate presence ("subjectivity") of the moment of comprehensive unity in the logic, which is itself the moment of immediate universality within the system as a whole. I point out these involutions of the larger movement in order to dispel the idea that Hegel's thought is built up from the bottom rather than being unfolded on many levels, controlled by an overall movement.

Mediation and Positing

Hegel says near the end of the logic that there is nothing, whether in actuality or thought, that is as simple and abstract as commonly imagined. Nothing exists as just brutely given and simply possessing one or two fully positive characteristics. Nothing exists that is just first and primary and on which other things depend without mutual relation. People intend to think about such things, but they cannot really succeed in doing so unless they stay on the level of imaginative pictures. Imagining that such things exist is possible only as long as we are ignorant of what is actually present (Science of Logic 2:489/829). What appears at first simple and immediate is actually complex and mediated. *Mediation* and *mediated* (*Vermittlung, vermittelt*) and the opposites *im-mediacy* and *im-mediate* (*Unvermittlung, unvermittelt*) are key terms throughout Hegel and especially in the logic. Everywhere Hegel tries to find mediation, to find the work of the negative, to find how what appears simple and immediate actually exists through complex mediations and interdependencies.

Literally, to "mediate" is to be in the middle, to connect two extremes. This meaning suggests that the items mediated already exist independently, but Hegel tries to show that everything is mediated, that nothing exists as immediate first. There is nothing that is first and independent, except the motion of the whole, but even that motion cannot exist without its mediated content. In the logic, mediation will involve the gradual development of categories to a point where there is nothing that is posited as first or independent.

Mediation is a matter of detail; the simple assertion that everything is mediated says very little. Hegel demands that one trace the way each supposed immediate being is really mediated, and those ways differ in different cases. It is this attention to detail that distinguishes Hegel's system from some later "hegelianisms" that settle for global statements about the inner relations connecting everything. Hegel would say such systems are taking the fact of universal mediation as itself something immediate, rather than showing it developing from other attempted systems and from the facts of the matter (*die Sache selbst*) in detail.

The verb *to posit* has been used a few times so far and will be used more in what follows. The English word is a standard coinage to translate the German *setzen*, which is a quite ordinary word meaning "to put or place something." The English translation harks back to the old use of *positive* in English, as in "positive law" as distinct from "natural law." Natural law was simply there working, while positive law was placed into force by an act of a legislative body or a ruler. After Fichte, *setzen* came to be used with a technical meaning that in Hegel is fairly wide. On its most general level it means that within some sort of system a difference (or a unity) is significant for the working of the system. Thus a large mass held together by gravity, such as the moon, does not posit any difference of whole from parts, whereas an animal does when it will save its life by gnawing off its tail caught in a trap. The distinction of whole from part makes a difference in the behavior of the animal. Not all differences need be so posited; in civil society the difference between those desires I have because I belong to a certain religious or ethnic tradition and those desires I have just as random whims makes no difference to the operation of the market. That difference is not posited as a difference within civil society. In the state as Hegel envisions it, that distinction between kinds of desires will be important for how a person's decisions are treated. The difference will be posited as such.

It is clear that the prime instance of "positing" occurs with systems that are conscious or at least self-regulating. Hegel uses the term analogously for other kinds of systems. This is more understandable than Hegel's use of the term when speaking about categories in the logic. One category is more developed than another because some difference or unity is posited in the one but not in the other. This is difficult to understand, since it is hard to think of logical categories "doing" anything, let alone positing differences in the way a concrete system might do.

It is tempting to say that for a logical category to posit a difference is for a thinker using the category to be consciously aware of the difference. Unfortunately, this is not adequate; either it makes the thinker the source of the structure of the category, or it begs the question. To say that the English language posits explicitly a distinction of singular and plural in every noun (which Japanese, for example, does not) is not merely to say that English speakers are aware of this difference. There is also the implication that the rules of English force speakers constantly to mark this distinction. The speakers did not create the rule; in a sense the rule helped create them as speakers. Language rules are not constraints imposed on an already existing flow of speech. The rules allow the speakers to be speakers and make a series of vocal events into speech. Something analogous can be said for Hegel's categories. They do not arise as products within or constraints upon a previously existing flow of thought; they make a sequence of psychic events into a flow of thought.

To say that a logical category posits a difference is to say that the structure of the category includes it explicitly. A category is not a simple thing; it is a pattern or structure with an internal multiplicity of contrasts, inclusions, exclusions, and mediations of other categories.

Talking of logical categories as if they were things on their own is dangerous. But still more dangerous is talking as if categories of thought were tools that we make and shape at will. English-speaking philosophy has a strong voluntaristic bent: when we talk about a structure we tend to ask whose decision made the structure what it is. In the early days with Locke and Newton, it was God's decision that made structures of the world and of mind what they were. Later these became social and individual choices. So we analyze language into rules and these into conventions and these into social choices and these into individual choices. All this presupposes a typically modern individual separate from the structures presented to him.

Hegel calls the logic a study of pure thought. This does not mean that there is some energy or process called pure thought above the categories and producing them by its acts. The final movement of the logic will be to define pure thought in terms of the categories. Hegel is deeply opposed to voluntarism in any form. If forced to choose, he would say that structure comes before willing rather than vice versa. But he does not want to be forced to choose, and he works to remove the sharp distinction between a static structure and a flowing force or energy or decision.

For Hegel, it is wrong to talk of thinkers as active and of logical categories as their products or tools. It would be more correct to say that what exists is categories and structures that are realized in actual thinkers and actual thoughts. Thinkers and thoughts are on the same level: both embody the logical categories. This formulation, while it does capture Hegel's Platonic sympathies, is still misleading. It suggests that we might first inventory the categories of thought and then tell another story, with its own structures, about how the categories are realized. This is what Hegel interprets Kant as doing. Kant understood the need for a deduction of the categories, but he surrounded that deduction with a separate story about things-in-themselves that located and explained the status of the categories while itself using uncriticized structures. For Hegel there is only one story, and questions of the location and the status of the categories and their relation to reality are all raised and answered within the categorial sequence. The final word on what the categories are and how they relate to what is other than them is provided in the final category of the series. This demands of the logical sequence a peculiar kind of self-reference and is one reason why the system must be circular.[5]

A Sample Movement: Form and Content

Hegel's criticisms of modernity involve the claim that the categories by which modern subjectivity understands itself are not ultimate in the logical sequence. In order to understand this criticism better, we will look at how Hegel goes about deriving, then passing beyond, the category pair form and content. The pair is obviously not chosen at random, since this distinction is crucial to elaborating the standard picture of modernity we saw in the first chapter. By observing how Hegel locates these categories within the logical sequence, we can see what kind of argument he uses to undermine their adequacy. It will turn out that no categories that share the general features of such a pair are adequate for describing even civil society, let alone the more comprehensive unity of the state. We will have to move from a discussion of form and content to Hegel's treatment of formal universality.

Hegel's discussion of form and content occurs in the course of the second large division of the logical sequence, the logic of essence. The categories of essence involve variations on the theme of foundation and what is supported by that foundation, distinctions within entities of independent and dependent aspects of their reality. Many of the categories discussed are quite familiar: form and content, form and matter, things and qualities, existence and appearance, things and their laws.[6]

In the essence section most categories occur in pairs. Reality is thought of as having some inner essence that is the foundation for an outer manifestation.

> the immediate being of things is thus conceived under the image of a rind or curtain behind which the essence lies hidden. . . . There is therefore something more to be done than merely rove from one quality to another, and merely advance from the qualitative to the quantitative, and vice versa [as was done in the first section of the logic, the logic of immediate being]; there is something permanent in things, and that permanent is in the first instance their essence. (Encyclopedia #112a)

The inner being of things will be at first their "essence" but then their "ground" or their "form" or their "law" and so on through many varieties of foundational relations. What complicates the picture is that the categories of essence do not really consist of a firm base plus a shifting manifestation or appearance. That is what is intended, but Hegel wants to show that in each case both poles end up depending on each other, and firm primacy cannot be assigned in either direction. Attempts to stabilize the relations and make one side the definite foundation keep failing and resulting in transitions to another pair of categories.[7]

Because of its emphasis on tortuous inner mediations, the second part of the logic is the most obscure, and this obscurity is compounded because this section exists in two quite distinct versions. I will follow the longer treatment in the *Science of Logic*, where the categories involving form are grouped together. I will discuss later what implications might follow from a difficulty in deciding which of the two versions is to be preferred.

Several category pairs involving form occur as the first part of a long chapter on ground. In this chapter the ground of something's being is posited as an immediate first, a foundation not itself posited or mediated by anything else. The category of form is introduced as one of a pair of categories called form and essence, developed out of an earlier sequence. This pair changes into the pair form and matter, which in turn changes to form and content. This then moves into the category of determinate ground and a series of other attempts to think grounds and conditions.

(a) Form and Essence: The first of the categories involving form is that of form and essence (Science of Logic 2:67/448). In this pair the categories involve a distinction between a basic inner self-identity appropriate to each thing, and its expression in determinate outer form. (Essence here means the inner self-relation and not yet a basic nature or essential quality. That conception comes later in the sequence.) The inner self-relation of the thing is taken as primary and the determinate outer character as secondary or posited. The distinction involved may seem somewhat crude, and it is so in comparison with the more explicit familiar categories to come. But the distinction of form from essence has arisen from a whole series of earlier attempts to think the self-identity of each thing in terms that go beyond simple immediate presence (a mode of thinking already tried and found wanting in the first large section of the logical sequence).

The pair form and essence is not satisfactory. The definite character making a thing what it is and separating it from other things is not just an outward and posited aspect based on some inner self-relation that is indeterminate yet different in each thing. Form should not be conceived as connected to the self-identity of the thing in a dependent, passive way. The relation ought to be reversed. Form provides the difference that makes self-identity possible. The self-identity is not the prior element; it is the result of the thing's having a definite form. Self-identity is to be thought of as passive, receiving definiteness and determination from form, now conceived as an active source of determination rather than as a dependent result. This switch in priority is the transition to the category pair form and matter.

(b) Form and Matter: With the transition to form and matter the previous pair, form and essence, appears as an abstract and inadequate way of thinking about the relations that are now explicitly posited in the new pair. One can look back and see that the earlier categories failed to posit a crucial distinction between what accounts for definiteness and what accounts for subsistence. In the previous pair each side consisted of definite identity and an enduring subsistence joined in an immediate union that failed to allow the thought of either real definiteness or grounded subsistence. The pair form and matter explicitly posits that distinction by assigning one side to each of its members.

Matter is the aspect of endurance, defined as indifferent to form. For example, the clay of the statue has no predisposition to be formed one way or another, though it must exist under some form. This is an idealization, of course, since real clay will not support some forms, for example, extremely thin, long shapes. To the extent that the clay imposes restrictions on what forms it will accept, it is not pure matter but matter already formed in some way. Pure matter would be pliable and passive, enduring and supporting whatever form it was given. In the ideal version, the form contributes definiteness and determinate quality, and the matter contributes endurance and subsistence. In their combination, each allows the other to exist.

Philosophers have argued about the precise relation of form to matter, about whether a pure matter is really possible, and about other technical questions that Hegel does not treat directly. What he does is argue that there is no primacy with either pole of the relation. The whole statue may be thought of equivalently as a realized form or as formed matter. The statue is each member of the pair made fully real. Each member "contains the whole relation," and neither can be taken as the foundation for the other. Hegel works this out in a lengthy three-part criticism of various ways to assign primacy to one side or the other.

(c) Form and Content: Since the effort in this chapter of the *Science of Logic* is toward finding a fixed ground in one of the members of the pair of categories, failure to do so with the pair form and matter will be the transition to a new pair. If form and matter are distinguishable, one should be the ground of the other, but their mutual relation prevents this. To think of form as a first and immediate ground fails because form is only thought of as relating to something else that is its own subsistence. To think of matter presupposes form, because matter relates to form as to its own determination. Determinate shape and enduring subsistence, which were apportioned to form and matter respectively, cannot be separated in this way. But neither can they just be thrown immediately together, as they were in the pair form and essence. To remedy this is the task of the new pair form and content. From that new position, the pair form and matter is shown to be inadequate, because it fails to posit explicitly the necessary unity it implies. That unity is explicitly posited as "content" (Science of Logic 2:74–5/454).

The true ground on which the determinate character and the permanence of the entity rests is found in the content exhibited by the entity. Content is definite, at first inward or implicit, and then expressed in some definite, outward combination of form and matter. One content can be expressed in various combinations of form and matter. For example the content that is a circle can be expressed in a diagram on a blackboard, an equation in a book, a bronze circle. The content of Romeo and Juliet can be expressed in a play, an opera, a ballet, a movie. Each expression is itself a whole of form and matter now seen as grounded in the unifying content it expresses.

The category of form and matter now appears as an abstraction from the more highly elaborated notion of a content that can be expressed. Indeed this distinction of form from content is close to the Greek notion of *eidos* (usually translated "form") that has potential and then actual existence. (Hegel does not introduce the pair potentiality and actuality until more conceptual machinery has been developed, since the current categories are still at an early stage concerning possible foundational relations.)

The pair form and matter was derived from the first pair, form and essence, because form and matter successfully posited as distinct what the earlier pair had lumped immediately together. The pair form and matter in turn gave way to a new pair that explicitly posited the unity present in the first pair and presupposed but ignored in the second. The result is not a return to the earlier stage but a new kind of unity containing both the separation and the unity of definite determination and subsistence. This new unity is hardly the last word, however, and in its turn will suffer divisions. The pair form and content will turn out to be unsatisfactory, because it lacks any real determination in its grounding relation. It posits unity and differences but loses any way of accounting for the definite nature of the content, which is now just accepted as a first immediate given in each case. "Content" expresses only the tautologous reference of every appearance to a ground that is just that same quality made internal. Hegel at this point makes the obvious reference to "dormitive powers." The attempt to think in terms of an inner foundation for the being of things has not yet succeeded, and the categorial sequence continues on into more refined and differentiated conditions and conditioning relations.[8]

Hegel's Pattern of Argument

We have just seen an example of Hegel's oft repeated movement. A set of categories itself resulting from previous stages is criticized because some distinction has not yet been posited explicitly. The criticism of the categories does not leave us groping for replacements; the criticism consists precisely in the positing of the distinction (or later the unity) that is not explicitly present in the old categories. That positing is at the same time a criticism of the old categories and the announcement of the next categories. This is the process Hegel calls "determinate negation." A new set of categories thus develops, explicitly positing the distinction in question by assigning it to separate things or spheres or aspects. The new categories are criticized in turn for treating the posited distinction as if it were ultimate, and a third set of categories is introduced explicitly positing both the distinction and the unity of the aspects or spheres in question.

In the categories involving form it was definiteness and subsistence that were immediate, then distinguished, then united. The categories appropriate to the transition from traditional society to civil society to state form another such sequence, where broadly speaking the aspects in question will be the universal process of social interaction and the particular social values or ways of life.

However, the kind of relation of form and content appropriate to civil society cannot be described by any of the three pairs we have just examined. These concern aspects of things, not the distinction within a (social or other) system of a formal process from its particular content. The categories needed to think this relation are developed in the third major section of the logic.

The account I have just given is very incomplete; each of the transitions I have mentioned contains more aspects and is accomplished in its own threefold move or longer. The logic demands Joyce's ultimate insomniac reader. But we can now begin to see what kind of argument Hegel wants to develop. The earlier categories of the logical sequence give way to more elaborated categories that make the earlier ones appear as abstract and too immediate. Hegel's books are difficult, but the difficulty changes during the course of the reading. Many of the early categories of the logical sequence are difficult to understand because they are so primitive. They are notably less complex than the everyday categories we use. They do not yet posit distinctions and unities and differences we are used to noting.

Hegel wants to show that our ordinary categories such as form and content come out of a sequence into which they fit somewhere in the middle. It is in developing the precursors of ordinary categories that Hegel finds his warrant to proceed beyond the ordinary to the final categories, which are less familiar and have a new difficulty because of their unusual totalization. Hegel tries to show that ordinary categories belong in a series that both accounts for them and carries beyond them. The series also allows him to correct ordinary ways of thinking. In the case of form and matter, Hegel's version is quite close to the ordinary, but in other cases it is more revisionary. Hegel is giving the correct version of form and matter according to its necessary place in the logical sequence; he is not trying to deduce the ordinary or the Aristotelian versions of that relation.

If this is the kind of argument Hegel is building, the beginning of the sequence will be of considerable importance, but that question is beyond the scope of this study. According to Hegel, there can be only one beginning—the poorest, most abstract category, "being"—and from it the process must be necessary.

The revisionary quality of Hegel's argument means that Hegel is not under the obligation of including in the logic every purported category of thought found in history. He does, however, need to argue that the logical sequence is complete and that the unincluded categories are either illusory attempts or illegitimate combinations of genuine categories.

It is tempting to speak of the logical series as a genetic process, but it is a mistake to do so. We speak of the later categories being derived from the earlier, but in fact the order of dependence is the reverse. In trying to think through the earlier categories we find that their independence breaks down and they enter our thinking as moments of the later categories. Exactly the same will be true with civil society, both in its logical structure and in its operation. The development Hegel traces is to show that civil society cannot be thought to exist without being included in a larger whole, which is the fuller community he calls the state.

More Involutions

Through the gyrations with the three pairs involving form, the notion of a foundational ground has moved from empty inner relations (the essence of form and essence) to a definite content allowing various forms to appear. This change overcomes the separation of ground from definiteness, which was posited at the beginning of the chapter. In terms of the larger movement of the essence division of the logic, various aspects that were too immediately together have been successfully posited as separate, but without destroying the unity of the foundational enterprise. In terms of the largest movement of the logic, essence has shed some of the immediacy it had at the beginning, but the distinctions implicit in that immediate unity have not all been explicitly posited. Once they are so posited, the movement will begin to turn toward positing comprehensive unity and leaving behind the search for an inner foundation.

This clarifies the way in which the logical sequence is composed of nested motions on various levels. Various small versions of form and matter that I did not summarize fail to articulate the relations intended in that pair. That pair itself fails to be the last word in the discussion of ground. Ground fails to be the last word in foundational enterprises that presuppose one pole is immediate. Those enterprises fail to embody the full foundational move attempted in the logic of essence. The logic of essence as a whole fails to embody . . . what? The structure of pure thought? A vision of what it means to be real? Hegel, at least, would claim that the logical sequence as a whole is not an attempt to articulate any particular vision or content but only the necessary structures of thought in their completeness and purity.

4

Categories for Modernity

Our explorations in Hegel's logic are being guided by his definition of civil society as "an association of members as self-sufficient individuals in a universality which because of their self-sufficiency is only formal" (Philosophy of Right #157). We need to know how Hegel develops the category of formal universality, why the self-sufficiency of the members makes the universality formal, and what the fuller category is into which formal universality will develop.

The answers to these questions are to be found in the third section of Hegel's logic, where he develops categories appropriate to wholes and systems.[1]

In the third section, Hegel has various names for the self-differentiating unity he is trying to think about: "the universal," "the concept," "the judgment," "the syllogism," "the absolute idea." These names are taken from traditional school logic and given first a Kantian then a Hegelian twist. They all play a role similar to the Greek notion of *logos*. For the Greeks, *logos* (speech, argument, reason, gathering together) names that common principle of definiteness and unity that makes thinking, speaking, and acting possible. Though it is explained differently by different thinkers, *logos* is the primal gathering that forms and allows unity within any sphere of beings or thought. Hegel's word that is translated as "concept" is *Begriff*, also a grasping and holding together. It too indicates the binding unity that allows any being, any thought, any action to be unified and definite, and so allows it to be at all. We will find later in

Heidegger a superficially similar but deeply opposed *logos*-doctrine of the gathering together that lets things be.

Throughout the section of the logic that we looked at briefly in the last chapter, categories come in pairs never able to resolve the dispute over which was the foundation and which was dependent. When complete mutual dependence of all aspects is explicitly posited, the logical sequence reaches its third stage of comprehensive unity.

Near the end of the logic of essence there is a recapitulation of Spinoza's category of an underlying substance that expresses itself in finite modes. Then Hegel moves to a variety of categories involving causality, law, and reciprocity. In the categories involving reciprocal interaction under law, the attempt to make one category basic is abandoned, and all the aspects are posited as mediated by their mutual interaction. This explicitly posits the lack of a first immediate foundation and replaces the demand for such a basic starting point with the movement of a whole constituted by mutual reciprocity (*Wechselwirkung*). At this stage each member is thought of as constituted by interaction with the others, but there is not yet any thought of the system as a whole distinguished from its members, and the whole remains indeterminate.

Here we begin to encounter categories that might be useful for thinking about civil society. We must progress, however, to categories that involve a way of thinking about mutual relations and particular content in terms of the whole system. To think about civil society we need to be able to distinguish a formal process of interaction from the particular content and particular interactions of its members. This requires a move to the third section of the logic, where the whole is posited as a third that is not identified with any one of its elements or with any one side of the oppositions it may contain. The emergence of this new kind of identity is one of the most crucial moves in the logical sequence, a move I have only tried to indicate here.[2]

Because identity and the whole are explicitly posited, all the categories in the third section concern totalities, although they all contain oppositions explicitly posited as posited within them. Compared with the abrupt changes of the first section and the tortuous play of the essence categories the third section makes comparatively easy reading. Hegel claims (Encyclopedia #273z) that the middle section of any dialectic is the most difficult because the comprehensive unity is neither present in immediate fashion, as in the first section, nor explicitly posited on its own, as in the third. In the second section the unifying bond shows only as external necessity or as the failure of the parts, taken on their own, to account for their own status and togetherness. This is the case with civil society, which occupies the middle in the triad family, civil society, state. Here the deeper unity shows at first only in the external necessities of market interaction.

In the third section of the logic, comprehensive unity becomes the central theme. There is development within a totality that is at first taken as positing its inner divisions and articulations too immediately, then too much in separation. This movement is repeated on many levels throughout the section.

Categories for Modernity

The third section of the logic provides the categories needed to grasp the modern situation. The categories provided in the second section were not sufficient. They do not give a way of thinking the relation of formally universal institutions and independent particular members. The free market is not a unification performed on indifferent matter; individuals bring their already determinate purposes to the market. Nor is the free market a tautologous manifestation of some inner content as suggested in the category of form and content. Although some discussions of modern subjectivity make it sound as if subjects had fixed inner desires and needs translated into external action, the relation of the free self to one's chosen self-identity cannot be thought of simply as an inner content given external existence. The insufficiency of the essence categories to describe modern formal selves and institutions is significant, because many discussions of modernity tend to stay within the perpetual tensions characteristic of Hegel's categories of essence. Weber's categories, for example, do not move on to the level of explicit totality.

Critics of Hegel attack just this move to the third section and its totalities. It seems to many interpreters that in the third section of any dialectic, especially in the logic, Hegel becomes unreal and leaves the tensions of our situation for a mythic reconciliation based on a postulated totality. Such critics favor a "so far and no further" approach to Hegel's thought. This approach is made all the more plausible by cosmological readings of Hegel that treat his discussion of the universal and its successors as the introduction of a large entity. Since we feel we cannot take the latter seriously, there is no need to deal with the former. Without the "incredible" Hegelian metaphysics we are left with polarities in the shifting relations characteristic of the level of essence.

Hegel's thought is too unified for us to follow it just so far and no further. The step we may not want to take has been long prepared and prefigured. If we want to disagree with Hegel's ultimate unification, we have to disagree more profoundly than by begging off at a certain point. Hegel's concepts need to be changed at their base, not cut off in the midst of their development.

In the third section of the logic, Hegel does discuss categories pertaining to questions of idealism and to a kind of ontological monism. But the logic itself makes no claims about these matters except to say that the categories by which we usually discuss them are inadequate. The effect is to avoid many questions that Hegel is usually taken to be answering directly. In the progress toward our goal of investigating what Hegel says about modernity, such issues of idealism and monism are red herrings. Here I am differing with Charles Taylor, for whom it is these issues, among others, that cause us to dismiss Hegel's prescription for modernity, keeping only his insightful diagnosis of its problems. I agree with Taylor in denying the encompassing unity to which Hegel appeals, but this denial is possible without forcing that unity into descriptions that Hegel would have rejected as involving insufficiently developed categories, such as idealism or ontological monism in their current Anglo-American meanings.

The Concept: Universal, Particular, Individual

The first large chapter of the third section of the *Science of Logic* is devoted to the concept (*das Begriff*), which explicitly posits the totality lacking in the categories of essence, even in the category of mutual interaction. I have kept the translation of *Be-griff* as "concept" in order to capture the connotation, albeit a learned one in English, of the Latin *con-ceptus*, "grasped together," which echoes the German etymology. John Burbidge's translation "comprehension" has much to recommend it, and I have used it occasionally in adjectival locutions. For the reasons Burbidge gives I have not used "notion" to translate *Begriff* (see Burbidge 1982, 252).

The three moments of the concept are the universal, the particular, and the individual. These terms are meant to parallel the traditional genus, species, and individual. In German the three terms are *das Allgemeine*, *das Besondere*, and *das Einzelne*, together with their appropriate adjectival and abstract forms. I have retained the traditional translations, but a word of caution is in order for those more familiar with the usage of the English words in contemporary analytic philosophy.

(a) By *universal*, Hegel is not referring to an abstract entity as distinguished from concrete individuals. From Hegel's point of view the universals debated in current discussions of nominalism and realism would be just another kind of immediate entity.

(b) About *particular*, the difficulty is that in one current technical usage the word has come to mean a definite individual entity, the bearer of properties. So one can speak about bare particulars and collections of particulars to be quantified over. Hegel uses *particular* in a more ordinary sense, as when we speak of a particular color of rose or a particular style of dress. *Particular* refers to the determinate character of an entity. The word is an echo of *quality* in the first section of the *Science of Logic* and of *form* in the second, but is meant as the fuller conception these terms only approach. Particularity means a definite content or quality defined over against other such qualities, but now that content is seen as a particularization of some universal unity.

(c) With regard to *individual*, similar cautions apply. In current English language discussions it often has meanings quite similar to *particular*. Hegel intends it closer to the ordinary sense, namely a thing in-dividual, un-divided, single, independent. Not everything in the world that can bear properties will be an individual in this full sense of the word. If universality implies for Hegel unity and commonality, particularity implies definiteness and distinction, and individuality implies subsistence, singleness, self-related independence, and self-sufficiency. Hegel's category of individuality has obvious connections with Aristotle's notion of individual substance but is meant as a successor to that notion.

We must be careful not to prejudge what counts as an individual for Hegel. On the categorial level one is not deciding what apparent individuals in the world are true individuals. There is no real parallel in Hegel to the enterprise of analytic ontology, which attempts to find out what words truly refer to real, particular individuals. Hegel uses his language with many levels of analogy, not disqualifying claims to individuality but placing them on various levels of completeness and totality.[3]

Hegel says of the three moments of the concept that they are completely interrelated.

Universality, particularity, and individuality are, taken in the abstract, the same as identity, difference, and ground [the three moments of reflection, in the *Encyclopedia* version of the logical sequence]. But the universal is the self-identical, with the express meaning that it simultaneously contains the particular and the individual. Again, the particular is the specific difference or determinateness, but with the meaning that it is in itself universal and is as an individual. Similarly the individual has the meaning that it is subject, basis, which involves the genus and species in itself and is substantial. Such is the posited inseparability of the moments of the concept in their difference. This is the clarity of the concept, in which no distinction makes a break or an opacity, but instead all remains transparent. (Encyclopedia #164)

Hegel's problem in introducing the universal is akin to Kant's problem in refuting Hume. Kant adds no additional impressions to the flow of experience Hume describes, only the unifying and unification worked by the categories. So Hegel adds no new things to the world, only the universal behind and within and expressed as the comprehensive unity of the world. At times one may feel that Hegel is legislating away the difficulties he has seen earlier, that the universal and its successors are magic formulas to banish the fear of separations. But Hegel thinks he has shown that definiteness and separation cannot be the last word but only one word in the process of comprehensive unity.

Sometimes Hegel uses images suggesting that the universal is some vaporous force or energy or life circulating through things. Hegel never entirely shook off the rhetorical influence of the romantic images he used in his youth, but he demands that such images be rethought through the logical categories, and not vice versa.

Hegel does not use *universal* to designate an abstract entity, such as cowness or the number nine. But his use of the term is not unrelated to this traditional meaning. In the old Porphyrian tree of generality we start with an individual object—say, Bossie the cow—and we move upward by abstracting: Bossie, Holstein, cow, cud-chewing animal, animal, living being, material being, entity. This ascent still describes Bossie at each step, but it leaves out more and more of the determinations that make her the unique individual she is, cows the unique species they are, and so on. Hegel has this to say about such universal concepts: "What are called concepts . . . for instance 'man,' 'house,' 'animal,' etc. are simple determinations and abstract representations [*einfach Bestimmungen und abstrakte Vorstellungen*]—abstractions that retain only the moment of universality from the concept and leave aside particularity and individuality, thus they do not develop into these other moments and so abstract from the [true] concept" (Encyclopedia #164z). It is only in the interrelation of all three moments in the concrete individual that the concept can become fully itself.

> The return [from the particular] to the universal is twofold: either through the abstraction which drops the particular and rises to the higher and the highest genus, or else through the individuality to which the universal in the particularity itself descends. Here is where the false path [*Abweg*] branches off and abstraction strays from the way of the concept and forsakes the truth. The higher and highest universal to which it raises itself are only an ever more contentless surface; the individuality it despises is the depth in which the concept grasps itself and is posited as concept. (Science of Logic 2:260/619)

Concepts formed on the false path are perfectly good empirical concepts, but their universality remains indifferent to content and without any philosophical necessity. The general concepts can be limited from without, by any chosen restrictions. "Cow" can be limited down into many arbitrarily chosen subclasses: male, female, white, standing, sitting, costly, friendly, and so on. Similarly, any feature of Bossie can be picked for abstractive highlighting and used to construct a tree of species and genera. There are no necessary criteria to tell us what aspects of things are the objective or necessary systematic content (Science of Logic 2:453/796). In this sense there are no essences for most of our empirical concepts.

There are, however, necessary structures for thought, and these can serve as criteria for correcting some ordinary conceptions, for example, conceptions of the state. Only the concept in the full Hegelian sense will contain the requisite necessary content, which will appear precisely in the interrelation of the three moments of universality, particularity, and individuality.

How is this interrelation to be thought? Hegel describes the universal as "a unity that is a unity with itself only through its negative

relating" to particularity and individuality, an "identity of the negative with itself" (Science of Logic 2:242/603). Most readers of Hegel
first run against the universal in the *Phenomenology of Spirit* chapter
on sense-certainty, where Hegel uses "the now" as his first example.

The now remains the same while its content changes, yet it is
the same only through that changing content. The now exists by
being distinguished from its past and its future content; now is day
not night, but the now is not identical with day since soon now will
be night and not day. A permanent now with one content would
lose the temporal motion essential to "nowness." The now is not an
"it," not an immediately present entity that is just simply present.
If we can speak of it at all, it is because we can think of it using a
complex scheme of negations. In one sense the now is its current
content, and in another it is not identical with that content.

Critics often point out that Hegel should treat the now as a de-
monstrative rather than a universal. Hegel is not saying, however,
that the now is a universal concept in the ordinary sense of the
term, but that it is a unity maintaining its identity through negations
and relations. In some ways it is akin to the activity and background
needed to perform demonstratives.

After introducing his example of the now Hegel concludes: "A
simple thing of this kind which is through negation, which is neither
this or that, a not-this, and is with equal indifference this as well as
that—such a thing we call a universal" (Phenomenology of Spirit
82/#60). In the *Science of Logic* Hegel uses the ego as an example of
a universal in his sense. The ego is a unity, but it is not a continuing,
immediately present object in consciousness, such as Hume searched
for in vain. Nor is the ego identical to any one item of experience
or a sequence of such experiences. It is not a positive item within
experience but the binding and unifying that make the items part
of experience. The ego is a unity through its negative relation to all
the particular items in the stream of experience—it is the unity that
is precisely not one of the items experienced—but the ego needs
that stream of items of experience in order to be at all. The unity
of the ego is achieved by the "not this" relation to all items of
experience, yet this is the relation binding these items as part of *my*
stream of experience. (Later we will see the state as a universal
maintaining its identity by a negative relation that limits various
interest groups yet relates positively to those groups by authorizing
their characteristics and powers as part of its articulated unity.)

These examples highlight the temptation to think of the universal as a kind of energy of cohesion keeping determinate parts together, visible only in its manifestations. But this still takes the universal as a positive entity rather than as the negatively related self-identity Hegel has in mind. Each of the three moments is and is thought through the others; this is different from the categories of essence, where the whole is not explicitly posited as such. Now the whole is posited neither as a first immediate foundation nor as a final result of independent parts. The third section of the logic works out this relation until all traces of immediacy are removed. In the relations of the three moments of the concept, no one moment is the first, as would be the case if the universal were some kind of dominant energy or soul. None is first and none is ultimate; their mutual distinction and relation are the basic movement within which the determinate moments exist, and the movement is only the motion separating and uniting these elements. There is no first and no last to be brought into a full presence as the foundation of all, but the circle itself can be made self-transparent and consciously lived within.

From Immediate Universality to Formal Universality

The lack of a first has an important result. Because each of the three moments exists in its distinction and motion with the others, if we were to try to separate the universal from the other two moments, we would get only the abstraction of unity and self-relation without determinate content. If one were to gaze into the universal moment, in order to see what depths it hides, one would find nothing. The now, apart from day and night, has no content; the ego apart from experience is only an empty relating. If we were to separate the particular content from the universal, the universal would be empty, only an abstract form of unity. Civil society is an example of the posited separation of the universal institution and the particular content, and the universal is formal and empty.

This begins to answer one of the questions with which we approached the logic. How does Hegel think that the modern self-sufficiency of particular individuals makes civil society a *formally* universal process? And how is that formality to be overcome without losing the achievement of individual freedom? Both questions are answered through the progression of the categories. The formal universal enters with the positing of the difference between universal and particular, and it is overcome with the positing of their unity within the structure of the mediations of the concept, a structure that is the "objective content" we have been searching for.

The progression from immediate universality to formal universality occupies the first sections of the chapter on the universal. In the social terms that are our concern, the immediate universal corresponds to the structure of a traditional society as Hegel has described it. In such a society the individual is defined by his or her social role, and that role is immediately perceived as supporting the common good. Differences within society are acknowledged but are held within a harmonious whole expressed in each of its parts. Hegel uses as his usual example the Greece of the Homeric poems, where each individual *is* his or her role and has firm trust in the unity of all roles with the social good. The logical pattern found here is the immediate unity of universal (the social whole), particular (this or that definite role), and individual (Antigone as a concrete person). These three moments can be distinguished but cannot be held apart; there are no social institutions that posit the differences explicitly. The three coalesce into an immediate unity; one leads to the other without any posited separation to be overcome.

Here we see the unity characteristic of the opening paragraphs of the chapter on the universal. The unity achieved at the end of the section on essence is first posited as the universal that contains all division and content immediately within it. The universal does not need to be contrasted with something else in order to have content. A traditional society has its own inner differentiated content; it does not achieve that content by contrast with the tribe over the river. Such contrasts, as Greek versus barbarian, are consequent upon the sense of identity developed within the articulated whole. In Hegelian terms: the universal is determinate in and for itself. Nor does such a unity demand polar oppositions such as are found in the essence section. A traditional society may contain many such oppositions, but they do not constitute its unity.

In this complex category the simple self-related unity of the whole includes the other moments within itself immediately. The content that differentiates and completes the whole is not some limitation from outside the universal but a positive progression within the whole's self-identity.

So why not end the logic here? Hegel may seem to have overcome the distinctions he set out to overcome, but this unity is all too immediate. The moments of universal, particular, and individual have so far been thought of only in terms of the universal as unity. But we know from the overall movement of the logical sequence that immediate unity is not the whole of what it means for something to be. The moments of the concept must be conceived in their difference as well as in their unity, and doing so will open up further developments.

Hegel claims that further progression is already implicit in the immediate unity. Since each of the moments is posited as immediately one with the universal, each of them is posited as sharing in the self-relation and self-sufficiency of the whole (Science of Logic 2:245/605). Just because the whole is thought of as immediately united, each moment can be the whole. The whole is to be taken in terms of particularity and individuality as well as of universal unity.

This leads to a subtle change. Previously the universal moment was thought of as the unity within which were the other two moments. But each moment, if it really is immediately united with the whole, is equal to the universal unity. Once we realize that the other moments share the wholeness, then the first way of thinking is no longer "the" way of thinking the whole; it is only one way of conceiving the unity of the whole, namely the way that emphasizes the moment of unity and immediate self-relation. There are other ways of conceiving the whole under the signs of particularity and individuality. In other words, the whole conceived of in the first case is only a particular kind of whole. The whole cannot be characterized primarily in terms of universal unity, for this is only one moment. The movement that is the whole must be characterized in terms of all three moments, not the dominance of any one of them.

To think this way, about the various, particular ways of conceiving the overall unity, is already to be under the sign of the second moment, which distinguishes the three moments in their different particular characters. We see here how Hegel bends the logical progression back on itself.

This all seems quite abstract. But recall that modernity was born by positing in institutions and individual selves the difference between particular individuals (with their particular desires and needs) and the universal, social body of customs and laws. Whether that difference was posited in religion by the Lutheran definition of the individual's direct relation to God, or by Descartes' doubt, or by the free market institutions, in all these cases a difference was made central to thought and action. But even though a difference was posited, the links between individuals and the links among the various moments of the concept were not broken; they still exist but are now devoid of content, purified and formal. In civil society, structures of mutual recognition are not done away with, but they become formal. In this case the traditional social whole of custom and roles comes to be seen as only one way to exist in society. It is seen as a way that overemphasizes the universal unity at the expense of the particular differences. There is another way to organize society in terms of particular differences and formally universal institutions. A new kind of overarching unity is available.

This is to think about unity with the emphasis on particularity. It is not a fragmenting of unity so much as a new kind of unity, a new relation of universal, particular, and individual that emphasizes the difference between universal and particular. "Insofar as the particularity of the difference [between particular and universal] is posited and so has being, the universal is the form in that difference and the particular is the content. The universal becomes formal in so far as the distinction [between particular and universal] is the essential [element posited]" (Science of Logic 2:248/608).

A new distinction between form and content has arisen as a result of distinguishing particular from universal. Here is Hegel's answer to the question of why modernity entails both individual rights and formal institutions. The unity of the community must be thought of as formal if all the content is placed on the side of the determinate particular members. In a traditional society the unity of the community is articulated "by nature" into elaborate social content. In modern society the whole can be distinguished from any particular content. In a second-level sense, the unity of the whole has become something particular, distinguishable as a particular kind of thing, unity as opposed to particular content, an empty and perforce formal process of interrelation and unity.

This new distinction between form and content is not like the distinction we saw in the essence section. It is not a form impressed on indifferent matter nor a content tautologically expressing itself. Rather, it is the thought of a social whole expressed in a collection of particular contents and in formal unifying institutions. Each needs the other, but their difference is posited within society; that is, the difference is built into the functioning of the institutions and into the decisions of the particular citizens. We recognize the form of civil society, an association whose unity is formal because its members are self-sufficiently particular. They do not depend on the whole to assign them their definite roles and content for their lives.

Because particular content and universal form have been posited as different from each other yet each the whole, there is in civil society no internal connection between the two, no principle in the formal institutions and no preadaptation in the particular content to account for the unity between them (Science of Logic 2:250/610). In civil society, particular desires and needs are not formed with the general welfare in mind, while on the other hand the pressures exerted on the individual by the market are felt as forces external to the desires one wishes to fulfill. This disjointedness is the great achievement of modernity. It frees the citizen from substantive unity with traditional ways of life that exist in immediate, universally valid identification with the social whole.

On the other hand, civil society brings problems resulting precisely from that separation of the particular citizen from the social whole. But no catalog of problems, however long, need convince a determined defender of modern separations. Hegel's most basic argument for the surpassing of civil society by the state lies in the logical progression. Just as it has led up to the structure appropriate to civil society, so it proceeds beyond that structure.

Moving Beyond the Categories of Civil Society

I am not suggesting that Hegel wrote his logic with civil society in mind. The logical sequence is supposed to be a pure development of categories in themselves. But when Hegel came to treat civil society, he had his logic in mind, as is clear from his definition of civil society in terms of formal universality.

What demands that the logical progression continue beyond the kind of unity exemplified in civil society? Hegel says that the difficulty is that "particularity is not present as totality" (Science of Logic 2:248/608). Particularity is definiteness defined in relation to other definiteness—for example, red as distinct from green, badger from cow, within their respective unities of color and animality. No one of these definite particulars can be said to express the whole. In civil society no one's particular desires or needs express the society's direction. No one particular determination is present as the totality of the universal. When taken together, the particulars remain without inner unity. Neither singly nor as an aggregate abstracted from the formal universal do the particulars express the whole.

For Hegel, to pause here would be to pretend an intermediate stage is final. The categories adequate for thinking civil society are found in the logical sequence at a stage where the particular and universal are *already* posited in their unity. Granted that the unity was posited only immediately and that it had to break down into the splits characteristic of civil society, yet that unity was already posited and the categories appropriate to civil society have ceased to posit that unity explicitly. This is why it is important for Hegel that the categories appropriate for describing civil society arise not during the endless tensions and polarities of the essence section but in the third part of the logical sequence, when overarching unity has already been affirmed.

The totality and unity in question have been affirmed as the conditions for the possibility of the divisions typical of civil society. It is not a question of building a new unity from the originally disparate parts provided by civil society but of positing explicitly a totality that has to be there in the first place in order to make civil society possible. The mutual identity and mediation of the moments of the whole are already in the logical sequence. That mediation cannot be made to go away; it must be posited explicitly along with the distinctions typical of civil society. Doing so is the transition to the new categories of individuality.

Describing civil society's kind of formal universality related to self-sufficient particulars, Hegel says: "What makes this universality abstract is that the mediation is only a condition and is not posited in itself. Because the mediation is not posited, the unity of the abstract [universality] has the form of immediacy, and the [partic-ular] content has the form of indifference to its universality. This is because the content is not the totality which is the universality of absolute negativity" (Science of Logic 2:249/609). Hegel's phrase here, "the content is not the totality," sounds similar to the phrase quoted above, "particularity is not present as totality." But now Hegel adds that the totality is "the universality of absolute negativity." The term *absolute negativity* means the motion in which there is no first and everything is mediated by everything else. Here this refers to the three moments of the concept: universal, particular, individual.

What is characteristic of the first kind of universality, correspond-ing to traditional society, is that the three moments are all in immediate unity. What is characteristic of the second kind of universality, corresponding to civil society, is that each moment is posited as particular and distinct. So the particular is posited as self-sufficient, only externally related to the unification worked upon it. Difference has been posited, but not mediation and unity. There needs to be a third stage where each moment is taken as mediated by the others.

The self-sufficiency characteristic of the members of civil society is a first attempt to have the freedom of true individuals but an attempt still too much caught up in being different from the whole. Its "freedom from" is too much defined in terms of opposition to be able to reach the self-completeness and independence characteristic of true individuality.

The dialectical transition to the fuller version of individuality occurs, as do most transitions in the third part of the logic, by a quiet development. Each of the moments of the concept is seen as self-related (because a moment of the universal) and determinate (because particular and defined as different from the other moments), but self-related determinateness is the independent status that Hegel calls individuality. Each of the three moments of the concept can be taken as self-related and complete in itself and therefore as embodying the other moments. The chapter on the individual discusses this achievement, which, however, produces another breakdown of the unity of the concept. Each of the moments seems self-complete, and the unity, which was at first the immediate unity of all three moments and then the unity of formally universal process and particular content, is now shattered into the thought of three different kinds of unity each complete in itself, each featuring the dominance of one of the moments.

In his chapters on judgment and syllogism, Hegel chronicles the return from this multiplicity to unity, but to a unity where all the separations and the mediations of the moments are explicitly posited. Full individuality is achieved only at the end of that long process. Its achievement is also the move into the categories of objectivity, an important development we will not examine here.

Hegel's treatment of individuality is more complex and includes more mediations and references to the whole than the categories deployed earlier in the logical sequence for thinking independent beings (for example, the categories of determinate being, limit, form and content, thing and appearance). If we ask which individuals in the world Hegel is talking about, the question is wrongly put. Hegel is discussing the categories appropriate to talking about individuals; he is not making an inventory of what seeming individuals in the world really exemplify these categories. We will see in the next chapter that it is wrong to treat the logic as a categorial system offered as a hypothesis for describing individuals in the world. This would be to locate the categorial sequence within a subjective act of application rather than to treat the categories as conditions valid in themselves for any thought.

Objective Content

It is in the development of the categories of individuality that Hegel finds the objective content needed to give him the structures of the larger community that will locate and limit civil society. Speaking of the level of individuality found in civil society Hegel says that "the difference between this individuality [which arises from the distinction of universal and particular] and the individuality of the concept is that in the former the individual as content and the universal as form are separated from one another. Just because the individual is not present as absolute form the universal is not present as the totality of form" (Science of Logic 2:261/620).

The puzzling phrase "absolute form" refers to the pattern of the various mediations among the three moments of the concept. The fuller version of individuality arises through thinking the individual as the full motion among the three moments. But what is that motion? Hegel works out the details of the mutual mediations in the chapters of the third part of the logic devoted to judgment and syllogism. In these chapters the separate unities that are the result of the dialectic of universal, particular, and individual combine and recombine. None of the three is taken as first or basic. These chapters show the three moments, now each considered as independent, enacting complex separations and unities, which gradually reintegrate themselves though a host of detailed mediations. The pattern developed is the "absolute form" and "the universal present as the totality of form." The absoluteness of this form consists not in some hypostatized ontological status but in its not needing to be thought of as related to a separate external content. All the needed divisions and content are provided within its mediations.

In the development, too long to be traced here, the absolute form is presented. That form provides the objective content that Hegel requires, because the absolute form has itself for content. "The absolute form has in its own self its content. . . . The content is simply and solely these determinations of the absolute form and nothing else—a content posited by the absolute form itself and consequently also adequate to it" (Science of Logic 2:231/592). This content is spelled out in the eighty or so pages of the larger logic devoted to judgment and syllogism; these provide progressively more adequate ways of thinking comprehensive unity while positing all the divisions and mediations that must be posited. (There are still more mediations involved in the absolute form; these are developed further on, but for our purposes the relations of universal, particular, and individual are sufficient. We will see how Hegel uses them to show what institutions the state should possess.)

The chapters on judgment and syllogism consist of lengthy, complex, and not wholly convincing correlations between traditional grammatical and logical terminology and ever more elaborated involutions of the three moments of the concept. I am not here concerned with the success or failure of Hegel's attempt to incorporate the terminology of the school logic of his time. What is important for us is the development of the absolute form. Ultimately this happens in the sections devoted to the syllogism.

A judgment (Ur-teil or "original division," in German) is a mediation that involves only two of the moments of the concept and does not bring them together within a third moment. Hegel speaks of a civil litigation as a judgment and of a crime as a different kind of judgment (Encyclopedia #173). In civil litigation one particular right comes in conflict with another; in crime the criminal's particular desire is asserted against the social whole and the universal institution of right in general. Two different logical patterns govern the separations and unities involved.

Syllogism for Hegel is a category for thinking a complex whole containing all three moments of the concept, each mediating the other. "Everything is a syllogism," says Hegel. That is, everything that is in some degree a self-sufficient whole must be thought of as having all the moments of the concept at play within it. Syllogism here refers to the mediations in the nature of things and not to the argument form used to express those mediations.[4]

It is worth pointing out that it is because of this need to express triple mediations, and not because of some mysterious intuitionism, that Hegel says propositions involving the dyadic relations of the subject-predicate form cannot express the results of dialectic. Hegel's speculative thought can only be expressed, he claims, in a series of propositions having some tension among them.

The chapter on syllogism proceeds until all the moments are posited as mediating one another. None is first, none is last; each is united with the each of the others through the thirds. The triple mediation of universal, particular, and individual is folded into itself twice to produce twenty-seven patterns of mediation. Each pattern contains all three moments with different moments taking the role of the mediating unity, and each of those unities is in turn thought according to each of the three moments. (See Düsing 1976, 267ff.) The various mediation patterns are named according to the old terminology of figures and moods of the Aristotelian syllogism, which is a tour de force Hegel can manage only partially to complete.

Hegel is providing a compendium of ways for thinking comprehensive and self-sufficient unity. In thinking about a situation we find in the world, if we discover just what mediations and divisions of the moments of the concept make its structure, we will know where it fits into the logical sequence and to what degree it is in fact a self-sufficient totality. If its pattern resembles some of the earlier ones in the chapter (or in the following chapters, those giving more explicit worldly analogues) we can see what remains to be mediated. For example, discussing diplomatic relations between states, Hegel observes that manner in which arguments are conducted over disputed territory allows almost any contingent fact (of language, inheritance, history, geography, and so on) to be cited as a reason why one nation rather than the other should have the territory. This shows that the whole formed in international law is not a system in which the universal specifies what particularities are to count in action and value and therefore is not a fully developed community that can stand on its own (Encyclopedia #184z). In a similar manner, civil society is less adequate than the state because the latter's pattern of interactions form a syllogism more complete in its logical structure.

Overcoming Modern Formalism

Hegel does not reject the modern emphasis on form, but tries to go it one better. What makes absolute form the overcoming of modernity is that absolute form cannot be posited as different from its content. One cannot posit this difference because the absolute form already includes that difference as something overcome. To try to make a new and more encompassing difference of form and content would be to fall back to a stage already posited and passed by.

There is an air of mystery about all this. Hegel would claim, however, that once one has advanced to thinking the universal at all, there is no choice but to go the rest of the way. To halt in the kind of divisions characteristic of modernity is to fail to express the very conditions that make those divisions possible. Once we are in the third section of the logic, we have already found posited the comprehensive unity that exists through a mutual mediation where nothing is independent, and there is no first element on which the rest are based. Modernity should be thought of, Hegel would argue, as a separation within an already posited but too immediate version of such a unity. The unity reasserts itself since it is the condition for modernity in the first place. That unity is not some simple immediacy that can be permanently transcended by making new divisions. It is the complex unity of the concept thought of as immediate, yes, but as the immediately universal and self-related with no immediacy within it. To fail to move beyond the categories characterizing modernity is willfully to avoid thought.

This account of Hegel's objective content must raise the suspicion that Hegel has not really overcome the division of form and content. I have been calling the objective content a series of patterns, and this suggests they are to be applied in an external way. The pattern is to be found embodied in various ways: as governmental institutions, for example, or religious systems. Doesn't this leave room for all the modern separations once again?

Hegel would deny this objection. What appears to be the separate content is only the form itself viewed as other to its motion, but "viewing as other" is something already encompassed within the form itself.

This is reiterated at the end of the logical sequence. The final category is the absolute idea, in which the logic explicitly incorporates the vocabulary of positing, immediacy, and mediation, which has been used in the exposition of the categories. The ultimate category describes its own mediations as the context of all determinations of thought. All other categories are seen as abstract and incomplete ways of thinking this most basic motion of thought itself. If we were able to view the earlier categories as immediate facts to be ordered, then we could view the method of the logical sequence as a form separated from them. But for Hegel there is no such separation. "For the method it is a matter of indifference whether its determinations are taken to be of form or of content. . . . Since it is the absolute form, the concept that knows itself and everything as concept, there is no content that could stand over against it and determine it to be a one-sided external form" (Science of Logic 2:501/ 839–40, cf. 2:485/825). Hegel claims that such an overarching motion, which comprehends itself, is the final condition for making any of the distinctions others take as ultimate. Such a comprehensive unity has already posited and overcome the dichotomies one might want to make. No ultimate distinction of form from content can be posited either within the logic as a whole or between the logical sequence and the reality "outside" it.

5

Applying Hegel's Logic

Before considering the details of Hegel's transition from civil society to state, we need to discuss how the logical sequence comes to be applied. Hegel is not performing conceptual analysis, seeking the necessary and sufficient conditions for the use of some concept. His work is revisionary in that he does not merely wish to clarify criteria already in force but suggests concepts to replace those we ordinarily use. Hegel does not analyze the concept of the state to show what institutions it must contain; rather, he analyzes the state as a concept (that is, as a certain kind of comprehensive unity) to show what mediations it must embody and thus what institutions it must contain. This may seem a verbal quibble, but the difference runs deep. In the one case he would be analyzing a concept formed by abstraction and empirical survey; in the other he is treating a concrete totality according to the necessary form for such totalities, where the form was derived from the pure progression of the logic.

The necessity Hegel appeals to comes from a kind of transcendental analysis. But here too we must be cautious. He is not producing a "transcendental argument" in one recent sense of that phrase. He is not saying that in order to apply category A we must already know how to apply category B. Strawson tries to build such arguments in his *Individuals*, and Charles Taylor tries to show how passages in Hegel's *Phenomenology of Spirit* can be interpreted as offering such arguments.[1]

77

The transcendental conditions Hegel deals with do not have to be known in order to be in force. Various categories contained in the logic have been elaborated into whole philosophical systems without the subsequent categories having been discovered. In using any earlier category in the logical sequence, one is thinking within a context that when posited as such will involve the later categories. The context does not have to be posited at the moment of use of the earlier category, but if it is not, there will be developments leading to that positing.

Hegel both applauds and criticizes Kant's efforts at transcendental deduction (Science of Logic 2:227/589). Kant glimpsed the absolute form but backed away from it to rest in a separation of form from content made within a story about subjectivity and things in themselves. His application of transcendental method remained within the framework of the subject-object relation. But though the subject-object relation is among the categories structuring pure thought, it is only one of many and not the highest or most encompassing. This theme informs Hegel's varied attacks on Kant's philosophy.

What then does a transcendental deduction look like in Hegel's version? It looks like the *Science of Logic*. The logical sequence is the journey to positing all that must be posited if the immediate beginning is to be as it is. Hegel argues that the sequence must begin where it does, and from there each step must be posited because it is already the condition that makes possible the earlier more abstract stages. In this process, content is not extracted from the earlier stages but is added to them from the unexplicit context that makes them possible. The content is the context posited as such. But that enabling context is not a group of entities or principles; it is the triple movement of thought that is the motion of positing. "The logical idea has itself as infinite form for its content" (Science of Logic 2:485/285).

Hegel and Finitude

Hegel does not deduce the logical sequence from axioms or remove it from the depths of some first principle. He takes it as he finds it arising from the movement of positing, the *Ur-teilen* of the universal. However, there is a dangerous misunderstanding to be avoided here. Being, essence, the concept, the universal, the absolute idea: none of these is a first formless entity that is then limited, or limits itself, to produce the articulations of our thought or our world. "The concept is not the abyss of formless substance. . . . Determination is not a limitation" (Science of Logic 2:242/603).

Hegel breaks with one of the basic traditions in Western philosophy, the tradition that sees definiteness and determination as arising through the limitation of some prior indefiniteness. Hegel does not derive the content of the logic by progressive limitations on some primal fullness. The closing categories of the logic do not point to some formless energy behind everything. Instead Hegel speaks of a complexly related motion that makes the space for thought.

That motion is infinite in the sense Hegel prefers; it is self-related and independent and contains a positing of its own other. In terms of the possibilities it opens up for our thought and action, however, that motion is finite in one usual sense of the word. There are not indefinitely many categories; there are not ever-new possibilities for thought and action.

The logical sequence gives conditions for our thought and action that open a finite set of possibilities. This is not to say that we cannot continue indefinitely into the future and that we will not have new experiences. But for Hegel the varieties of overall structure we have available are finite. For all his optimism Hegel does not believe in endless progress. To do so one would have to envision the possibilities before us as indefinitely open, so that given any current set of definite structures and institutions, we could carve out from those still indefinite possibilities before us some new creative opportunity. Note that I have invoked the modern subject separated from the possibilities that lie before the judging eye. Endless progress as an ideal demands indefinite possibilities and the correspondingly emptily defined subject to advance through them. Hegel believes in neither. Our subjectivity happens within the logical sequence and its limited repertory of possibilities. We happen within the definite historical manifestations of the logical forms, again limited. Hegel believes that we are at a privileged point in history, the time when all this becomes clear, the end of history insofar as it has been a development toward that clarity. What becomes clear, however, is not an endless future of ever new forms for thought and action but the limited rational forms for human action. Those forms have content within them; they specify institutions and social roles. They are not like the endlessly open, formally rational rules and institutions of modernity.

I insist on this point because it will be important when we make comparisons with Heidegger, who is a great proponent of finitude. Hegel also embraces finitude, a kind of finitude that goes against crucial modern presuppositions.

Hegel breaks with a long tradition in philosophy, going back to Plato and the pre-Socratics, which sees the definite shapes of things as due to a limit imposed on some formless possibilities. The Greeks usually expressed the tradition of determination by limitation in pairs of principles, one of limit and the other of formless possibility, as in Aristotle's principles of form and matter or actuality and potentiality. In Plato there is the dyad of limit and unlimited, which reappears in neoplatonic thought.

In Christian philosophy this tradition was adapted with difficulty to the notion of creation. The crucial question was whether any limits were imposed on God's creative decisions. The more rationalist tradition, represented by Aquinas, who has his own version of determination by limitation in the distinction of essence and existence, argued that God's own nature as rational imposed limits on what he could create. He could not, for example, change the laws of logic or mathematics. The more radical voluntarist tradition, represented by Ockham, argued that it was God's creative decision that first established whatever limits or patterns things might have. God could create anything he wished. We see this tradition at work in Descartes's claim that God could have created a world in which two and two made five (Descartes 1972, 2:248).

Much of modern thought continues the idea of indefinite possibilities open to a deciding will. It is against this background that social choices are acted out, and it is the indefinite openness of the possibilities we face that makes it imperative for us to find a criterion to choose among them. Debates ensue about whether the criterion is to be rational or emotional. Hegel challenges the presupposition of the debates. We are in fact already enmeshed in a finite set of possibilities; indeed we *are* the conscious openness of that set of possibilities. We do not stand opposite an indefinitely open field of possibilities that waits for our creative act of decisive limitation. We find ourselves within a set of already moving structures and possibilities with their operative norms and values not indefinitely open to revision. Those possibilities and structures have changed in the course of history; now we are at the time where the law of those changes has become clear, but that does not mean we are free from the motion of the concept. We can now live it with a transparent rationality, but that does not make us lords of its motion.

It may be that this break with the tradition that contrasts limited forms with indefinite possibility will provide a way to envision a postmodern situation.

Hegel does have his own discussion of determination through limitation, in the dialectic of limitation and ought (*Sollen* and *Grenze*) in the first part of the logic. But this is surpassed in the later treatments of determination in terms of essence and then in terms of the motion of the concept and absolute idea. I emphasize Hegel's departure from the tradition of determination by limitation, but he also departs from the major alternative tradition in the West, stemming from the Greek atomists, which takes some basic determinations as simply given and the foundation for everything else. Hegel's doctrine of the absolute idea as the form of its own motion having itself for content is an attempt to find an origin for determination that is neither a limitation on a first formless principle nor an acceptance of basic given determinations. We can see this, for example, in his refusal to trace the basic outlines of a political constitution either to some act of a social or individual will or to some fixed grounding in the nature of man's given drives and preferences.

Success in the Logical Enterprise

In the last few pages I have tried to give some sense of what Hegel is aiming at in his logic. If he succeeds, he will have overcome modernity at its roots. Hegel rests his case on the necessity of the beginning of the logical sequence and the subsequent necessity of the sequence itself. The beginning is derived in the *Phenomenology of Spirit* and in the introductory essays to the *Science of Logic*. The success of that derivation is controversial; I pass over that dispute to look at the logical sequence itself.

There are probably fewer transitions in the *Science of Logic* that make the reader immediately uneasy than there are in the *Phenomenology of Spirit*. Nevertheless we need to understand how we would go about deciding whether Hegel has achieved the required necessity for the logical sequence as a whole.[2]

I mentioned earlier that the logic exists in two versions. Hegel wrote the *Science of Logic* during his time as a school principal in Nürnberg. The first volume was published in 1812, a second in 1813, and a third in 1816. Hegel reworked the material for the various editions of the *Encyclopedia* published during the next two decades. In 1831 a revised version of the logic of being was published, but Hegel died before he could complete revisions of the other two sections. For those we have the compressed *Encyclopedia* versions but no revised long treatment. This is unfortunate, since the *Encyclopedia* versions, especially of the logic of essence, are quite different from the older, longer treatment.

To follow our earlier example, the various pairs involving form are widely displaced in the shorter logic. The treatment of form and essence has disappeared entirely. In the larger logic the categories involving form are treated as *less* developed categories that are part of the development toward more familiar category pairs such as a thing and its properties or reality and appearance. In the *Encyclopedia* version the categories involving form show up after these standard categories. In the new version the form categories are held to be *more* developed, that is, they posit differences and unities that the familiar categories are now said not to posit explicitly.

The new locations of the categories involving form are quite insightful when studied in detail, but then so were the old locations. Each version suggests interesting and significant relations among our ways of thinking. There is no immediate reason to prefer one version over the other. The reader has no obvious perception that the later version is the better. The revised first volume of the large logic is generally quite close to the abbreviated treatment in the 1830 edition of the *Encyclopedia*, so perhaps in his planned revision of the rest of the large logic Hegel would have followed the *Encyclopedia* version. But we should be able to tell on other than biographical grounds which is better. Since Hegel believes that the necessary series gives us a warrant for moving beyond the more ordinary categories in the middle of the sequence to the final unified categories at its end, there ought to be a recognizably superior presentation of that necessary sequence. It is a tribute to Hegel's intelligence that the various versions all give us insightful material for thought. But it casts doubts on Hegel's claims when we cannot tell *on our own* which version is better.

In his revisions Hegel did not tamper with the overall movement of the logical sequence on its highest levels, which defines the nature of the sequence and the system. But unless Hegel is to be judged guilty of separating form and content, we cannot say that the arrangement of the categories on the finer scale is only a matter of appropriateness and not of necessity. Although the finer details of the logic are not the support for the larger movement, they are the place where it is made more and more adequately. They ought to have their own necessity.

But it is on their level that we do not easily find criteria for judgment. The several proposed arrangements seem illuminating; none seems decisive; each seems helpful; it is not clear how one would decide how to improve one or the other. The only possible criterion must be the higher-level movement itself. Can we judge whether a given arrangement on the level of finer detail better carries out the larger movement of the logic as a whole? This criterion seems plausible until one tries to apply it. Then it becomes unclear which version indeed does better. Yet this is the only way in which a judgment could be made, if it could be made at all.[3]

Saying that the overall movement of the logic is to be the key to decisions about which version of the finer detail is the true and necessary sequence does not finish the matter. The larger movement itself is supposed to be derived within the logical sequence; there are supposed to be no external criteria. But if we cannot be sure just how the details of the sequence are to go except by presupposing the larger motion, then Hegel has failed to achieve the desired necessity. If there is no way to judge the various versions on their own terms, then Hegel's logic will begin to look more like Kant's metaphysical deduction than his transcendental deduction. That is, it will be a systematizing and enlightening arrangement of material found in language, thought, and history but not a necessary derivation of *the* necessary categories of *any* thought. The overall three-part movement of the logic, from being through essence to the concept and idea, will begin to look less like the necessary movement of thought and more like a clue for the arrangement of historical material, a clue Hegel derives, in a way that he does not account for in the system, from his own historical situation.[4]

The success of Hegel's enterprise depends crucially on the status of the overall movement of the logic, the movement from immediacy through posited separation to posited comprehensive unity, which is repeated again and again and involuted upon itself to make the categories of the logical sequence. It may be that this movement, and the project of circular self-grounding it implies, expresses one particular understanding of reason and of what it means to be real, an understanding that is not self-grounded but is the historical gift of Hegel's situation. This is the nub of Heidegger's criticism of Hegel, which we will be examining later. [5]

How Is Hegel's Logic to Be "Applied"?

At the beginning of my treatment of the logic I spoke briefly about a common view of its relation to the discussion of civil society. In this view Hegel offers in the *Philosophy of Right*, on the one hand, trenchant observations on the development of the modern world and an acute awareness of its problems. The logic, on the other hand, is viewed as a failed attempt to give Hegel's thoughts on modernity the metaphysical backing of a monistic idealism no one today can take seriously. It is best left aside. (See Quinton 1975; Taylor 1979, 97.)

In contrast to this view, I have argued that it is the logical development that provides Hegel's treatment of modernity with whatever force and necessity it has beyond a catalog of harms and complaints. If we question the logical development, we should also question the descriptions that these critics so appreciate, since the descriptions are structured around categories developed within the logical sequence.

Before we look at Hegel's discussion of civil society and its relation to the encompassing state, we need to be clear what relations he thinks the logic has to "the real world." It is important to realize that he is not making ontological claims, nor is he strictly speaking "applying" the categories of the logical sequence to something outside them.

Hegel says that logic cannot and should not contain that reality (*Realität*) which is the content of the further parts of philosophy, the sciences of nature and spirit. The concrete philosophical sciences are a more real (*reeller*) form of the logical idea than the logic itself (Science of Logic 2:231–2/592). The word *real* needs some comment here, since Hegel uses it in a traditional meaning, found in the Middle Ages and up through Kant's time, which differs from the usual English meaning. According to the old meaning, we can say that Bossie is more real than the concept of a cow, not because Bossie is external and the concept internal but because there is more to Bossie, more things we can say about her, more content to her. Even two abstract concepts can be distinguished as more or less real in this sense if one has more determinate content than the other (as "violet" compared with "color"). A more real concept is one with a more differentiated and complex content. It is in this sense that Leibniz and Kant speak of God as the most real of beings, because God's concept contains the content of all other beings.

Hegel's discussions of concrete reality remain philosophical sciences; he does not intend them as empirical studies. They continue the development of the logical categories but now in their posited otherness in nature and history. This is not easy to understand, and it is not helped by Hegel's vague and metaphorical descriptions of the relation of the logical idea to concrete reality. Here is a typical passage: "Logic exhibits the elevation of the idea to that level from which it becomes the creator of nature and passes over to the form of a concrete immediacy whose concept, however, breaks up this shape again in order to realize itself as concrete spirit" (Science of Logic 2:232/592).

What does this talk about the logical idea as the creator of nature mean? This is perhaps the murkiest single issue in Hegel interpretation. Opinions range from traditional theism to very austere category transitions (see White 1983, 85–89). My own interpretation moves in the latter direction. For our purposes in this study it is not necessary to resolve this problem in full; we need only emphasize that the transition from the logic to the more real sciences is not a move *outside* the categories of the logic. Hegel is not developing a set of categories that is then applied to some foreign entities or embodied in some concrete material. In his effort to show the congruence of his thought with traditional Christianity Hegel uses metaphors which suggest this kind of transition, but such a transition is inappropriate for the structure he develops.

The logic's strategy is overarching and encompassing unity. Its relation to concrete reality cannot be the relation of something whole and complete (the categorial sequence) to something else whole and complete (concrete reality). The *Phenomenology of Spirit* and the logic itself attempt to undermine the categories used to structure such a distinction.

These concrete sciences do, of course, present themselves in a more real form of the idea than logic does; but this is not by turning back again to the reality abandoned by consciousness which has risen above its mode as appearance to the level of science [this refers to the argument of the *Phenomenology of Spirit* which is meant to disqualify the pattern subjects-facing-objects as the only way thought can think about itself in its relation to otherness] nor by reverting to the use of forms such as the categories and concepts of reflection whose finitude and untruth have been demonstrated in [the essence section of] the logic. (Science of Logic 2:231/592)

For one who has been caught up in the logical progression there is no place outside the logical idea to which it might be applied or in which it might be embodied. What happens in the transition to concrete reality can only be a further thinking of the logical idea in terms of itself.

According to the logic, nothing can be conceived as a full independent reality except through the motion of the absolute form. This is true of the absolute form itself. It is tempting, but mistaken, to imagine that thinking the logical sequence happens on a meta-level from which the categories will be applied to reality. In such a case worry about the status of this meta-level would suggest a meta-meta-level above it. These are the moves of the kind of reflection Hegel attacks in the *Phenomenology of Spirit* and in the essence section of the *Science of Logic*. Such reflection implies a highest (or lowest) level of thought that is just there, immediate, and an external reality that is also immediately there. For Hegel nothing is immediate, in thought or in actuality. Thought and its relation to reality must be thought in terms of the motion of the absolute form: universality (the logic), particularity (the logical categories spread out in otherness in nature), individuality (the logical categories as forming self-aware individuals, spirit). Each of these moments exists through the others; no one moment is "first." This is most completely expressed in the doctrine of the triple syllogism (Encyclopedia #574–77) where logic, nature, and spirit are explicitly mediated by one another. This doctrine is designed to frustrate readers who want to surround the system with questions about its application to some space of objects outside it. For Hegel, banning such questions is an important move beyond Kant, who surrounded his deduction of the categories with a story about things in themselves. The absolute form of the motion of the concept and idea provides its own space within itself for any transitions and applications that must be made.

When the logical sequence is thought through according to its own pattern, the whole contents of the world and self-consciousness are included, at least in their necessary aspects. There is no application of the completed categorial sequence to a foreign realm. This relentless extension of encompassing unity is meant to forestall questions of the kind we usually ask about causes and mechanisms. There is no change or transition which requires an external cause; we are thinking the necessary structure of the whole within which we find ourselves by thinking the necessary structure of pure thought. For Hegel, our yearning for explanatory mechanisms reflects a failure to understand how the logical categories are more fundamental than any explanation we could give of their transition to nature and spirit. Whatever account one gave beyond the logical sequence would be structured in terms taken from prior stages within that sequence and would not get behind or outside it to talk about its application or embodiment.

This is transcendental philosophy with a vengeance, overcoming Kant's failure to carry his revolution all the way. In his lectures on the proofs for the existence of God, Hegel says that his logic can be read as an extended version of the ontological argument for God. But this does not mean that the logic develops a set of categories and then proves they exist in reality as well as in the mind, as the traditional ontological argument attempts to do. Hegel says that his attempt is not structured according to those discredited dichotomies of internal mind and external reality. Rather, he is elevating our awareness of our own existence to an awareness of our full necessary conditions and context. There is no move from inside to outside.

We become able to recognize our full conditions of possibility. Those conditions do not involve the Kantian distinctions of thought from reality in itself. In this sense Hegel never makes ontological claims. To do so would be to admit a separation between a mentally derived set of categories and an external reality, adding a subjectivity outside the categories to do the claiming or applying. Talk of ontological claims presupposes modern subjectivity, lord of its mental constructions and facing a world of data to be interpreted. For Hegel we are involved in a whole we can come to recognize; we cannot get outside. We do not claim the existence of spirit; we discover it as we come to be aware of the full context within which we exist. Becoming aware of that context is not an empirical investigation but an awareness of the conditions of possibility for our thought. And it is part of the motion of spirit that we should discover it.

We would expect that the "absolute knowledge" attained at the end of the *Phenomenology of Spirit* and worked out in the system would be a definitive ontology stating what is real and what is not. Instead it is a transcendental deduction of what is valid. This does

reject metaphysical options whose categories Hegel finds inade-
quately developed. But it proposes no set of categories to be tested
against the world. That kind of application and testing is one of the
options rejected. Because of the encompassing unity involved, there
is no contrast of the valid categories with another realm of existing
reality. There is only the further working out of the categories in
terms of themselves into more and more "real" (that is, more and
more determinate) content. The otherness of concrete reality is
involved within the logical sequence.

Absolute knowledge is not some last and largest horizon of interpretation within which we see the true content of the world, not a
guaranteed horizon surrounding a self engaged in interpreting its
world. It is rather the transparency of the motion of pure thought
that is the event of having a world, of having any particular horizon
of interpretation. That motion will be found repeated and involuted
as the essential content of the world, but it is the motion of the
event of there being world and thought at all.

Is Hegel Really Doing A Priori Philosophy?

Hegel's relentless overarching of any dichotomies we want to bring
against his system from outside suggests an obvious objection: how
convenient that the necessary categories for thinking the logical idea
should eventuate in nineteenth century science, society, and thought!
Isn't there a covert empirical survey under all the logical double-
talk? Isn't Hegel really getting the "objective content" he wants by
looking around him and then adjusting his system accordingly?

The objection suggests the following dilemma: Hegel is doing
either an improbable deduction of all content from some first principles or else a covert empirical survey. This dilemma depends on
the separation of universal from particular. But Hegel believes he
has overcome that separation. In his system there are no first principles; there is only the motion of the concept and the idea, where
nothing is first and, correspondingly, nothing is last. There are no
one-way dependencies. While the system will make assertions about
politics and art and other concrete matters, they are part of the
larger circular movement of the system, not its application or its
conclusions.

The objection requires a closer look at Hegel's attitude toward
history, and this will bring us nearer the question of civil society. It
is true that Hegel finds the content he needs around him and does

not deduce it a priori. Hegel is an a priori philosopher in the sense that he wants to find necessity in many features of the world. But he is not a predictive philosopher. He never claimed to be able to deduce concrete content from some first principles. If we tried to make the universal or the concept or the idea a first principle, take it in isolation, and gaze into it to see what we could deduce from it, we would find it empty.

We must avoid a false dichotomy between logic and history, as if each were complete on its own. Hegel is not applying a nonhistorical theory to historical material nor finding within history parallels to a nonhistorical scheme already existing complete in some mental realm.

On the other hand, the understanding attained in the logic and system is not for Hegel available at just any time. It is not a point of view available to a freely deciding modern subject, not a position a subject can take on objects simply by defining itself in a certain way. It is the self-understanding of the motion of thought. Our comprehension of the logical sequence is not an outside event happening contingently to that sequence, or to us as outside observers. To recognize the absolute content is to recognize ourselves as implicated within it, to recognize our comprehension itself as one moment within that motion.

Though the logical sequence is not made possible through history (rather the reverse), our comprehension of that sequence, as a moment within it, has logical presuppositions within the sequence that are equivalent to natural and historical prerequisites. We have to be in a spatio-temporal world, to have bodies exhibiting sufficient organic unity, and we have to be in a certain historical situation with certain purified modes of mutual recognition allowing us to think about ourselves in new ways. History must have developed structurally to the point where it both exemplifies and allows us to perceive the logical forms in their completeness. The concrete totality in which we come to presence is already differentiated by the time when we can conceive the task of tracing its differentiations; we do not have to think up or think out the differentiated content on our own.

By the point when we reach our understanding of the logical idea and the progression of spirit, that same logical content must have already developed around us in certain definite forms of politics, economics, language, art, and philosophy that express the same logical categories we are coming to understand. This may seem to be putting ourselves unjustifiably at the center, but it is only a consequence of trying to think out in terms of the logic the conditions that make possible the comprehension of the logic. It is no more (and no less) egotistical than the use of the anthropic principle in some recent cosmology.

These considerations show that Hegel approaches the historical world with a guarantee from the logic that what he finds will express the movement of the concept and idea. He does not seek in foreign content lying around him evidence to validate or apply the logic. He is already persuaded of its validity from its internal progress. This leaves him free to take up content from what is around him. Any attempt to think concrete content up on his own would betray the encompassing unity of the logic itself.[6]

So Hegel is neither bringing foreign content into the light of the logical sequence nor extending that sequence deductively to generate content. He is working within an encompassing unity to bring to consciousness the movements of that unity in a variety of more particular areas. When he talks about politics and economics, he is not exactly applying a theory to practice but illuminating the already working structure we are within. And the act of illumination is part of the working of that structure.

In the *Philosophy of Right* Hegel claims to be developing the ideas of right and freedom from within themselves and, at the same time, to be developing speculative analogues of common political and ethical categories. Because of their speculative solidity his categories can be used to criticize and refine common understanding of what is going on. But this is not exactly to apply his categories so much as to show them already at work. Hegel does not deduce an ideal constitution from his theories. He finds in current practice the principles by which constitutions can be developed expressing the shape of spirit now available. He does not offer a new constitution; what he suggests is already present, at least in principle, in post-Napoleonic Europe. He uses the logical movement of the concept to disengage from the welter of current practices those truly appropriate to our stage of spirit. Our awareness of the structure of the modern world is not an outside event but part of the workings of that world, and our criticisms of inadequate understandings are part of the progress of that world. Unlike Marx, however, Hegel attributes no causal efficacy to this understanding. Spirit develops on its own and does not need our comprehension to accomplish what will be made transparent through our achieved knowledge.

Thus Hegel does not feel he is offering "his" solution for the problems of modernity. He has thought up no solution. He has the logic that enables him to see the solution that is already being worked out in the world; he supplies self-consciousness, not new ideas.

The danger in this procedure is most evident in Hegel's philosophy of nature. There he seems merely to wrap the logical categories around the results of his contemporary science in a way that adds no further intelligibility to the scientific results. When he deals with social and political matters, on the other hand, there is a sense of new insight. Perhaps this is because social and political inquiry was not so developed at his time—or at ours. Or perhaps it is because Hegel was more passionate about social and political matters. Or perhaps it shows that we are looking for something other than the speculative grounding Hegel was trying to provide. He is not concerned with learning new facts but with bringing unity and justification by demonstrating the indwelling patterns of the motion of spirit.

I have now answered in a roundabout way the objection that Hegel is hiding a covert empirical survey under his speculative process. He does look about him and pick his content from what he finds, but that survey is internal to, guided by, and guaranteed by the speculative process of which it is itself a part.

We should briefly consider another objection, one that is in some ways the reverse of the one just considered. Why is it that Hegel's system gives us *only* the content of the current world and its history? Think of Spinoza's absolute substance with its infinite attributes, only a few of which we know. Hegel's speculative totality may seem poverty-stricken in comparison. His spirit cannot be infinitely rich with continuously new basic possibilities. As I noted earlier, for Hegel the infinite self-relation of spirit authorizes a certain finite but guaranteed set of possibilities that are not chosen from among a wider set. There may be infinite amounts of empirical detail to be studied, but there are no different overall structures of time and space or of history and the state. Otherwise the self-transparency of spirit would be compromised. In an important sense, Hegel's world is finite.

My constant appeals to the overarching and encompassing quality of Hegel's claims does not mean that these claims are correct. But we need to be reminded of this kind of claim. In fact it furnishes one main alternative to the permanent residence in dichotomy offered by Weber and like theorists of modernity. Nor is Hegel's type of claim absent today. It appears in doctrines about the inescapability of language, in pragmatic wholisms that refuse the absoluteness of formal meta-levels, in poststructural thought. All of these, and to a modest extent even their chaste siblings such as Quine, make a move similar to Hegel's. They substitute for a final descriptive language in a subject-object framework a movement that enfolds within itself any attempt to establish a place beyond itself. There is less totalization, less self-transparency than Hegel would prefer, but in many thinkers today something like Hegel's general strategy persists.

Transcendental Philosophy and Reality

We have been considering the opinion, prevalent in many presentations of Hegel, that the logic represents an unfortunate metaphysical excrescence on some interesting social analysis. Among some thinkers familiar with transcendental philosophy, on the other hand, it is the logic that seems the sturdy part of Hegel's endeavor, while the social analysis needs to be better linked to the speculative strengths.

Klaus Hartmann and his collaborators, and in a somewhat different way Kenley Dove and his, have argued that Hegel's logic is a transcendental justification of categories. I have benefited from this work, and although the idiom I have used to discuss the logic differs, the substance is often similar. Hartmann also offers a sophisticated reanalysis of the *Philosophy of Right*. Somewhat like Taylor he finds the civil society section of the *Philosophy of Right* more convincing than its overcoming in the state, but unlike Taylor he offers suggestions for improving the discussion of the state to bring it into better connection with what he takes the logic to have proven.[7]

Hegel's "spirit" has been interpreted in many ways. I have resisted what I called the cosmological, or large entity, interpretation in favor of a more transcendental approach. There remains a difference between what I have suggested and the interpretations advanced by the scholars mentioned above. After discussing the logical sequence as a transcendental analysis and justification of categories, these interpreters go on to distinguish that sequence from its embodiment in the real world. But they do not seem to make this distinction along Hegelian lines. In discussing the logic, Hartmann argues that its aim is to develop valid categories. That validity is to be sharply distinguished from existence. The dialectic of categories provides a justification for certain modes of thought that should become normative for our social endeavors. It also tells us how to think about the relation of the categories to the world—from the side of the categorial sequence. The realities of society and history do not always seem to correspond to what we have thought out in the logical sequence. Hartmann and others do not share Hegel's faith in the overarching unity of thought and reality. The world may not correspond to what we discover in our transcendental investigations. It may be that we will be unable to make it so correspond. If not, we can say, with Fichte, "At least we have philosophized."

For Hartmann as for Hegel, philosophy is its own age comprehended in thought; it is possible that in the future changes will necessitate a new justification of new categories. Transcendental analysis is a reconstructive activity performed on the categories that have resulted from centuries of thought; it is not likely that they will be significantly changed, but it is possible. It is also possible that changes in society will reveal new dimensions, new phenomena whose categories will need to be validated. The structure of our thought needs to be arranged according to the overall architectonic of the logic. This architectonic expresses the permanent demands of reason for a total grounding that can be accomplished only through the circular process Hegel has discovered. That process and its overall movement will not change, but as history goes on, different materials might have to be arranged into the chain of self-coincident grounding. [8]

While I agree with much Hartmann says about the inner structure of the logical sequence, his views about the status of the logic within the system seem to invoke dichotomies that Hegel would reject. There is too much of an outside to the logical sequence. Thought and reality, norm and achievement are held apart in a way Hegel would never accept.

Hartmann and others would reply that Hegel purchases his overarching unity and his confidence in the perfect embodiment of the categories he discovers only at the price of positing an unjustified metaphysical absolute. I have suggested earlier that this is not the case, that the overarching unity of the system obtains enough hold on existence as we recognize the complete conditions of possibility for ourselves as thinkers.

It seems to me a mistake to take Hegel as ever positing the existence of any being, even of the world-spirit. To do so presumes there is a space outside the logical sequence where that positing could be done, and this is to deny the encompassing unity of the whole. While it is true that Hegel's lecture series on history, art, religion, and philosophy do not share the systematic rigor of the central books, they do not demand an external teleology such as Hartmann claims to find. They are attempts to think about the logical sequence in its otherness, but that otherness is not its presence in some foreign metaphysically posited realm. I take Hegel to be making much stronger claims for the power of transcendental analysis, claims so strong that there is no need to add a metaphysical appendix, as Hartmann accuses Hegel of doing, and no need to make a distinction between the transcendental analysis and its contingent embodiment, as Hartmann himself does.

On the question of what Hegel was doing, Hartmann does not seem to go far enough. On the more important issue of what is possible for our thinking today, Hartmann's proposal is more cautious and more acceptable than Hegel's. In fact, Hartmann is not so much trying to interpret Hegel as to correct him and make him useful today. He takes the idea of categorial justification to be the core of Hegel's thought, but a core betrayed by Hegel's full system. Corrected and made more rigorous, Hegel can be important today, especially in giving us categorial justification for social thought. This depends, however, on the success of the (re)construction of the logical sequence, a task concerning which I have already indicated my doubts.

In this chapter I have tried to show how Hegel can be a foundationalist thinker while not positing any "first" to be a foundation. Not even the logic taken by itself can be said to be an unqualified first principle from which nature and spirit are derived. To the degree that it can be so taken, the logic presents no steady first content to be inspected, but only the motion of the concept and the idea. That motion is not presented to our intuition or held as an object to inspect, but is something we acknowledge by finding ourselves within it. The self-transparency of that motion is not the clarity of a clear and distinct idea.[9]

In recent times antifoundationalist thought, which actively fights the positing of any first or any totality, has become increasingly popular. This leads to a debate, which will occupy us later, between

Hegel's totalizing thought and Heidegger's attack on "metaphysics."
Is the project of justification and self-grounding expressed in the
overall architectonic of the logic, which expresses what Hartmann
calls "the demands of reason," something timelessly necessary and
available to us, or does it belong to a historical space we might no
longer fully inhabit?

6

Civil Society and State

Hegel's confidence in overcoming the problems of modernity stems from his belief that the conditions that make a problem possible also bring about the solution. In terms of Hegel's logic the separation of formal universal and particular content is possible only because of the already posited unity of the three moments of the concept. In terms of concrete life, civil society and its culture are possible only because of the already existing wider community of the state. Hegel's solutions are not prescriptions for the future so much as narrations of the development already built into the problematic institutions and ways of life. Civil society first appears in its purity as something opposed to and posited as separate from its matrix in the state. But within civil society and the kinds of life it fosters Hegel finds self-transcending movements that lead to positing the unity of civil society and state.[1]

In this chapter we will examine the move from civil society to state. Members of civil society, as needy individuals capable of contracting with others, can choose to contract for whatever they desire. "[The] individuals in their independent freedom . . . have themselves in their particularity and their conscious being for themselves [*Fürsichsein*] as their goal—a system of social atoms. The [social and ethical] substance becomes in this way only a general mediating connection of independent units [*Extremen*] and their particular interests" (Encyclopedia #523). In civil society the social whole makes no demands except that individuals respect the freedom of others.

Because of the formal nature of the structures of mutual recognition in civil society, each self can distinguish his or her free choice from the particular content of his or her contingent desires, needs, and satisfactions. This separation liberates the individual from immediate identification with particular social roles. Yet in producing this liberation, civil society also produces a series of economic, psychological, and cultural harms that stem from the same separation.

Proponents of civil society contend that the harms are the price of freedom. Hegel argues that the freedom of the individual demands the fuller community of the state. The logical categories behind civil society arise within a larger process and cannot be taken as themselves complete and independent. If we confuse civil society and state, we will conceive freedom in terms of the separation of particular from universal, and this will leave freedom empty. If there were such a thing as a pure civil society, the citizens would live with an empty freedom that was in reality the tyranny of particular desires and contingent whims. If in fact our lives have more direction and purpose, as they do, then we are not living in a pure civil society but in a deeper totality that the categories of civil society will not describe correctly. That deeper totality is not yet fully posited as united with civil society.

The two forms of community must be carefully distinguished.

If the state is confused with civil society, and if the state's specific end is laid down as the security and protection of property and personal freedom, then the interest of the individuals as such becomes the ultimate end of their association, and it follows that membership in the state is something optional. But the state's relation to the individual is quite different from this. Since the state is spirit objectified, it is only as one of its members that the individual himself has objectivity, truth [Wahrheit], and ethical life. . . . The individual's calling [Bestimmung] is to live a universal life. His further particular satisfactions, activity, and mode of conduct have this substantial and universally valid life as their starting point and their result. (Philosophy of Right #258z)[2]

Paradoxically, the problem Hegel sees with the free citizen of civil society, who has been liberated from tradition, is that he is not free enough. He is still beholden to the contingent content of his desires and the external fate generated by the decisions of others on the market. He needs objective content to give him a rationally valid yet free way of life.

Objective Content and Freedom

To see what this demand for an objectively valid way of life implies, we need to extend what was said earlier about Hegel's conception of freedom. The will is a process of self-withdrawal that affirms my nonidentity with any particular item among my desires, needs, and impulses. The other moment of freedom is a self-determination whereby I posit a desire or goal as mine. But how do I determine what to posit as my goal from among the multiplicity available? "An impulse is simply a unidirectional urge and thus has no measuring rod in itself, so the determination of its subordination or sacrifice [to some other goal] is the contingent decision of the arbitrary will which, in deciding, may proceed either by using intelligence to calculate which impulse will give most satisfaction, or else in accordance with any other optional consideration" (Philosophy of Right #17z).

The key term here is *optional*. Hegel does not think that choosing some formal rule to apply to our desires, as in modern decision theory and its rules of maximization or satisficing, makes for fully rational choice. There are many possible rules and no way to derive only one of them from the definition of freedom, as Kant tried to do. The choice remains arbitrary. In such a case

> the subject is the activity of satisfying desires, *formal rationality*, as it translates them from the subjectivity of the content, which is purpose, into objectivity. . . . The will as thinking and in itself free distinguishes itself from the particularity of its desires and places itself as the simple subjectivity of thinking above this manifold content. . . . The will is at the standpoint from which it can choose among inclinations. . . . However the content on which this formally universal will decides itself is still nothing other than desires and inclinations. The will becomes actual only as subjective and contingent. (Encyclopedia #475–78; italics added)

This kind of decision, though it is made with the principles of formal rationality, is still not fully rational, because the content remains contingent, "infinite in form only" (Philosophy of Right #14). "At this stage, freedom of the will is arbitrariness [*Willkür*] . . . contingency manifesting itself as will" (Philosophy of Right #15).

This kind of freedom is still too much like a random process. It is not true self-determination, because the self involved is empty. "Its content is not intrinsic to its self-determining activity as such" (Philosophy of Right #25). The idea of an empty self freely giving itself content is an illusion; it results only in domination by whatever content happens to be contingently present. For there to be full self-determination there has to be something in the self that can serve as a measure and be actualized in a free decision. Yet that something within us must be more than a contingent fact about us. It must be both our own and also valid in a noncontingent way. Hegel agrees with Kant in calling this intimate but universally valid something within freedom "rationality." Without some rational guidance at one with our deepest selves, our choices cease to be ours in the special sense needed to separate freedom as our *own* acts from random acts that happen to happen within us (Philosophy of Right #15z).

In Kant's case the categorical imperative was to express the nature of our deepest rational selves, but it remained caught in the duality of universal form and particular content. Modern attempts to derive formal rules for rational decision making also fail because of this separation, which leaves them either powerlessly general or useful but arbitrarily chosen from a number of possible rules. In any case they remain tied to contingent content for their inputs and weightings. For Hegel the needed rationality must be found in the mediations of universal, particular, and individual through which any self exists. These are to provide a more concrete rationality that overcomes the separations characteristic of Kantian and utilitarian reason.

Freedom and Custom

The task is to recognize our freedom as involving the absolute form of the movement among all the moments of the concept, not just the separation of formal universal from particular content. How is this to be done? How does the self come to know and participate within all the mediations of the concept? What mental gymnastics lead to that awareness?

It is not a matter of individual awareness, and there are no mental gymnastics I can perform alone that will achieve this freedom.

To see freedom as involving the whole motion of the concept is to see it as no longer a problem simply of my will and my desires. I as a single individual can never embody all the moments of the concept, because I cannot stand related to myself as a universally valid content. While I can stand "opposite" myself by reflection, this produces only the separation of pure freedom from particular desires that remains "caprice" (Encyclopedia #469z).

Only by finding my place within the structures of mutual recognition of a rationally structured community can I find content
both universalized and particularized in a way more effective than
my private thought alone could perform. Such a community will
appear as a way of life with customs to be followed.

The question which are the good inclinations and how are the inclinations to be subordinated to one another changes into the exposition of
what relationships spirit brings forth as it develops into objective spirit, a
development in which the content loses its contingency and arbitrariness. The discussion of the true intrinsic worth of the impulses, inclinations, and passions is thus essentially the theory of legal, moral, and
social duties. (Encyclopedia #474z)

True freedom exists as a customary moral life [*Sittlichkeit*] in which the
will does not have subjective or selfish content but universal content for
its goals. (Encyclopedia #469)

The state grasps society not only under legal relations but mediates . . .
the unity within custom, culture, and the general manner of thought
and action. (in Ritter 1982, 123)

Everything hinges on living within a social whole whose divisions
into roles and ways of life is itself inherently rational in the sense
that it is derived from the motions of the concept. It will not do to
have a rationality of adaptation and maximization—that would be
civil society again—or a substantive rationality of immediately accepted goals—that would be traditional society. Hegel tries to affirm
a rationality at the base of society and of individual freedom that is
both substantive and formal. It is substantive because there are
definite structures and ways of life that are accepted as rational. It
is formal because those structures come from the absolute form of
the mediations within the logical concept. It is not one of Weber's
two kinds of rationality because it partakes of both and because in
it nothing is immediate, neither the structures, the process, the
particular content, nor the individual selves.

Through this mediation Hegel hopes to resolve the dilemma of
empty choice versus brutely contingent content. Alasdair MacIntyre
in *After Virtue*, concerned to validate the need for tradition and attack
the formal self, faces this dilemma. He appeals to the fact that we
are always within some historical tradition, so that the question of
naked choice does not arise. This answer, which has affinities with
what Heidegger will say, cannot satisfy Hegel. For him modernity

has brought an unavoidable new stance toward tradition. To be true to modern freedom we cannot just appeal to our insertion into this or that historical tradition; we must demand rational justification. But that justification must be in terms of the full rationality revealed in the logic and not the formal rationality of principles applied to contingencies. We always stand already within the motions of the concept; in that motion is a set of mediations among the three moments that must be present in a fully developed social whole. Any social totality that needs to be judged according to its rationality will contain these mediations more or less adequately, so we will be able to judge it.

The rational content of the social whole is to be found within its structures of mutual recognition. Individual selves exist self-consciously only through their mutual recognition of one another, and this demands structures by which such recognition can be mediated. In civil society these structures are quite formal, but in the state they have considerable content. How far does this content extend? The constitution, the general lines of the division of labor, the overall personalities of certain groups within the state, even something of the national characters of the different states—all these Hegel finds by examining the various forms of mediation among universal, particular, and individual. Further peculiarities of this or that nation or group are contingent, destined to interact, grow, and perish in the movement of history.

Hegel's way of finding content for a deeper yet rational community takes up and modernizes an old Greek move. Plato and Aristotle and the Stoics wanted to re-found the social whole on the citizens' shared possession of a common *logos*. At the core of each person is reason, the *logos* which provides a shared movement and a shared content that can bind the citizens together. This bond is neither contingent nor arbitrarily created. Hegel too uses this strategy, but he purges it of what he takes to be an insufficient respect for freedom. Plato could say that when we went into ourselves, we found there an openness to the patterns at the basis of reality. It is more important to Plato that we conform to those patterns than that we do so freely. Hegel will say that the patterns that are the basis of reality demand that our conformity with them be through our own individual choice and particularity.[3]

Hegel follows Kant in seeing freedom as more concerned with true self-determination than with multiplicity of options. While Hegel insists that a citizen must have a number of options and be free to choose his own way of life, he does not view every increase in the number of options as necessarily an increase in freedom. To be free is to be self-determined, but the self involved is not a naked chooser facing indefinite possibilities. There are limited options available within the rational structure of the community; this finite set articulates the mediations at the basis of social and individual life.

Hegel carries out the exposition of social content mostly on the political level. The state's economic patterns are those of civil society but are kept from unrestricted expansion by governmental regulation and by the social culture of the groups involved. The ways of life available in the rational state express the basic mediations of the moments of the concept: universal, particular, individual. Each division within the state expresses one of these moments as mediating and mediated by the others. On the highest level this is expressed in the divisions of governmental powers and the political organization of the state. The same mediations occur again in the basic division of labor, and they occur in finer detail in intermediate-level social groupings. Below this the rational form is harder to distinguish in contingent detail; Hegel has nothing to say about why one neighborhood has the custom of monthly block parties while another celebrates only at Christmas. But the essential modes of mutual recognition for basic social roles and identity are to be derived from the mediations of the absolute form.

The Syllogisms of the State

Hegel's treatment of the syllogism provides the details for the absolute form of the concept, where each moment of the concept is mediated and mediating in turn. Hegel treats the state as a system in which each moment is in turn the central mediating unity. The three moments of the concept are present: the universal is the social whole, the particular is each person's definite needs and desires, and the individual is each citizen as an independent free person. Hegel summarizes the mediations involved as follows:

In the practical sphere the state is a system of three syllogisms:

(1) the individual (the person) comes together with the universal (society, right, law, government) through his particularity (his physical and spiritual needs which when fully developed for themselves result in civil society).

(2) the will and activity of individuals are the mediating unity through which needs are given satisfaction within society, right, etc., and society, right, etc. are filled out and given actuality.

(3) however, the universal (state, government, right) is the substantial middle place [*Mitte*] in which the individuals and their satisfactions have and maintain their reality, mediation, and permanence.

Each of the determinations, when the mediation brings it together with the other extreme, comes together with itself, produces itself, and this production is its self-preservation. It is only through the nature of this coming together, through this triple syllogism of the same terms, that any whole can be truly understood in its organization. (Encyclopedia #198)

Both civil society and state contain all three mediations, but they do so differently. In civil society the unity is undifferentiated, and all difference comes from the unrelated particular content brought into the system by individuals. In the state the unity is differentiated and contains particular content built into the way individuals recognize one another in the social whole. The mediations can be contrasted as follows:

1. The particular brings together the individual and the universal:

In civil society: an individual's particular needs and desires are what link him to the social whole through the market.

In the state: a person's needs and desires fit or come to fit his chosen place within a rationally articulated social whole composed of subcommunities that have particular ways of life embodying various sets of needs and desires.

2. The individual brings together the universal and the particular:

In civil society: when the individual makes decisions based on his own needs and desires, his will and action bring about his own particular satisfactions, and his decisions also help make actual the social universal as a system governed by economic law and based on each individual seeking his own particular good and respecting the freedom of others.

In the state: when the individual makes decisions based on his objective position in the community and the way of life he has adopted there, his will and action bring about his own particular satisfactions, and his decisions also help make actual the articulated state based on each individual seeking the common good of all by seeking his particular good, which he knows to be rationally connected to the good of all.

3. The universal brings together the particular and the individual:

In civil society: The social whole is a clear space constituted by formal modes of mutual recognition. In this space individuals interact with others through their particular needs and desires. The social whole puts only external constraints on the individuals' particular needs and desires.

In the state: The social whole is a complexly articulated whole of different structures of mutual recognition that create a variety of particular social spaces within which individuals can live. These particular substantive modes of interaction grow naturally from civil society, expressing natural groupings of self-interest, and they also express the rational divisions of the state. This variety is not unlimited; it stems from the detailed mediations of the concept. When an individual chooses his mode of life, he internalizes the identity offered by a group. This helps order his desires and impulses from within. Knowing and participating in the articulation of the state, he can will the common good and his own good at the same time.

The mediations of the concept are embodied in differentiated structures of mutual recognition within the state. The individual can find a mode of life that is both his own particular choice and an articulation of the community rational in the Hegelian sense. The civil society merely provides a space and protects individuals' rights. The state provides more structure; Hegel calls it "the architectonic of life's rationality, which sets determinate limits to the different circles of public life and their rights, uses the strict accuracy of measurement which holds together every pillar, arch, and buttress and thereby produces the strength of the whole out of the harmony of the parts" (Philosophy of Right, Preface p. 9/p. 6). Statements like this earned Hegel his reputation for submerging the individual in the social whole. His intent is to bring both individual and community to their fullest development together. This does involve limiting freedom as it is understood in civil society. Those who attack Hegel for absorbing the individual usually differ with him about what it means to be a free individual with definite content in one's life. Or one might agree with his notion of freedom but complain about the institutional structures he suggests.[4] Hegel has no intention of advocating totalitarianism, although his institutional suggestions do not always well embody his intentions. He means to stake out a position that is neither the old absolutism of the central power nor the infinitely divisive freedom of the French Revolution and civil society.

In terms of current debates within the United States, it is misleading to view Hegel as favoring either laissez-faire or government activism. Such debates presume that private interests and government are two sides, each complete in itself and acting externally on the other. Hegel questions this presupposition.

For him the state is not external to civil society; it makes explicit the rationality that emerges within civil society. Just as in the logical sequence the categories corresponding to civil society are possible only on the basis of the already posited unity of the universal, so civil society is possible only if grounded in a larger community. If we try to think about or live within civil society ignoring that grounding, we end up with impossible tensions. A pure civil society is an idealization like a frictionless plane; it does not exist as described. It exists within a larger community, as "economic man" always has. What is distinctively modern is that civil society has been posited as free and separate within the whole. In the Hegelian state both the distinctiveness and the unity of state and civil society are to be posited. This state is modern because it recognizes the relative independence of civil society and its freedoms in a way earlier forms of polity did not and could not. The state is not civil society but the posited unity of civil society with its larger social context. The state is not an alternative to civil society. Neither a free civil society nor a modern state can exist without the other.

The Self-Transcendence of Civil Society

The mistake of many modern theorists, Hegel thinks, is to see the state as only civil society writ large. Hegel argues against the adequacy of civil society as a social whole. He looks at the dangers of such a society, as we saw in the second chapter. He analyzes the logical sequence of categories behind social totalities and applies this analysis to the notions of freedom and individuality, as we have seen in this chapter. Finally, he tries to show how within civil society posited as distinct from older forms of polity there are self-transcending developments that lead to the explicit positing of the unity of civil society and state. "The philosophic proof of the concept of the state is this development of ethical life from its immediate phase through civil society, the phase of division, to the state, which then reveals itself as the true ground of these phases. A proof in philosophical science can only be a development of this kind" (Philosophy of Right #155).

In the family an individual is immediately united with a particular role, for example, as mother or son. For Hegel the family is not a sphere of freedom, because the individual's will and insight are not involved in the determination of the particularity of his or her role. To say, as some do now, that relations among all the members of the family ought to be matters of contract would be to destroy the family as a separate sphere of life and to absorb it into the patterns of civil society. Just as Hegel argues for the state as a sphere beyond yet including civil society, so he argues for the family as a necessary sphere of life within the state but not reducible to civil relationships. Given the dialectical patterns, this also shows that although Hegel uses words such as *family* and *organism* to describe the state, he does not take them literally. They indicate too immediate a connection of the individual with his particular role. The state is meant to include freedom in a way that these less complete spheres do not.

Hegel perceives many self-transcending tendencies within civil society. I have organized them into seven categories.

First: The external restraints imposed by the market force the individual to face up to the social whole, at least in terms of external necessity and other people's desires. The individual cannot remain totally sunk in the particularity of his own impulses; he must order and chose among them so he can successfully meet his needs. In doing so he is strengthening his sense of himself as an individual who is more than a collection of particular impulses. Civil society helps "educate particularity up to subjectivity" (Philosophy of Right #186–87z).

Second: in civil society, interaction with others soon becomes a need on its own and not merely a means to satisfying one's physical needs (Philosophy of Right #192–94).

Third: the labor necessary to fulfill one's needs increases both the sense of self and the sense of integration into the whole (Philosophy of Right #197–200).

The first three developments begin to undercut the purely atomistic life of the members of civil society. The next two developments consider civil society as a whole.

Fourth: Civil society involves structures of mutual recognition, whereby each person recognizes the other as recognizing himself as a free person capable of choice and contract. The formally universal validity of these structures must be posited as such within civil society. This is done in the administration of justice. Fraud and tort are not just private offences against the aggrieved individual; they offend the basic structures of civil society itself. The result is that in the administration of justice civil society is explicitly posited as a whole within the life and action of its members. "In civil society the idea is lost in particularity and has fallen asunder with the separation of inward and outward. In the administration of justice, however, civil society returns to its concept, to the unity of the implicit universal with the subjective particular, although here the latter is only that present in single cases and the universality in question is that of abstract right" (Philosophy of Right #229).

The administration of justice corresponds to what some have called "the minimal state." In Hegel's eyes this is not a state at all but a feature of civil society. A real state is not an expanded version of this civil governance but a new medium of interaction involving a different kind of communal and personal identity. This view could be used to formulate a Hegelian answer to Nozick's question of how a government dare do more than be a minimal state (1974, 334).

Fifth: Besides dealing with wrongdoers, the civil authority supervises some contingencies affecting the society as a whole. Hegel departs from a laissez-faire model when he develops the civil function he calls *Polizei*. (The name is a reminder of the Greek *polis*, "city, community"; see Riedel [1970, 57] and Foster [1968, 157].) This function is the posited unity of particular individuality and formal universality. This civil authority looks after contingencies that would impede the rights of citizens to participate in exchange. For instance, in case of a conflict over the price of basic commodities that are essential for all consumers, this civil governance would take appropriate action (Philosophy of Right #231–38). Also, civil society becomes a kind of universal family, because it undermines all other substantial social ties. Thus the particular person has a right to look to civil authority for some guarantees of education, protection against extravagance with family capital, and remedies against extreme poverty (Philosophy of Right #238–46). The argument Hegel gives for this protective welfare function somewhat begs the question against a radical individualism that would claim that undermining substantial ties leads properly to self-responsible atomic individuals. What Hegel says here would have to be supplemented by his general attack on atomistic theories of society.

Hegel does not believe that economic affairs tend to equilibrium. The best the civil authority can do is mitigate the effects of continual overproduction, underconsumption, and disparities of wealth. The economy contains unresolvable economic tensions that must be taken into the deeper unity of the state, where they will be harmonized politically, not economically.[5]

Such tensions cannot be eliminated. This is one of those places where the power of the negative remains painful. Some persons are sacrificed to the well-being of all by being caught in mechanical labor or extreme poverty, and there is no solution within the unity of the state. This reminds us that the state is not the deepest unity in Hegel's world; there remains world history as a process (itself full of the power of the negative) and the reconciliation found in art, religion, and philosophy.

The final group of self-transcending tendencies within civil society highlights the differentiation that develops within the formal unity of civil society.

Sixth: People in civil society find themselves in groups with others who share their interests and means of livelihood. Such groups form out of shared individual self-interest that develops from the division of labor. These groups are the highest form of nongovernmental organization within civil society, and they become the lowest form of particular group recognized by the state. They thus play a double role. They are freely formed but also rationally necessary (Philosophy of Right #206z). They are rational by civil society's standards, since they are organized to foster particular interests, and they are rational by state standards, since they are permanent articulations of necessary divisions of labor and reflect the mediations of the universal. By building its system of representation on these groups and giving them political functions, the state encompasses civil society. In these double-faced groups the "a priori" of the concept meets the "empirical" of particular interest.

Hegel envisions such groups along the lines of industrywide associations, more reminiscent of medieval guilds than of modern trade unions. He calls them *Korporationen*.[6] By joining such a group the individual lives within a community with a definite way of life; he is no longer a purely particular individual (Philosophy of Right #207). The group provides the individual with a way of life that is communal and rational on the larger level, yet stems from his free choice. The individual's contingent choice is turned into a protected right to work and so acquires a universal aspect recognized by society. The social whole becomes less external and formal, and the individual's particular identity now includes a reference to the whole. "As the family was the first, so the corporation is the second ethical root of the state, the one planted in civil society" (Philosophy of Right #255).

Seventh: There is a second type of division within civil society that is taken up within the state. Hegel calls the groups in question *Stände*, which is usually translated "estates," since they are not quite what we call "classes." Hegel distinguishes three such groups, which arise through the division of labor. The substantive estate is linked to the immediate givenness of the land, family spirit, and natural rhythms; it includes agricultural laborers and landowners. The reflective estate seeks private interest; it includes business owners and workers. The corporations mentioned above are mostly subgroups within this estate. The universal estate works directly for the common good; it includes civil servants, jurists, teachers. These estates are not organizations with their own independent structure, as are the corporations. The division of estates is used to structure the legislative body within the state.

The points just covered show how Hegel thinks that civil society, posited as distinct from older forms of community, itself develops toward positing the social whole within which civil society exists. Civil society educates its members to a level of conscious universality, and it develops the internal divisions that will provide the rational structure of the state.

The Success of the Hegelian State

Hegel seeks a new community in which the life lived by "economic man" will be changed into a striving for the common good.

The state is the actuality of concrete freedom. But concrete freedom consists in this, that personal individuality and its particular interests not only achieve their complete development and gain explicit recognition for their right . . . but, for one thing, they also pass over of their own accord into the interest of the universal, and for another thing, they know and will the universal. . . . They take it as their end and aim and are active in its pursuit. The result is that the universal does not prevail or achieve completion except along with particular interests and through the cooperation of particular knowing and willing; individuals do not live as private persons for their own ends alone, but in the very act of willing these they will the universal in the light of the universal. (Philosophy of Right #260)

Hegel develops a fairly detailed outline of the constitution of the rational state. He aims at countering various extreme conservative or radical suggestions current at his time. While he thought that the basic principles for organizing the modern state could be discerned in the political changes after the French Revolution, his specific constitutional proposals do not echo the structure of any particular European country. He was certainly influenced by the Prussian government of his day, especially its more liberal form before the Carlsbad Decrees, but he was no apologist for any one system.

The feature that relates most closely to our question about modern subjectivity is that individuals enter the state through their objective particularity, that is, through the values and way of life they share in a group.

The member of the state is a member of . . . a group . . . and it is only as characterized in this objective way that he comes under consideration when we are dealing with the state. (Philosophy of Right #308z)

The circles of association in civil society are already communities. To picture these communities as once more breaking up into a mere conglomeration of individuals as soon as they enter the field of politics, the field of the highest concrete universality, is to hold civil and political life apart from one another and as it were to hang political life in the air, because its basis could then only be the abstract individuality of caprice and opinion. Hence it would be grounded on chance and not on what is absolutely stable and justified. (Philosophy of Right #303z)

If we compare what Hegel says with the standard American justifications for treating individuals politically in abstraction from their group affiliations, we see how voluntaristic is the theory of American democracy: the form of the state results from common willing, whereas Hegel contends the form of the state is what makes possible a common will. The American system would seem to Hegel "tantamount to a proposal to put the democratic element without any rational form into the organism of the state, although it is only in virtue of the possession of such a form that the state is an organism at all" (Philosophy of Right #308z). It would be interesting to consider from the perspective of Hegel's argument the increasing dominance in the United States of targeted political appeals and single-issue political groups. Hegel believes that undifferentiated suffrage leads to voter indifference and to a sense of powerlessness, which put elections into the hands of small caucuses (Philosophy of Right #331).

The details of the political arrangements Hegel envisions in the rational state have been widely criticized. I will not try to discuss the details of his constitutional proposals, except as several of them are useful for a critical perspective on his argument as a whole. It is possible to agree with the overall argument and disagree with much that Hegel proposes in detail. For example, Klaus Hartmann has argued that the Philosophy of Right fails in its detailed suggestions because Hegel has dealt only with the logical progression from civil society to state and not with the interrelations of the two. According to Hartmann, Hegel describes the arising of the state out of civil society, and while he succeeds in showing that the more encompassing community is demanded, he does not treat the complex social whole which results. Instead he treats civil society as one kind of totality and the state as another, without going into the relations that arise when they coexist and mutually influence each other. Hegel tries to rectify this by descending to details in his description of the state, but he succeeds only in losing its categorial character in the process. Hartmann proposes a different way of concluding the Philosophy of Right that deals with the interaction of civil society and state and changes the treatment of sovereignty within the state. For instance he and his collaborators suggest that the proper conclusion concerning representation is not the system of estates but a parliamentary democracy with political parties. Although I do not find this specific suggestion convincing in the context of Hegel's argument, there is much merit in Hartmann's overall criticism.[7]

Hartmann's basic line of criticism can be restated in terms of my earlier worries about the connection between overall movement and detailed content within the categorial sequence. In his concern to show that civil society cannot be taken as an adequate theory of the social whole, Hegel has neglected to describe the more complex social totality he proposes. We get an economic discussion of civil society and a political discussion of the state but not enough on how state and civil society are to interact. The logical sequence does underlie the crucial moves. This means that any vagueness in the criteria for success in the logical endeavor reappears in the Philosophy of Right when it comes to questions of detail. The overall movement of the absolute form, mediating universal, particular, and individual with one another, is repeated on many levels in the *Philosophy of Right*. This movement depends on the overall architectonic of the logic. But just as it is unclear in detail how the logical sequence is to proceed, so it is unclear what would count as a conclusive justification of detailed political and social institutions in terms of the larger movement within the *Philosophy of Right*. Different sets of institutions seem generally adequate, but none seems convincing as "the" right set to articulate the overall movement. As in the logical sequence, the overall movement and the detailed movements are not connected closely enough, and this makes the overall movement, the purported absolute form, itself something particular.

It will be helpful to look at several general ways in which the details of Hegel's state might be criticized. These raise issues that will be useful for relating Hegel and Heidegger.

First, the transition between civil society and state is supposed to come about through the two-faced institutions, the corporations and estates, which arise freely in civil society yet express the rational structure of the state. But what kind of connection do they provide? It is plausible to see civil society generating groupings of some kind, but do they develop of themselves into the elements of the state? Manfred Riedel (1970) has argued that these groups do not fulfill the role Hegel assigns to them. They develop in terms of civil society and its aggregate good, not the state and its common good. While it is true that the state needs these groupings in order to actualize its structure, the dependence is not mutual. The groups do not need the state's authorization in order to be what they are within civil society. Nor do they have of themselves any tendency to move to that authorized status. The state's enfolding of these groups seems to respond to the state's needs, not civil society's. It may be true that viewed from outside with an eye to totality and harmony, the state "should" be there to contain the excesses of civil society and its harmful effects on human identity. But these are not *problems* from within civil society. They are simply effects. It is not easy to show that civil society fails *by its own standards* in any way that demands a transition to the state. Civil society succeeds: it allows the sway of particular interests, it generates wealth, it protects freedom. To ask more is to place external demands upon it.

The logical sequence of categories that go beyond those of civil society does not seem to be internally expressed in this transition but imposed from outside. The two-faced groups are meant to express the self-transcendence of civil society, but they only show its inner differentiation. They do not by themselves demand the new type of larger political unity that is the state.[8]

Second, it is important to the political community of the state that individuals do not simply pursue their selfish interests. They act knowing that their particular desires and ways of life fit into the common good. In a traditional society members trust that their own social roles and the universal good fit together. That trust is an immediate feeling; it was destroyed when individual freedom was more strongly affirmed and the difference between particular interest and common good was posited within the life of the citizens. In civil society that difference is affirmed. In the state the unity of particular and common good is again posited, but in a modern way. That is, the citizen has "the right of insight." The citizen has the right to know the unity of particular interest and common good as something rationally clear, not just as an object of immediate trust or blind faith.[9]

In the passage quoted earlier the citizens were said to "will the universal in the light of the universal" (Philosophy of Right #260). Hegel wants the citizens to be able to find in their own particularity the universal. It is doubtful that his proposed arrangements successfully grant the right of insight. The citizens participate in government through voting and through public opinion. The various representatives are elected from the corporations. Such suffrage through local and familiar organizations would probably increase the sense of participation and the feeling that one's interests were being represented, but the elections are not of tremendous import. Elected magistrates work with the bureaucracy, which has its own traditions and values. Elected deputies are not bound to vote their constituencies' views, nor does the legislative body called the Estates have that much power. It functions more as an organ of mediation and conciliation and publicity than as a true legislature (Philosophy of Right #301–02).

The power called "legislative" actually resides in the interaction of the king, the bureaucracy, and the Estates. Hegel does not believe in the separation of powers after the American model, since this posits only separation and forces the various functions to face one another externally. Though he distinguishes the usual three powers of government, he refuses to assign each to a single body (Philosophy of Right #273).

Public discussion is not expected to have great effect in the state. Perhaps surprisingly for one who champions the right of insight, Hegel agrees with Plato that the multitude cannot distinguish truth from falsity (Philosophy of Right #279, #305z). Freedom of speech is guaranteed, but since the constitution is rational, the government is stable, and debates in the Estates are publicized, the citizens are left with little to say and no illusions that what they say is of great importance (Philosophy of Right #319).[10]

How then does the average citizen get the consciousness that the state is indeed rational and that in his free decisions he is "willing the universal in the light of the universal" instead of only pursuing selfish interest? He can keep in touch with debates in the Estates to see that his interests are being served, but this does not assure him about the rationality of the whole system. For this, the citizens have religion and patriotism.

The guarantee of the constitution . . . lies in the spirit of the whole people, namely in the determinate way [differentiated and structured] in which it has the self-consciousness of its reason. Religion is this consciousness in its absolute substantiality. (Encyclopedia #540)

[Patriotism is] the *trust* that my interest is contained and preserved [in] the state's interest. (Philosophy of Right #268, italics added; cf. Philosophy of Right #270a)

Hegel here faces the problem confronted by others who find the basis of political unity in some deeper shared *logos*, reason, or will different from the surface consciousness of the average citizen. The problem is to show that the so-called deeper element really is common and not just another particular interest masquerading as universal.

Hegel's state possesses, for the average citizen, no guarantees against false consciousness. The citizen cannot know, he can only trust that the state is rational. Given what Hegel has said about necessary mediation through the individual, if the average citizen cannot know that the state is rational in Hegel's sense, then the state is *not* rational in Hegel's sense.

It is instructive in this regard to consider Hegel's doctrine of the monarch. The king is the subjectivity of the state, the individual who says "I will" and unifies the whole articulated structure. But in a properly run state, Hegel says, the king does not have to make decisions for himself. He is bound by his counselors and merely signs his name (Philosophy of Right #279a, #280a). It would seem that for the average citizen also, *political* freedom (as distinguished from his economic and personal freedom to choose a way of life) mostly consists in ratifying what is decided by others.

Third, as the wider and deeper community, the state is supposed to put limits on the functioning of civil society. Not every possible commercial transaction or kind of satisfaction will be allowed. This is in part due to bureaucratic management for welfare purposes. A more pervasive limitation stems from the values shared by the citizens. The particular ways of living within various groups and within the nation as a whole discourage some choices and encourage others. The ways of life within the nation and its subcommunities are tied to the overall rational division of labor and social action that stems from the logical sequence as it appears in the structure of the state. But these ways of life, like all rational structures, are embodied in contingent ways of living.

Just as the various subgroups have their ways of life, for each nation as a whole there is a character and spirit that make a people French or German or Japanese. Most states will eventually adopt the modern rational constitution, and the differences between their political structures will be minimal. The differences of national spirit will remain very important, however, as a focus for loyalty and a check on the unbridled expansion of civil society's self-interested psychology. The national spirit must be kept active in the political consciousness of the citizens, lest politics degenerate into mere competition of various self-interested groups.

The values and ways of life that check self-interest will not be effective if they are only the result of reflective calculation and decisions made by distanced modern subjects. They provide the moment of immediacy in the citizen's relation to the state. Granted that ways of life and their values have arisen through history and are not immutable, it remains true that for the members of the group they should be found in immediately given customs and ways of living that also harmonize with and embody their free choice.

Commentators have often smiled at the peculiar political role Hegel assigns to the agricultural estate, but that role touches a deep modern problem. Hegel feels there must be somewhere in the state an immediate identification with values that give the state as a whole its particular spirit. He finds this in the agricultural life. The landed gentry form the upper house of the Estates and are given special access to appointive office. Their property is entailed so that they are assured of a livelihood and insulated from the selfish strivings of civil society. They live a life in contact with the land, with natural rhythms and the family.

Their mode of life owes comparatively little to reflection and indepen-dence of will. . . . This estate has the substantial disposition of an ethical life that is immediate, resting on family relationship and trust. . . . The agricultural estate will always retain a mode of life which is patriarchal and the substantial frame of mind proper to such a life. The member of this estate accepts unreflectively what is given him . . . living in faith and confidence. . . . This is the simple attitude of mind not concentrated on the struggle for riches. (Philosophy of Right #203, 203a)

Hegel's picture of an idealized peasant mentality may be naive, but the problem he is struggling with is very real: can we find substantial values that escape the corrosion of civil society? We are familiar today with similar longings for norms provided by the life of non-economic man.

Hegel was aware that the forces of industrialization were begin-ning to infect the agricultural class even as he idealized it.[11] This infection has only increased since Hegel's time; agribusiness and the scientifically manipulative approach to nature push agricultural life more and more into line with civil society. When the old peasant immediacy is destroyed, will reflective and willful attitudes dominate and reduce the agricultural life to one more item to be judged for its efficiency? Are there in the community no values to be celebrated without an edge of irony or a sidelong appraising glance?

Heidegger, in his approach to modernity, assumes that this loss has now become virtually complete. He worries about the result, and he looks back to the peasant mentality as a sign of what might yet come after the sway of modern subjectivity.

It might seem that Hegel's attention to the particular national characters of the various states is misplaced. Let the nations join into one world state and these particularities will be less important. A world-state would be just human and not French or German. Hegel would reply that there is no universal without particularity and consequent plurality. The only rational modern world-state, as distinct from a replay of the ancient empires, would be the formal rationality of civil society, with all its problems. In such a world the possibility for a deeper human identity is reduced, not enhanced. The particularity of the various states, with their own substantive national values, must remain and be mediated only by the processes of history, not by any larger political structure.

A worldwide civil society may be the direction in which we are headed today. Nationalism has remained a formidable power in our world. Nevertheless, rather than the various nation states enfolding and limiting civil society, history seems to show civil society enfolding the state. Rather than a testimony to a hidden rationality within civil society, the process by which the state authorizes as political agents various groups that arise within civil society may be a tribute to the adaptability of the state as one particular interest among others within the larger context of civil society.[12]

What has been at stake in these criticisms of Hegel's state is neither his ingenuity in inventing political structures nor his power to predict the future. What is in question is Hegel's totality and the relation of his logic to the world. He was committed to discerning in contemporary affairs the movement of the logical sequence. Given his limited success, it is tempting to save the program by moving up in generality and decreasing the audacity of the claims involved. But this threatens to change his careful balances into a tautologous separation of form and content. On the other hand, Hegel's insistence on the overarching universal stands as a rebuke to our own tendency to accept as ultimate the standard modern separations. Hegel forces us to ask if these separations are made possible because we live even now on another level as well, a level where those separations cannot be posited as final. We will see in Heidegger a different attempt to think in this manner, an attempt that repudiates the Hegelian universal and its logic.

7

Heidegger and the Modern World

Hegel's active career occupied the first thirty years of the nineteenth century, Heidegger's, the middle fifty years of the twentieth. The worlds they faced were both "modern," but after revolutions, world wars, Darwin, Freud, Auschwitz, and developments in technology, the worlds are hardly the same. Yet for all the differences between Hegel's time and our own, comparisons are possible and the continuities are obvious. We still describe our situation in terms that would be familiar to Hegel from his discussions of civil society and modern subjectivity.

There is a sense, though, in which our world results from failures in the reconciliation Hegel described as taking place. Universal, particular, and individual do not seem smoothly mediated in the structures of mutual recognition by which we live. Civil society has not been integrated into the modern state. Men do not find their lives rational enough in either the formal or the Hegelian sense. The power of the negative does not seem to be held within any reconciling unity. Hegel believed in the negative, the necessity of war, and spoke of history as a "slaughter bench" (Reason in History chap. 3, sec. 2a), but he also expected that sheer wasteful tragedy would no longer dominate our thoughts about how history moved. [1]

We turn now to Heidegger's discussion of modernity. We will move through the same topics as we did with Hegel: Heidegger's description of the modern world, his discussion of the conditions that make modernity possible, and then how this is meant to be applied in our life in the modern world. Because Heidegger's thought is deliberately less systematic than Hegel's, the various topics will interpenetrate more, and the exposition will retrace itself, introducing more detail and depth each time. I will bring in Weber and Hegel occasionally along the way but reserve the major comparisons until later.

Rather than repeating points made earlier in the discussions of Weber and Hegel, I will concentrate more on those aspects of Heidegger's description of modernity that add something to what we have seen so far. It is important to note that while we will first be considering Heidegger's characterization of modernity in terms of subjectivity, in his essays of the 1950s and 1960s he somewhat changes his description. In his essays on technology he prefers to speak of *das Gestell*, a difficult term whose translation we will discuss later, as crucial to modernity. While Heidegger does not abandon his treatment of modernity in terms of subjectivity, neither does he claim it to be the whole picture, as seemed the case earlier. Nonetheless, the theme of subjectivity continues, and it is important to us because it parallels what we have already seen and because Heidegger finds in Hegel a culmination, not an overcoming, of modern subjectivity.

The Homeless World

Like Hegel, Heidegger tries to show that modernity is located within a context and made possible by conditions such that the standard modern dualities cannot be taken as the last word. But while Hegel wants to correct and trim the pretensions of modernity, keeping its basic movement intact, Heidegger laments what he sees as the general direction of modern times. Hegel is confident problems are being overcome, even if the power of the negative will persist. It is Heidegger who speaks in the tone one might expect from Hegel's comment on the owl of Minerva in the preface to the *Philosophy of Right*. Heidegger seems a voice of gloom, but he means to offer hope. He fears we must endure an age of iron, yet as he often quotes, from Hölderlin, "Where the danger is, there grows the saving power." The dangers of the modern world are also an opening to new possibilities that go beyond the previous Western tradition.

Heidegger offers a description of the modern world that is similar, at least on the surface, to that we have found in Weber and in Hegel. Modernity is characterized by a distanced subjectivity that stands over against objects, judging and manipulating them for its own chosen goals. Heidegger condemns the endless "more" that results from this empty subject's efforts to affirm its identity and power over objects, especially in the expansion of civil society. Like Hegel, Heidegger traces the origin of modern subjectivity to something more fundamental in the process by which the world comes to have the meaningful shape it has.

In the modern world that Heidegger describes, civil society is swallowing up the state. All elements of tradition are being undermined or turned into marketable products to be chosen by willful consumers. Heidegger speaks of the "calculative thinking" that dominates our life and attributes to it the same basic structure as Weber's formal rationality. "Whenever we plan, research, and organize, we always reckon with conditions that are given. We take them into account with the calculated intention of their serving specific purposes. Thus we can count on definite results. . . . Thinking computes ever new, ever more promising and at the same time more economical possibilities. Calculative thinking races from one prospect to the next. Calculative thinking never stops, never collects itself" (Memorial Address 14–15/46). The results of such thinking are familiar: things are converted into commodities, nature is treated only as an instrument, and evils are to be solved by more calculation. This is the thinking one would expect from the members of civil society. For Heidegger this need not be the thinking of atomized individuals, as it is for Hegel. It could be mobilized by a socialist state as well as by bourgeois individuals.

There is nothing wrong with this thinking in itself. "Such thought is indispensable" (Memorial Address 14/46). What makes it destructive is the homelessness behind it, analogous to the loss of substantive content described by Weber. Calculation is in the service of empty subjectivity.

The partly conceded, partly denied homelessness of man with regard to his essence is replaced by the organized global conquest of the earth and the thrust into space. . . . The historical course of our era entertains the illusion that man, having become free for his humanity, has freely taken the universe into his power and disposition. The right way seems to have been found. All that is needed is to proceed rightly and thus to establish the dominion of calculated correctness [Gerechtigkeit] as the supreme representative of the will-to-will. (Nietzsche 2:395/4:248)

The willful emptiness of modern man manifests itself for Heidegger in such symptoms as the blending of war and peace into a constant state of mobilization, the reduction of true distance and nearness to a bland availability, the decay of art and of book publishing into fashionable commodity marketing, and the loss of the university's role as a place of centering and thought. He regards the solutions usually offered, such as a search for new values, careful planning to control the increase of technology, or more sensitive social engineering, as manifestations of the basic problem of manipulative subjectivity.

Heidegger's Characterizations of Modernity

In his essay "The Age of the World Picture" Heidegger lists five characteristics of the modern world: the mathematical science of nature, machine technology, the loss of the gods, the attempt at universal cultural formation for everyone, and the conversion of the realm of art to that of aesthetic experience. All of these have in common the relation of man's dominating subjectivity to some realm of objects he defines or enjoys. The first three traits could without too much trouble be translated into Weber's terminology as the disenchantment of the world and the dominance of formal rationality. The last two resemble Weber's prescription for what little hope modern man has of keeping life humane and escaping the iron cage of formal rationality and bureaucratic administration. For Heidegger such attempts at "culture" and "art" are only part of the problem; there must be another way out of the iron cage.

Unlike Weber, Heidegger does not interpret the changes that constitute modernity as happening in the beliefs and attitudes that individual subjects have about the world. Weber's methodological individualism is an expression of modernity and not a universal insight about the structure of man and society. The conditions that make possible any particular age in its difference from other ages are prior to the individual subject, though they could not "be" without him. Thus far Heidegger agrees with Hegel, but in specifying the conditions their views diverge.

In order to show how Heidegger goes about his analyses, I will examine two of his proffered characteristics of modernity. In "The Age of the World Picture" he cites the conversion of the realm of art to that of aesthetic experience. Works of art enter our world as objects used to stimulate a special kind of experience. A business develops for marketing such stimuli. In this development the more original function of art is lost. Art at one time could open up or change the world in which men live. (It would not be correct to speak of art as expressing the world in which men live; "expression" involves an inner-outer dichotomy Heidegger wants to avoid—which he finds throughout Hegel's treatment of art.) Instead of changing the way things are open and available to us, art now manipulates our feelings. The whole phenomenon of art is absorbed into a way of thinking and living centered on the subject-object division. Besides the art business, this produces the endless debates in modern aesthetic theory about the nature of the inner experiences involved in art, whether they are cognitive or emotive, how they link with sensible stimuli, and so on.

Heidegger's procedure here involves two moves. Through descriptive analysis and discussion of Greek ideas about art and language, he tries to drive home the point that modern ways of experiencing works of art and thinking about these matters are not the only possible ways. Then, through an inquiry about the conditions for any such experience and way of thinking, he tries to show that our deepest relation with the arising of a meaningful world cannot be thought in subject-object terms.

Art has not always been lived or thought about in the modern manner. Heidegger cites the Greek notion of art and its correlative notion of how the beings that surround us came to be meaningfully present. For the Greeks, he argues, to encounter something as real was to encounter it as coming to presence with other beings in the open space provided by *physis* (usually translated "nature"). Nature was encountered not as the sum total of objects and laws, in the modern manner, but as the process by which things rise out of hiddenness into the luminous clarity that reveals them in their order and their tensions. For the Greeks man with his perceptions and theories did not bring the world out of hiddenness nor collect it together into an order. Man's task was to harmonize himself with what was revealed. Art, therefore, was not involved with man's subjective responses, symbolizing them or stimulating them. Art was the skillful making present again of some thing or action that was already present on its own in the natural encounter.

Heidegger is talking about what is usually referred to as the theory of art as imitation (*mimesis*), but he is trying to describe it without speaking of a distanced subject who first internalizes an object in perception and then creates in an external medium some representation that reproduces the original inner experience. He tries to reformulate the Greek theory of art so as to make plain that the subject-object manner of thought is not the correct way to approach it.

The fact that the Greeks encountered art differently does not, of course, show that the modern way is wrong or inadequate. Heidegger's ultimate claim will be that the very large scale historical differences he points to cannot be judged in terms of their correctness or incorrectness. Nonetheless he wants to show that the moderns deny their own deeper context in a more thorough manner than did the Greeks. Although I have not tried to summarize his view here, he also tries to show that there is no simple opposition between Greek and modern; the modern way brings to fruition certain aspects of what started with the Greeks.

What I have just outlined is typical of Heidegger's method when he begins his treatments of modernity. He takes some current phenomenon or idea, sees it as expressing the subject-object split (or later, "technology" in his special sense), and contrasts it with the analogous Greek phenomenon or idea in order to show that the modern way is not self-evidently the only way to experience or think. He also tries to show the dependence of the modern way on the emphasis on presence that began with the Greeks. He then typically moves on to discuss the conditions that make the modern experience (and the Greek) possible.

Heidegger wants to question the obviousness of the subject-object way of thinking about language and art. He tries to develop alternatives to most of the standard basic concepts we use to think about the nature of our experience, including the concept of "experience" itself. "The guiding notions which under the names 'expression,' 'experience,' and 'consciousness' determine modern thinking, were to be put in question" (Dialogue on Language 130/36).

In the "Dialogue on Language" Heidegger worries that the modern Western subjectivist approach to art and to language may be corrupting Asians' attempts to think about the nature of art and language within their own tradition. In that dialogue and other essays he tries to develop a conception of the functioning of art and language that does not appeal to the standard modern picture of inner experiences expressed by some external sensible sign. The replacements he suggests for such basic concepts are proposed as more fundamental descriptions of our situation, although the role such new descriptions are to play in our lives remains difficult to specify.

Being and Time remains Heidegger's most sustained attempt to develop alternatives for the standard Western vocabulary centered on "consciousness," "experience," and the subject-object split. Heidegger never abandoned the basic moves made in *Being and Time*, but he came to feel that the wholesale creation of an organized new vocabulary was not helpful. In his later works he continually introduces new terms without systematizing them, avoiding, as best he can, hardening his terms into technical jargon. But the moves and gestures he encourages remain similar despite the continual new vocabulary. His later essays on language bring him into the neighborhood of Wittgenstein's attempt to think the nature of language without appeal to an inner mental realm. Heidegger's way is perhaps not as liable to behavioristic interpretations as Wittgenstein's, but neither is it as easy to link to discussions in the social sciences.

I turn now to a second and more obvious mark of modernity, the predominance of science and technology. It is clear that these play a larger role in Heidegger's understanding of our times than they did in Hegel's appraisal of his. For Hegel the new science was part of the liberation of man's understanding from the restrictions imposed by traditional society. The sciences provide man a new means to analyze and control nature, but they are not the last word. They describe nature under a particular type of abstraction on the level of understanding (*Verstand*), which must be complemented with the wider intelligibility of the inner essence of nature revealed by dialectical reason (*Vernunft*). Recent claims that science could describe reality exhaustively would have seemed to Hegel old-fashioned remnants of pre-Kantian thought; he argues against such claims in his philosophy of nature and in chapter 5 of the *Phenomenology of Spirit*. As for technology, Hegel did emphasize that machine manufacture and control of nature were key modern developments. The extent of recent technological developments might surprise him but would not require any radical change in his views. For him science and technology play a very important if subordinate role in characterizing modernity.

Heidegger, though he agrees with Hegel that modern science happens because of changes in something deeper in man's way of being, makes science and technology crucially important for his description of modernity. In "The Age of the World Picture" he gives three characteristics of modern science: the use of theories to delineate a realm of objects in advance, careful exploration of the realm of objects, and ceaseless organized activity. What is modern lies in the rigor with which these are carried out, a rigor that shows the domination of objects by the activity of the subject. I will consider each characteristic briefly.

(a) Delineation in advance (*Vorgehen*): Science involves creating theories that open a range of possible objects for investigation. Definitions and axioms create interrelated variables whose values range over defined possibilities as observation dictates. Only what is verified according to the structure of the theory will be allowed to count as true and real. For many today this might seem a straightforward description of cognitive process in any age, but for Heidegger it is a specifically modern mode of knowing. People did not previously interpret their theory (*theoria*, "looking at") as an act of their own that opened up a rigorously delineated realm for exploration. Instead they saw it as a way of conforming more closely, within an already naturally opened horizon, to things whose characters and behavior had only been anticipated in general.

By talking about the prior delineation of a realm of objects, Heidegger means to undercut the distinction between natural sciences and sciences of man (*Natur-* and *Geisteswissenschaften*). Done in the modern fashion, history predelineates its objects just as much as does physics. Only those events or causes that fit the delineation will be allowed to count as true.

In trying to assimilate mathematical and nonmathematical sciences to a single basic cognitive approach (for which he appropriates the Greek phrase *ta mathematika*, "the things known in advance"), Heidegger may well lose something of the specific nature of the mathematical sciences properly so called (see Kolb 1983). Nor does Heidegger's discussion of science in "The Age of the World Picture" fit as well with recent investigations in the philosophy of science as do some other aspects of his thought.

(b) Exploration of the range of objects (*Verfahren*): Objects are made manifest by and within the predelineated possibilities projected by the theory. The changes that objects undergo are defined and made understandable by the laws of the theory. Objects and their changes are made manifest and clear (*er-klärt*, "explained"). This happens through experiment and observation. Modern experiment is different from the previous approach to nature. Before, people watched things acting in order to see their natures revealed in their operations. Now people make things act in forced circumstances to reveal normally hidden qualities and laws. The distinction is not just that modern people push nature around more. The pushing happens because moderns have rigorous advance projections of the range of behavior expected from objects described in detail, while the ancients had only general expectations and counted on nature to reveal itself.

Just as Heidegger generalizes over the natural and social sciences, so here he effectively reduces all modes of explanation to a version of explanation by subsumption under laws. He is so automatically antireductionist that he does not explicitly deal with the issues raised by reductive explanation. So parts of his discussion of science beg questions that are very much open today, especially those dealing with multiple descriptions of the same entity. [2]

(c) Constant organized activity (*Betrieb*): Nature is encountered as offering the data for a total picture of the world in ever increasing detail; this dictates the institutional structure science will take. Modern science is not an Aristotelian assemblage of analogous sciences nor a Baconian collection of observations. Precise organization of the various subordinate spheres is part of the exactness of modern science. As a controlled exploration, science is always moving into more finely delineated ranges of objects. These specialized investigations interact to produce yet further developments. Science becomes a constantly busy, constantly expanding work of specialists in research establishments linked by communication networks and dependent on careful apportionment of resources. The elaborate institutional structure and the ever-expanding activity is all part of "the making secure of the precedence of methodology over whatever is" (The Age of the World Picture 78/125).

This is a typically Heideggerean move. Rather than seeing the activity and expansion of science as something to be explained in the everyday context of society and institutions (for example, as a response to social needs or a result of the politics of governmental support), Heidegger sees the way science is institutionalized as a consequence of a particular encounter with nature. This encounter is made possible by a historically specific understanding of the way nature is to stand revealed in its particular kind of reality.

Heidegger uses the Kantian word *Vorstellung* ("presentation, putting before, pro-posing") to express the essence of modern science. In contrast to earlier encounters with the world, modern science is based on nature set out before us as a collection of objects. Entities are certified as real if they can appear directly or indirectly before the judging eye of the distanced subject. To say that something is real is to say that it is available for that subject. This does not imply that things are only my representations of them, as in Berkeley or Schopenhauer. Things are independent objects, but to be an independent object means that a thing has the kind of reality that allows it to be pro-posed in objective fashion to the subject. Its whole reality can be made open to objective inspection. Its reality is its lying there in a field of entities able to support a set of objective facts. It is constantly available to be represented in a rigorous way. None of this says that the object will be easy to find, that difficult research may not be needed, that everything will be discovered; the point has to do with the meaning of the reality the object is projected to have whether found or not.

To the objection that he is overplaying the role of the subject, that man is still dependent on what nature deigns to show, Heidegger replies that the "nature" appealed to in the objection is itself another predelineated object defined in the modern fashion. This nature is merely the sum of known and as yet unknown objects and their laws; this is quite different from the older notion of nature as *physis*, the emergence from hiddenness that could never be wholly captured.

Nevertheless, in the modern experience of nature the Greek origin can still be seen at work. The constant presence and luminosity Plato and Aristotle attributed to the intelligible core of reality has now been transmuted into the constant availability of natural objects to the objectifying gaze and manipulation exercised by the distant modern subject. Heidegger has to do some fancy and not always convincing footwork, however, to claim that his description of the modern subject's mastery over things does not also fit ancient thinkers such as the Greek Sophists. Heidegger somewhat ignores the manipulative side of Protagoras and Gorgias and the technological side of Greek civilization generally. (See The Age of the World Picture app. 8; Nietzsche 2/4, sec. 14.)

The Modern Encounter with Things

The discussion of science shows how Heidegger understands the modern encounter with reality. A thing is affirmed as real if it can be revealed to a subject using the method of rigorous predelineation of a range of objects. It is not just that this is a peculiarly modern method of revealing the world, but that the idea of having a method for that purpose is peculiarly modern. The ancients had methods in the crafts, including the crafts of thought and words, but they had no method for revealing the world. The world revealed itself. Man's task was to conform to the world revealed or to make it present anew in art.

For the ancients it was *physis*, the emerging from concealment, by which things were gathered into the open where they could be encountered. This is the *logos* as well. Although *logos* is usually defined with words referring to speech and thought, the verb from which *logos* is derived has the connotation of gathering together and laying out. For the Greeks man was within the *logos*. Modern man believes himself the source or center of the gathering, the *logos*, performed by his conceptual tools.

As I pointed out earlier, Hegel's *Begriff*, the concept, has etymological analogies to the Greek *logos* as "that which gathers together and lays out." Many of the fundamental differences between Hegel and Heidegger can be located by posing for each of them this double question: "As a condition for there being a meaningful world, what is it that gathers what together?"

Formerly, says Heidegger, man was pulled into the space where things were gathered into presence on their own. It was man's tragic glory to be pulled within the conflict-filled space of nature's presence and absence, full of the strife and tension in mysterious harmony of which Heraclitus speaks.

With Plato and Aristotle *physis* is smoothed down into a harmony always, in principle, available to the eye of the mind. Darkness, strife, and temporality become signs of lesser reality that declines from the constantly reliable core of things. In modern times Hegel may bring back a needed emphasis on the dark, the absent, the negative, but Heidegger complains that Hegel brings these back only to catch them up all the more firmly in the massive presence of reality to itself that has been the growing theme since Plato.

Varying Understandings of the Being of Things

The changes in our understanding found in Plato and Aristotle were not mistakes they made. The history of men's various understandings of the reality of things is not a history of interpretations made by men. Man's encounter with reality is different in different epochs, but it is man-encountering-reality that changes: man's self-understanding, the mode of encounter, the reality things are understood to possess, all change. It is not a matter of a fixed subject assigning different interpretations to things.

This talk of varying encounters with the reality of things can be confusing. The first temptation, given recent philosophy, is to read Heidegger as talking about how different ages set up different lists of what kinds of entities are taken to really exist. It is true that such lists vary, but Heidegger is not talking about them so much as about what is meant when one says "is" or "really exists." In the context of most contemporary discussions, the answer to such a query seems obvious. How we determine what exists may be difficult, but existence is merely something's being there outside us. Existence is a yes or no business; there is not much more to be said. Heidegger thinks there is a great deal more to be said, and the modern discussions of existence are not the only way men have understood the being of the world.

The difficulty in comprehending what Heidegger is trying to say is similar to the difficulty in understanding Hegel's claim that there have been different kinds of individuality in history. When Hegel talks about what it was like to be an individual in a Greek city-state, we tend to read him as talking about different subjective beliefs and attitudes held by an individual subject in the modern sense. The core meaning of individuality seems the same throughout history. That core meaning is described by Weber's methodological individualism in terms of the individual center of consciousness stripped of value presuppositions and confronting a world of objects that have to be given meaning by individual and social constructs. That core meaning allows people to have at different times different attitudes and beliefs about themselves and their individuality, about their relation to other people and to their society as a whole. In modern times people have come to think of themselves in terms of that core meaning of individuality alone, without accretions from substantive value systems.

Hegel is saying something more radical. What it meant to be Antigone or Creon cannot be understood by taking modern individuals and changing their beliefs and attitudes. It was not just these subjective possessions but the structures of mutual recognition that were different. "Being an individual" is a social and interactive role that is prior to any subjective beliefs I may have. Viewed as separated from any such social framework, man is not a modern free individual but only a certain kind of flexible animal. Structures of mutual recognition make self-conscious individuality possible, and they change throughout history. Creon and Antigone are not modern individuals under their different clothing. What underlies the varying forms of individuality is not Weber's methodological individualism and its subject-object presuppositions but the logical movement of universal, particular, and individual in their mutual mediation.

Heidegger's claims about how the being of things is understood makes a similar antimodern point. When we hear him talking about different ways of understanding in history, using the example of the Greeks, we are tempted to infer that the Greeks had a different set of subjective beliefs about objects. There is an unchanging core meaning of "to be" in terms of neutral, factual, objective existence stripped of all subjective accretions. Just as with individuality, the modern slimmed-down notion seems to offer the key to history. Moderns experience the core notion directly, whereas traditional peoples overlaid it with subjective beliefs stemming from substantive presuppositions in their cultures.

Just as for Hegel it is wrong to take the modern form of individuality as the historical core of all such forms, however, so for Heidegger it is wrong to take the modern meaning of "to be" as historically constant. Just as for Hegel modern individuality does not account for its own conditions, let alone for the earlier forms, so for Heidegger the modern account of reality, as neutral factual being, does not account for its own conditions nor the occurrence of other understandings. How the world is revealed is not to be explained in terms of subjects confronting neutral objects. Nor is the modern understanding of objective existence so stripped-down and purified as it seems. It has its own content, which will turn out to be a certain interpretation of time, subjectivity, will, ordering, power—everything Heidegger assembles under the name "technology."

There are further complications, because for Heidegger all the understandings of being that are accessible to us in the West are connected with what started with the Greeks, as we saw hinted in the brief discussion of Plato and Aristotle above. Thus in a way we can understand earlier ages of the West from our own standpoint. But the manner in which this is done is quite different from assuming a single unchanging core understanding throughout history.

Besides, the history of the encounter with things in the West is only one such history. There have been others. We can enter into a dialogue with the other traditions, but this is a matter that requires more delicacy of intellectual touch than is typical of Western attempts to understand others. As befits his historical and finitist position Heidegger is very cautious about such matters.

Heidegger suspects that it is only in the West that the fate of "metaphysics" has been laid upon us. Perhaps only in the West has the encounter with things and the way they appear been fated to be experienced in terms of "being." In a nonmetaphysical mode of living, non-Western or post-Western, the notions of being and reality and existence would not occupy such central roles, and the understanding of what it means for things to be revealed would be achieved in other terms. Heidegger may be making an attempt at these other terms in his discussions of the fourfold, although I will suggest a more complex interpretation of the role of this puzzling terminology. One should be careful not to read as an idealistic move the suggestion that we might abandon discourse centered on being and existence; for Heidegger, discourse centering on consciousness is just a variant of the modern Western approach.

Preconceptual Understandings

Why are we supposed to resist the temptation to interpret man's different understandings of what it means for things to be as if they were different interpretations made by human subjects of a neutral reality? Why not see these various understandings as equivalent to the "conceptual schemes" often discussed today?

Conceptual schemes and other tools of explicit understanding are secondary, Heidegger thinks. The encounter with things happens first on a more basic level, out of which we form our conceptual tools and erect our explicit propositions. It is on this level that human "being" can be referred to as *Dasein*, the "being-there" of the "world," our "being-in-the-world." This more basic level cannot be described in terms of a subject consciously or unconsciously accepting propositions. We are rooted on this level, and it is capable of changes which alter our understanding of what it means for things to be, and our understanding of ourselves.

Heidegger attacks the supposition that concepts and propositions are the only way to structure an encounter with the world.

[We must question the presupposition] that knowledge equals judgment, truth equals judgedness equals objectivity equals valid sense. (Basic Problems 286/201)

In order for something to be a possible about-which for an assertion, it must already be somehow given for the assertion as unveiled and accessible. Assertion does not as such primarily unveil; instead, it is always, in its sense, already related to something antecedently given as unveiled. . . . So far as it exists, the Dasein is always already dwelling with some being or other which is uncovered in some way or other¹and in some degree or other. And not only is this being with which the Dasein dwells uncovered, but that being which is the Dasein itself is also at the same time unveiled. . . . Only a being that exists, that *is* in the manner of being-in-the-world, understands that which is, beings. Insofar as what is is understood, something of the nature of significance-contexts is articulated by means of this understanding. These contexts are potentially expressible in words. (Basic Problems 295–97/208)

For Heidegger, concepts and propositions are not the basic means for making things available to us as meaningful. Propositions select and make explicit meaning that is already lived with in another way.³

To talk of a realm of meaning prior to the articulation of propositions tends to confuse English-speaking philosophers. Our standard model for such a realm is provided by Locke and Hume, and that model has been seriously questioned. Heidegger does not mean to speak of such a realm of immediately given data, either atomistic sense data or a flowing sensory continuum. Nor is he talking about some prior realm where concepts are possessed independently of their role in propositions.

The prior way in which things are made available as meaningful is not an intuition of sense data or contact with subsistent meanings. Heidegger talks about our being-in-the-world. Significance is found in the world in which we are always already involved. A "world" is not a collection of objects for a subject; it is a texture of things and possibilities in which we are involved in action and ongoing purpose. Things are encountered in our actions as fitting into a texture; they lead on to other things revealed within possibilities for action. The possibilities we find ourselves among are not direct objects of awareness; they are not objects for us as subjects. They are present in a sideways manner as the horizon within which we comprehend practically the things we are dealing with. The "world" is the texture of lived possibilities that reveal the things around us *as* having this or that character. A doorknob is *for* turning; turning is for entering; entering is for talking, and so on in many directions and dimensions at once.

The words *as* and *for* are not used here as an explicit attribution of qualities to objects, but as the kind of understanding one has by living around things as they are revealed. The usual oppositions and dichotomies we use to speak of our situation (subject and object, thing and qualities) do not occur as such on this basic level of involvement; they report ways of thinking and acting that arise out of this level but are not its constitutive structure. Obviously there are precursors of subject, object, and quality, but these precursors do not stand separate and opposed so as to admit the application of either the standard modern picture of experience or the metaphysical analysis of substrate and quality.

Our meanings and purposes are not first chosen and then laid upon objects to create a significant world; we are able to talk or act only because we are within and relying upon the texture of the revealed world and the possibilities it holds open. We presuppose it for our language and our action. Nothing we do on our own can alter it as a whole. This is because in an important sense it is not a whole, not something we can gather into view. It is not simply a set of items in the background, as if each item were present and waiting to be made the central focus or as if the whole could be grouped together in a large overview. Significance is not for Heidegger a present relation between present entities. It is a matter of possibilities lived *as possibilities*, that is, as not present and yet as influencing and molding presence. The world stands as the texture of distances and absences and possibilities that create significance. It is the always presupposed context of any viewing, the structure of absences, that makes possible any meaningful presence.

Therefore, though it is true that propositions can report and articulate the world, Heidegger would object to the claim that all the significance involved in our world could be mapped into a set of propositions. Propositions articulate from within a field of significance that is not a collection of things made present to us. The world has no boundaries and is not already divided up to fit propositions. So there is no clear way of judging that it has been "all" expressed in a set of propositions. Sets of propositions are themselves items made meaningful within the world, not a replacement for or summary of the world.

The Space for Understanding

We can encounter things because within our world we have an understanding of their particular kind of being, of what sort of things they are. When I hold a pencil in my hand, my dealings with it unfold within an understanding of what it is used for and what kind of activity I am engaged in, as well as a more general understanding of what kind of thing a tool is and what kind of activity communication is. Different kinds of things, tools, actions, historical acts, natural things, human bodies, and so on all have their unique "horizons" of possibilities within the world. To understand one of these things is to be able to encounter it against the horizon of possibilities that gives it meaning and to be able to link oneself with the possibilities involved in its way of being. This kind of understanding is how we are in the world; it is not an act we reflectively perform later. Or better, it is the foundation of the acts we reflectively perform. In this basic sense, understanding means to project oneself upon a possibility (see *Being and Time* sec. 31–32; Kockelmans 1984, 33, 45–46). This understanding is not something we do but something we are. To be in the world is to be the locus of understanding and possibility.

Talk of projection sounds subjectivist, and Heidegger later avoids the term for this reason, but in *Being and Time* he does not intend the term to mean something we send out from an inner realm towards the world. There is no inner self to project out of; we exist as the opening of possibility and understanding with things. That opening is constituted by the lived intersection of the three dimensions of time, properly understood. Since meaning and possibility involve the future, the terminology of "projecting" is not entirely inappropriate, as long as the Cartesian connotations are put aside. We live as projects toward future possibilities on the basis of what is revealed.

For Heidegger there is a mutual dependence; neither the world nor our projects are absolutely first. The world, as a texture of significances and possibilities, needs us as the "place" where it "happens." On the other hand, it is the world as a field of possibilities that solicits our projects and shapes lived time. The world surpasses our projects, which are a response to what we find ourselves among. Heidegger will speak of a "call" that we hear addressed to us; this is the world encountered as a texture of significance that our projects do not exhaust and that opens ways for us. The world is lived as already significant, surpassing what we can project or what we can explicitly say. Its meaning is never completely explicit, always "yet to come," because it is never captured or exhausted but continually opens up to and encourages our further responses. It is the open space within which we are always already in motion. We are, Heidegger says, "thrown projects" (*geworfene Entwürfe*).

Within the open space granted to us, presence and absence in the ordinary sense are possible. But the open space itself, the world, is a kind of making present through absence. The various kinds of "presence" involved need to be disentangled. In the ordinary sense, John is present here in the room or absent on a trip to Canada. Heidegger wants to contrast this with what he takes to be a prior sense in which John's absence in Canada is a mode of presence. Even though he is away, John is involved in the texture of significance that is our world. The possibilities of his presence and absence in the ordinary sense are woven into the world. That weaving is a deeper sense of presence. John is, Heidegger would say, "revealed" to us. A being or an aspect of a being that was in the correlative deeper sense "absent" or "unrevealed" would not be in our world, *and* there would be no hole left by its absence, no expectations or possibilities unfulfilled.

Heidegger is concerned to recognize the conditions for this deeper presence or revelation of things. "From *Being and Time* (1927) to *Time and Being* (1962) Heidegger has sought . . . to think the Same as the nexus of temporality and Dasein, as the luminous clearing and concealing of being, and as the event which engages man to the presencing of whatever is present" (Krell 1975, 8–9).

It is a major contention of *Being and Time* and *The Basic Problems of Phenomenology* that in any understanding of the being of things the dimensions of lived time are the crucial feature. The modes of being of things are not a final term of our understanding but are themselves articulated upon a further horizon of understanding. All modes of being are suitably schematized unities of the temporal dimensions of past, present, and future, when these are understood more basically than in the standard picture of a set of instants marching in a line. Modes of being are determinate modes of presence and absence. This includes the mode of eternity discussed by the ancients, as well as the modern mode of neutral factual presence. The arguments Heidegger gives for this claim that time is the horizon against which any mode of being is articulated are too complex to summarize briefly; the best short presentation is in *The Basic Problems of Phenomenology*, section 21.[4]

What it means to understand the being of things is to be within the world in which they stand revealed and which they hold together as intersections in a tissue of possibilities that defines and reveals them. The world is not indefinite openness but a limited texture, though it has no boundaries. The limitation is partly qualitative (the Greek world is not our own) and partly existential, concerned with the closure of death as the possibility that ends possibility. This means that the world cannot be thought of as a field available for some total presence. There is no total understanding of the being of things that could encompass all others in perfect clarity. Every revelation of things is limited, but there is no totality of which it is a part.

The self is a being too. The conditions for its revelation, for our understanding, obtain in this case as well. We come to presence to ourselves within the world and with a particular understanding of what it means to be a self. There is no pure access to the self; we find ourselves in the world. We *find* ourselves there; we do not choose or manufacture or insert ourselves there. We find *ourselves* there; what we are is the nodal point of the lived possibilities that open up the world. Those possibilities have a definite character; we do not first start with indefinite possibilities that we then narrow down to those that fit or define the world around us.

Nor do we possess some pure access to ourselves through our ability to reflect on ourselves. "Reflection, in the sense of a turning back [upon ourselves], is only one mode of self-apprehension but not the mode of primary self-disclosure" (Basic Problems 225/159). Heidegger thinks this consequence of his position on understanding undermines all philosophies that make self-reflection the primary act of the self, which he interprets modern philosophy, including Hegel, to do.

We do not possess ourselves or things within some indefinite openness that is to be determined by experience. Our texture of possibilities is limited. Our world is not limited to a fixed number of things in just so many relations; there are no boundaries of that sort. But our world is limited in that it is articulated within certain definite temporal structures and not others. To be human is to come into being in the midst of an opened-out context of significance that has a definite character. The ideal of a pure openness to things, unlimited access and pure transparency, is an illusion based on the predominance of one particular temporal structure that emphasizes presence over the other temporal dimensions. We become, in the language of *Being and Time*, "authentic" when we cease to flee the finitude of the world we find ourselves within. Instead we actively take up the possibilities open to us, retrieving what is as yet unthought and unsaid within them and creatively cooperating with what has been granted us to be.

All this will clearly play an important role in Heidegger's dealings with modern subjectivity. He denies the modern subject its desired role as purified and distant. The very formality and purity of modern subjectivity are its substantive content. Modern purified subjectivity with its correlative world of objects is not the essence of what it is to be human, but only one possible reflective characterization of our being-in-the-world. Our rootedness in the world cannot be described in modern categories. Those categories are themselves rooted in a particular way of being-in-the-world structured by a distinctive understanding of the being of things and a distinctive mode of temporality. Modern subjectivity as it describes itself (for example, in Weber's categories) misdescribes itself by overlooking its being-in-the-world, which cannot be captured in modern terms. But this is not simply a mistake or the influence of a bad intellectual tradition. It is not something we can correct by changing our words. Our forgetting our rootedness is not accidental. It arises, and the categories of subjectivity arise, from the particular character of modern being-in-the-world. Heidegger describes this modern world in terms of subjectivity and technology as understandings of the being of things. It is to those understandings that we now turn.

Modernity and Subjectivity

In his lectures on Nietzsche, Heidegger said: "Western history has now begun to enter into the completion of that period we call the *modern*, and which is defined by the fact that man becomes the measure and the center of beings. Man is what lies at the bottom of all beings; that is, in modern terms, at the bottom of all objectification and representability" (Nietzsche 2:61/4:28).

When Heidegger says that in the present age man has become the foundation and measure, he does not mean merely that we tend to think in subject-object categories. Modern subjectivity runs deeper than this or that set of conceptual tools. Preconceptually, the world we find ourselves within is already such that in our actions subjectivity becomes central. We experience things as gathered together into the present moment for significance and accessibility. We experience this gathering-place as subjectivity. Various modern thinkers have named that subjectivity in terms of our perceptions, our representations, our theories, our language, our experience. (In contrast, approaches that call themselves postmodern often insist how much that place is not under our rigorous control.)

Descartes's quest for certainty typifies the modern self searching out and bringing all other beings into ordered and controlled representation before its critical eye. The self secures its own reality from doubt by its methodical treatment of its experience. Though this rigorous study of the world seems an absorption in objective reality, the self is constantly affirming its role as gatherer and judge. Knowledge of objective reality is a special mode of self-relation.

In this way the self is not just one pole of the subject-object relation; it is the foundation of that relation.

All that is, is now either what is real [*das Wirkliche*] as the object or what works the real [*das Wirkende*] as the objectifying within which the objectivity of the object takes shape. Objectifying, in representing, in setting before, delivers up the object to the *ego cogito*. In that delivering up, the ego proves to be that which underlies its own activity (the delivering up that sets before, i.e., proves itself to be the *subjectum* [in the old sense of "that which underlies and supports"]. The subject is subject for itself. The essence of consciousness is self-consciousness. (Nietzsche's Word 236/100)

In the time of the Greeks what came to presence had validity on its own, and man strove to conform responsibly to what was gathered together with him into the open space. In modernity, the reverse obtains. A thing has certified reality only if its being is the sort that can be represented in a rigorous way by man's subjectivity. Thought is no longer open receptivity but active assembling, *co-agitatio*, as Heidegger puns on Descartes. Subjects define themselves as having a mental life, an inner activity composed of thinkings, *co-agitationes*, where self and object are whipped into shape, made to reveal themselves in an orderly way within carefully prepared fields of possibilities. No more the incalculable tragic divisions of the Greek world; nature will be written in the book of mathematics, and man as object will soon find his place there too. Instead of openness for what comes to presence on its own, things are regimented into appearance before the modern judging subject.

In 1929 Heidegger and Ernst Cassirer conducted a debate at Davos, Switzerland. During one of his speeches, Heidegger said, "Since antiquity, the problem of being has been . . . interpreted with reference to time, and time has always been attributed to the subject" (Davos 37). As we saw earlier, Heidegger contends that temporality is the horizon upon which the various modes of being are understood. Here he reminds us that temporality has traditionally been interpreted as centered in the subject, which possesses memory, present perception, and anticipation. From Plato's *Philebus* and Augustine's *Confessions* time has been seen as gathered together in our subjectivity. In *Being and Time* Heidegger tries to retrieve a more original phenomenon of temporality whereby the activity of the subject is referred to lived time, rather than vice versa. What concerns us now is Heidegger's statement that the subject has been at the root of Western interpretations of the reality of things almost from the very beginning.

Heidegger strengthens his interpretation of history by a series of studies of major thinkers. He discusses, for example, the Platonic encounter with the reality of things as *idea* ("thing seen") and *eidos* ("form," the shape that emerges into visibility), the invisible essence that emerges into our intellectual sight. The intellect can know this constantly present and operative foundation of our life and all reality. The relevant structure of temporality is in terms of constantly available presence, and it includes reference to the eye of the mind, which will finally develop into the modern guaranteeing of all things before the judgment of the self-present subject. "Then the *idea* [the Greek understanding of a thing's being as its emergence into open sensible and intellectual visibility] becomes the *perceptum* of a *perceptio* [what is perceived by a perception], becomes what the representing of man brings before itself, precisely as what makes the to-be-represented possible in its representedness. Now the essence of *idea* changes from visuality and presence to representedness and the one who is representing" (Nietzsche 2:230/4:174). There is a close parallel with Hegel here, for he also sees the modern subject-object distinction developing from a distinction proposed by the Greeks, that between unchanging universal and changing particular, which is coordinate with the distinction of intellect and sense. This is not the same as the distinction Heidegger discusses, but is closely related. For Hegel as well as for Heidegger the Greeks stand to us in a relation of both contrast and ancestry. One of Heidegger's most difficult tasks is to talk about the changes he sees in history without becoming Hegel. He wants there to be some connection, some necessity in the history from the Greeks to today, yet he wants no part of Hegel's dialectical development (see Haar 1980).

In some of his essays on modernity ("The Age of the World Picture" and "The Question Concerning Technology," among others) Heidegger offers an unpersuasive account of how this historical development may have come about. He suggests that the changes in religious faith at the end of the Middle Ages forced the self, which had earlier found its self-certainty in God, to turn inward in search of the guaranteed presence that was involved in the Greek-descended understanding of the self's being. Modern subjectivity is born in this drive for a self-guaranteed certainty of its own reality. This account leaves it unclear if the initial decline of faith was caused by historical events or by some less obvious prior change in the understanding of being. Heidegger's general approach makes the first alternative unlikely, but the second begs the question of how the change occurred. Nor is it clear why the loss of faith would lead to a search for self-founded certainty rather than to other kinds of guarantee. Nor does Heidegger account for the various modern attempts to turn away from certainty and guarantees altogether, as in Montaigne or Hume.

The awkwardness of this sparse account (compared, for instance, with Blumenberg's extensive narrative (1983)) suggests that Heidegger is not really interested in tracing the changes from the Greeks to today in terms of locatable historical events or structural pressures within systems of thought. For him, changes in the understanding of being are primary. They condition ideas and historical events and are not conditioned by them. In various later essays he reworks his historical account to make all the relevant changes occur on a level prior to ordinary historical events. This is reminiscent of the priority Hegel gives to the logical progression over its presence in history. Heidegger would disdain this parallel, but I will urge it as an important objection to both thinkers.

We come now to the last aspect of Heidegger's account of modernity in terms of subjectivity, something that has little parallel in Hegel's explicit texts but which Heidegger thinks expresses a determining influence on all modern life and thought, including Hegel's. Some of Heidegger's most intricate historical analyses go toward establishing the thesis that the core of modern subjectivity lies in the understanding of the reality of things in terms of will, as ultimately expressed in Nietzsche's doctrine of the will-to-power.

When Descartes turns inward, he discovers his self as a constantly present entity that guarantees the presence of other things. The self is always co-present with any other mental content. Its constantly available self-presence is paradigmatic of what it means for something to be. The self that Descartes discovers is not merely present; it actively affirms its own presence as the being that gives other things their measure. From this perspective the difference between Descartes's immaterial souls and material objects is less than would appear, since both kinds of entities have constant available presence as their fundamental mode of being. But the self goes beyond this in actively relating itself to itself. Heidegger contends that the modern self affirms itself in and through giving measure to other beings. To be a subject in the modern sense is precisely to be capable of bringing things to presence before oneself, to be able to represent the world to oneself as a collection of objects. This representation is a making present under the discipline of the subject's view to form an orderly picture of the world. Modern subjectivity exists as a subject when it imposes order. To impose a self-originated order on other things is an act of will. Modern subjectivity's self-affirmation expresses its power to control the conditions of representation; the modern self in its judgmental role affirms itself as will.

It is only by emphasizing the Descartes of the *Rules* over the Descartes of the *Principles* that Heidegger can say some of the things he does. It is doubtful if Heidegger successfully justifies his claim that the modern self becomes the central entity in all modern metaphysical schemes. In Descartes the self may be the first entity whose reality is assured, but it is not metaphysically basic in the order of causality or even in the order of analogy. This is true for other thinkers who, like Descartes, deploy the Aristotelian distinction between what is basic in knowledge and what is basic in reality. In a sense, Heidegger tries to make Descartes more "modern" than he really is.

Heidegger is claiming more than that modern subjects are essentially wills imposing a willed rigor on the appearance of other beings. The being of all beings is understood in terms of will. This is not to assert panpsychism. Heidegger claims that the understanding of being as will does not arise by analogy with human willing but is prior to our self-understanding.

Even if the essence of willing which is thought here is obscure in many respects, perhaps even necessarily obscure, we can see that, from the metaphysics of Schelling and Hegel, back beyond Kant and Leibniz to Descartes, [any] being as such is thought as will. Of course, that does not mean that the subjective experience of human will is transposed onto beings as a whole. Rather, it indicates the very reverse, that man first of all comes to know himself as a willing subject in an essential sense on the basis of a still unelucidated experience of beings as such in the sense of a willing that has yet to be thought. (Nietzsche 2:342–43/4:205)

The understanding of being in terms of will is meant to cut deeper than the division of subjects from objects. It culminates in the Nietzschean conception, which entails no subjects and no objects but only contending dynamic forces and their spheres of ready control. This can be seen in many popular current visions of the world.

Heidegger's more general historical claim about being and will is plausible, for some nineteenth-century thinkers, but it is not obviously true for the period before the nineteenth century. Descartes does have a doctrine that makes will central to reality, but it concerns God. The primacy of the will in human subjectivity, which Descartes accepts, is a diminished version of its primacy in God, who can will even the truths of mathematics to be different. Many early modern thinkers accepted from the medieval voluntarists a sharp dichotomy between the determining activity of the will and the passive determinate results of willing. Most existent things are passive results of willing, not active centers. Only later is this dichotomy consciously attacked by Leibniz and Kant in their theories of nature, and by the post-Kantian thinkers more generally. Heidegger ignores how the earlier thinkers, Descartes and the empiricists, keep this sharp division between those beings that exercise will and those that are passive resistances to or results of willing. The first class includes the divine will and its imitation in man's subjectivity; the second includes physical atoms, ideas and impressions, extended substance, and the like. Heidegger ignores these examples and relies on Leibniz, who with his doctrine of the monad as the unity of perception and appetite is professedly working against the generally accepted division.

Early and late in his writings Heidegger opposes the centrality of the will. Though his own thought of the *Being and Time* period has been considered voluntaristic in its emphasis on resolve and authenticity, he meant to dethrone traditional conceptions of the will in favor of seeing man as a more dispersed tension that never comes together into full self-certainty or self-presence. Man exists in a spread-out temporality that can achieve what appears to be the self-presence and will of the modern self only by being implicitly already involved in the project of ignoring its own dispersed temporality.

Heidegger's discussion of modernity in terms of will carries us to the threshold of his later descriptions in terms of technology, which clarify and somewhat change the picture presented in the previous treatment. Before moving to these later descriptions it will be helpful to draw one further implication from Heidegger's treatment of subjectivity.

Because of what he says about subjectivity and will, Heidegger can explain the persistence of issues that Hegel thought had been overcome. For Hegel, modernity was the age of civil society and the bourgeois or romantic individual. In the *Phenomenology of Spirit* he does consider other relations of the individual to the social whole, and the typical epistemological and ethical problems that develop out of the subject-object stance. But bourgeois individualism remains the basic form of modern life; other forms are holdovers from earlier times now being reduced to moments within a social and intellectual whole that transcends them.

Heidegger sees individualism as only one of the sheaf of possibilities opened up for modern life; for him modern subjectivity and will can be lived without much change of principle by both bourgeois individuals and collectivist societies. The persistent unresolvable debates over the typical modern issues in politics or religion or philosophy show that the underlying modern understanding of being remains in force despite many differences of articulation.

The constant arguments that occupy modern thought seem to Heidegger all agitations within the same confines. Disputes about whether the individual will or the social will sets the standards for life presume the reduction of all human modes of being-in-the-world to one mode characterized by representation and will. Debates about the source of "values" for life presuppose the reduction of all encounters with things to experiences had by a subject; in that context values appear as a peculiar sort of object to be held on to. (Previously there were no values as experienced objects to be debated about; there were ways of life and things that called man to paths of action within the world revealed.) Epistemological problems about fundamental certitudes in experience cannot occur before "experience" has been created by the reduction of all the ways things come to presence into a uniform string of representations for a distanced subject. (The Greeks did not "have experiences.") Modern disputes concern typically modern problems that arise within the modern understanding of being and subjectivity. They should not be read back into history, nor should we try to solve them in their own terms. Insofar as is possible, such problems should be abandoned for new kinds of thinking.

The new beginning of thought, however, will not be something that we do on our own. Nor will some dialectic of history do it for us. Yet there is something about modernity that makes this new beginning possible. What that potentially innovative feature of modernity might be is not obvious from Heidegger's discussion of modernity in terms of subjectivity. To see the side of modernity that prepares its own overcoming we must turn to the characterization of modernity in terms of technology.

Modernity and Technology

In the decades after the second world war Heidegger's writings on modernity come to center on the term *das Gestell* which he uses "as the explicit key expression for the nature of modern technology" (Origin of the Work of Art 97/84). When Heidegger speaks here of technology, he means more than machines. They are a metonym for the particular field of possibilities he denotes as *das Technik*. He is careful to distinguish machine technology from the mathematical science of nature, but he reverses the common understanding of their relation. For him the term *technology* involves a particular understanding of the being of man and of things, opening possibilities for particular kinds of activities in the world. This understanding of how beings exist, and the consequent possibilities, calls for natural science as the appropriate way of making available the things in the world. Technology is not an external application of a science that is already a complete enterprise on its own. Today's science can exist only because nature is now revealed as existing in a way that makes possible and calls for the scientific approach to nature. This leads to a civilization supported by technical devices, yet the essence of technology lies not in the devices but in the way man and things are brought into presence together. Heidegger wants to explore that essence, that call for man and things to come to presence as they do. He names it *das Gestell*.

This word is difficult to translate. In its ordinary meaning it signifies frameworks that hold things ready: bookcases, racks, holders. Etymologically it contains the prefix *ge-* which can mean a collectivity (as in *Gebirge*, "mountain range," from *ge-* and *Berg*, "mountain"). This is followed by the root *stell*, "to put or place" (which we have already seen in the word *Vorstellung* in the discussion of subjectivity). Thus *Gestell* could mean a collection of puttings or placings. Heidegger defines the word (*Vier Seminare* 129) as the bringing together (*Zusammenbringen*) of all the modes of *stellen*, where *stellen* has the additional connotation of "to put a demand on" (*Herausfordern*). The word *Gestell* shows something of this meaning in existing compounds such as *Gestellungsbefehl*, "mobilization order," and *Gestellung*, "reporting for military duty." The military connotation is useful, since the military is a realm where everything is supposed to be set in order waiting to be used at a moment's notice. This complete and instant availability is much of what Heidegger has in mind by *Gestell* but the accent on hierarchy found in the military needs to be removed. *Gestell* is the call to encounter beings as available for ordering and willful use but without a central will that is itself exempt from such availability. This is the world of objects available to a subject but with the central subject removed and everything reduced to open availability.[5]

Albert Hofstadter has used the English translation "enframing" in his versions of Heidegger's essays (see his note, in Hofstadter 1971, xv). Emphasizing the complex of meanings around the German *stellen* William Richardson has essayed "pos-ure" (1981, 66, n. 24). Theodore Kisiel suggests "com-posite," stressing the "provocative positing" involved (see his translators' note, Marx 1971, 176n). Joseph Kockelmans uses "the com-positing" (1984, 229, 237). The Italian scholar Gianni Vattimo uses *im-pozitione* (Vattimo 1980). This suggests the English "im-position," which I will use, generally in the phrase "universal imposition" to remind us that all beings without exception stand revealed under this call. One defect of this, as of the other translations, is the connotation of a struggle against resistance, whereas Heidegger does not mean *Gestell* to imply resistance that is actively put down. Everything is open and available. Heidegger uses the term *Bestellbarkeit* for this quality; I will translate it by "total availability."

In talking about universal imposition commentators sometimes refer to our age in distinction to others, as one might speak of the age of romanticism or the age of reason. Strictly the word refers not to our age but to the call that opens the space for this age. As we will see later, there is a somewhat paradoxical aspect to its use, since in order to understand what we are saying we must already have experienced ourselves in a somewhat different way than the age calls us to do. To name our age in terms of universal imposition is already to be on the road to overcoming it.

Modernity characterized as universal imposition seems different from the domination of subjectivity discussed earlier. The central subject has been removed from the world. The will-to-power has become generalized, without any specific origin or locus. While the understanding of being as will provides a clear bridge between the two characterizations, it is not clear what Heidegger is doing with his later discussion. Is he saying that universal imposition was underneath subjectivity all along? Or does he think that the modern age comes in two stages, the first characterized by the domination of subjectivity and the second by universal imposition? (See Gillespie 1984, 124–26; Kockelmans 1984, chap. 9–11). While Heidegger does cast the analysis of universal imposition backward over the early modern period, its main focus is our contemporary age, which Heidegger describes as qualitatively different from the period stretching from Descartes to Hegel.

Nietzsche is the transition from the preparatory portion of modernity (historically speaking the time between 1600 and 1900) to the beginning of modernity's fulfillment [Vollendung]. We do not know the temporal dimensions of that fulfillment. (Nietzsche 1:477)

The further modern technology unfolds, the more the objectivity of objects changes into a standing ready for use [Beständlichkeit]. Already today there are no more objects (nothing that is a being in so far as it stands fast opposite a subject which takes it in view)—there are only things standing ready. (Vier Seminare 105–106; cf. 126)

In this culmination of modernity the being of things is no longer experienced in terms of objects certified before our rigorous subjectivity. Things no longer stand over against us; they stand by, standing ready.

Everything is ordered to stand by, to be immediately on hand, indeed to stand there just so that it may be on call for a further ordering. Whatever is ordered about in this way has its own standing. We call it the standing reserve [*Bestand*]. The word expresses something, and something more essential than mere "stock." The name "standing reserve" . . . designates nothing less than the way in which everything comes to presence. . . . Whatever stands by in the sense of standing reserve no longer stands over against us as an object. (The Question Concerning Technology 16/17)

Everything faces everything else as ready for ordering and use. Within our own activity the subjectivity analysis can still be applied to some extent, but Heidegger now emphasizes mutual total availability. Men too belong as standing reserve ready for human engineering.

The modern meaning of being has been purified and generalized. Instead of seeing man as the projecting center of a willful rigor that makes things reveal themselves within predelineated outlines, Heidegger speaks of a general "attack" and a "challenging revealing" that sets upon beings and makes them stand ready for ordering. This is similar to the interpretation of being as will imposing order that was discussed at the end of the last chapter. But now instead of seeing every entity as a center of active force that works on those around it, every entity is encountered as open and pliable for an ordering that proceeds without any center from which an ordering force radiates.

In the earlier phase of modernity the "attack" by which things were ordered into rigor and clarity could still be attributed to man's subjectivity. But with universal imposition we are to realize that the "attack" is not due to the way any particular being behaves. It is due to the call, the particular open field of possibilities and the way beings are revealed as such. Man behaves in a dominating or exploitative way because he too is challenged by the same call.

Only to the extent that man for his part is already challenged to exploit the energies of nature can this ordering revealing happen. If man is challenged, ordered, to do this, then does not man himself belong even more originally than nature among those things which stand by for use? The current talk about human resources, about the supply of patients for a clinic, gives evidence of this. The forester who in the wood measures the felled timber and to all appearances walks the same forest path in the same way as did his grandfather is today commanded by profit-making in the lumber industry, whether he knows it or not. He is made subordinate to the orderability of cellulose, which for its part is challenged forth by the need for paper, which is then delivered to newspapers and illustrated magazines. The latter, in their turn, set public opinion to swallowing what is printed, so that a set configuration of opinion becomes available on demand. (The Question Concerning Technology 17–18/18)

Man finds himself challenged to investigate and manipulate nature, but he is not an autonomous bestower of meaning. In important distinction to the earlier analysis of modernity, man's self-certainty is no longer the goal of his projects. If one could speak of there being an overall goal, it would be that the whole world possess the certainty of ready order, but this is not an order for some central inspector or user. The Cartesian subject stood in the center; now there is no center from or to which the call for availability and ordering can be traced. Man has been claimed within the overall way things are called to come to presence. Man does, though, have a special role as that receptive locus that makes all this possible, as we will see when we speak of the mutual need of man and the propriative event.

In the world of universal imposition all is orderly, but we should not be deceived: the "attack" on things continues as thoroughly as in the world of domineering subjectivity. The use of nature need not be violent and disruptive. As the example of the forester shows, what is crucial is that nature be experienced as a vast reservoir of materials for use, whether they be ores and timber to be consumed or unspoiled vistas to be sold to the tourist industry. In such cases the older kinds of encounter with nature have become impossible.[6]

Our world of universal imposition carries out fully the understanding of the being of things in terms of presence that has been with the West since the Greeks. Our world fulfills the Platonic desire for the essential being of things to be open and steadily present, but we have no transcendent dimension or any goal for *eros*. We have Hegelian mutual connection and transparency but without dialectical tension and depth. It is the achieved will-to-power but without Nietzsche's contention and shifting perspective. This world would be familiar to Comte: open facts ready for recording and manipulation but without Comte's religion of humanity.

We must beware of taking "universal imposition" or "standing reserve" as names for social and psychological phenomena. This would put the whole discussion into typically modern terms about objects getting meaning though psychological beliefs or social practices. Heidegger is trying to characterize the conditions for the occurrence of those modern beliefs and practices. Universal imposition is not just a new set of concepts or a new set of social relations, although it conditions all such psychological or social frameworks. It is the opening of a particular way in which things and men are made available to one another. It grants the space within which social institutions are lived. These institutions will be conditioned by the space granted them to be, but not vice versa. That open space is a preconceptual, prepropositional happening. It is the final triumph of the temporal dimension of presence, so that even past and future are revealed as things to be made present by research or planning. This is not a scheme or conceptual tool we have thought up; it is the space within which thinking is revealed as the making of conceptual tools.

Even though Heidegger's discussion is meant to be be presocial and prepsychological, it has similarities to a Hegelian or Marxist discussion of structures of mutual recognition that set the possibilities for individual self-affirmation. Since there is no exploiting class, the picture seems closer to Hegel than to Marx. Yet because Heidegger's discussion is presocial, there is no obvious place to intervene in order to change the bad features of modernity. There is no place to apply revolutionary leverage. Could it be that this picture is ideological, hiding the existence of concrete exploiters who are the prime movers of the system? Heidegger would answer such an attack by saying that we cannot attribute to the action of some particular entities what is in fact a question of the overall field within which any entity comes to presence. Like Foucault's "disciplinary society" (Foucault 1979) Heidegger's universal imposition has no first actors, only a constant ordering of roles and beings that fit together within a field that is not the product of any of them.

It is important for Heidegger that this be so, for universal imposition cannot have within itself any dialectical tensions. This is true of all the epochs in Heidegger's history of the understandings of being; they do not lead to one another because of dialectical tensions or deficiencies in the earlier stages. In addition, universal imposition has a special completeness. As the culmination of the drive to total presence and availability that has dominated the West since the Greeks, universal imposition has nowhere to go. There are no further transformations of the Greek legacy to reveal. Heidegger treats all the seeming tensions within modernity as themselves movements within the space opened up by universal imposition. The meaning of being as total availability cannot change on its own, nor can what goes on within it change that space. Attempts to plan and master technology obviously stay within the modern space of order and control; Heidegger feels the same about current religious movements and other changes sometimes cited as signs of a new age.

In wondering whether there can be transformative tensions within the structure of universal imposition, we touch on the question of the relative priority of dialectic and phenomenology. For Heidegger dialectic is simply a particular kind of movement within a prior space itself untouchable by dialectical gyrations. A dialectical account of modernity misses the essence of our world just as much as a social scientific account, and for the same reason: neither is aware of the basic meaning of being that lets it be what it is. This question of the priority of dialectic and phenomenology will recur as we continue with Heidegger's account of the opening of the space within which we find ourselves.

Putting Modernity in Its Place

Heidegger does not suggest that we try to change or escape modernity. Nor does he try to incorporate it into a fuller totality after the Hegelian manner. Nevertheless he does not want us to believe that subjectivity and universal imposition are the final words on the human situation. There is a sense in which modernity can be overcome.

Like Hegel, Heidegger finds that modernity is made possible by conditions that cannot be described using the standard modern dichotomies. Also like Hegel, he does not think that it is simply a matter of personal or social decision whether or not the modern age gives way to an age more in touch with its own basic conditions of possibility. Near the close of his essay "The Age of the World Picture," after describing the modern age in terms of subjectivity, Heidegger declares:

Man cannot of himself abandon the destining of his modern essence or abolish it by fiat. But man can, as he thinks ahead, ponder this: to be a [dominating and representing] subject . . . has not always been the sole possibility belonging to the essence of historical man . . . nor will it always be. A fleeting cloud shadow over a concealed land, such is the darkening which truth as the certainty of subjectivity . . . lays over a disclosing event that it remains denied to subjectivity itself to experience. (The Age of the World Picture 103/153)

Although we cannot change the modern age by fiat, we can understand its historical and finite nature. This may lead us to encounter an "event" that modern subjectivity cannot experience, an event that may become less hidden in a subsequent age. The present chapter will explore Heidegger's development of this theme: the event of unconcealment.

To be aware that modern subjectivity is not the only possibility for historical man is to abandon the idea that distanced subjectivity is the constant essence of human selfhood throughout history. This by itself is not enough to overcome the modern age. Even if it is not the only way, modern subjectivity could still be the highest or the best or the most useful way for historical man to be. Heidegger argues, however, that any standard we might use to make such a judgment of excellence would itself be within the current way to be and therefore have no suprahistorical validity.

So far, Heidegger's point resembles historical relativism. But Heidegger is not a relativist in the ordinary sense. Strictly defined, relativism claims that the thought and values of a given epoch are not absolutely valid, because they are relative to something else that is not a set of thoughts and values. Changes in this base cause changes in thoughts and values. Many relativists accept something like Weber's methodological individualism as a constant structure whose content varies throughout history. Others speak of a very general social structure whose changes are the basis for changes in individual cases. Others make the course of history itself a basis to be accepted. Heidegger does not admit these kinds of relativism. They all postulate some basis that remains constantly present through its own changes, acting as the foundation for changes in beliefs and values. But for Heidegger all entities are revealed within the limited texture of fields of possibility that is the world. The world is not an entity present to us within the world. If worlds vary, as they do throughout history, there can be no basic entity outside the world to be made present as the cause of the changes. Nothing is constantly revealed in only one way—not selves, societies, economics, history, or anything else that could be the base to which beliefs and values were relative.

Nor is Heidegger a relativist in the sense that he wants us to give up hope for anything more than what we have and spend our time understanding our historical era. Relativism can have quite absolutist consequences, when it urges us to accept and not question the era we find ourselves within. Heidegger is not urging us to settle down within the horizons open to us, content in the knowledge that all other horizons are equally relative. He is not calling for us to take consciousness of our relative situation, as if that could function as a foundation and base for our age. This is not the kind of living within our finitude that Heidegger will recommend (see Vattimo 1980).

If anything can be said to endure throughout history, for Heidegger it will not be the structure of any entity such as human subjectivity or society. He makes some universal claims about history, but he tries to avoid a position above it all in the way that Hegel demanded. Yet the question will remain to what extent Heidegger can avoid distinguishing some constant structure from its varying historical content.

The Privileged Position of the Modern Age

This chapter started with a quotation asserting that modern subjectivity is not the only possible way for man to be in history. In other places Heidegger makes analogous claims about universal imposition and total availability: there are other possible calls, other possible ways for things to come to presence. Our age is one among many, but it is privileged in certain ways. The present age has special features linked to the dominance of universal imposition. It is not the only or the best way to be, whatever that might mean, but it is the *last* way in the working out of the history that began with the Greeks. Whatever follows will be from a new beginning.

We touch here on the theme Heidegger announces in his essays on the end of philosophy and the end of metaphysics. He argues that history has worked out all the variations of the destiny that the West has lived out since the Greeks. This claim is difficult to evaluate since he never gives any satisfactory way to test the "all," which would seem to demand the kind of suprahistorical view of possible alternatives that he rejects. A better reason for his claim lies in the character of the age itself. There is a peculiar completeness to the leveling out accomplished in the age of universal imposition. Even the dominant subjectivity Heidegger earlier talked about disappears into the general availability of things to be ordered. There is no first being that imposes order on the rest. Unlike earlier ages in the history of the West, our age offers no highest being to be the ultimate ground. We cannot displace the wonder about what allows beings to come to presence.

In past ages this wonder at the occurrence of the open space that let things be revealed could be turned into the question of what cause or reason supported all other beings in existence. For the metaphysical tradition, there was always some being (God, nature, atoms and the void, the principles of reason, the modern subject, the laws of science, and so on) that guaranteed the others and was itself constantly available *as* so grounding the others. The highest being both supported the availability of other beings and was itself available as a being fulfilling that role.

In our age highest beings decay. Ours is the world that results after God has died. Heidegger interprets Nietzsche's saying to mean that there is no foundation any more, neither God nor any of his substitutes. In the world of total availability no one being grounds all the rest. Everything is functional; there is no highest. In a sense this is the culmination of the West's metaphysical drive: the meaning of reality is pure available presence. Everything, humans included, seems to be in plain view. There are no hidden dimensions that are anything more than a lack of information.

This leveled out availability provides a unique entrance into that which has been obscured since the beginning. Our age is the most thorough concealment of something that has been hidden throughout the history of the West, and yet our age needs nothing to complete itself. But that lack of need hides a deeper need. This age opens a way for us, because without a highest being the two questions hitherto held together can come apart. We have a chance to experience that even in the absence of a grounding highest being there still remains the question about the occurrence of the open field that allows presence and absence. How do we come to have the understanding of being we do? What opens out the world in which we are always already in motion?

This question is not a question about causes and effects, for that is a specific mode of understanding being. It is not a historical question, at least not as modern history is written, for universal imposition has leveled out our notion of historical explanation to functional differences within formal rationality. What kind of question is it? In the modern age we have a chance to find out. Precisely because we are called to universal imposition and total availability without any highest being calling us, we have a chance to take the step back that will enable us to encounter a context and condition that cannot be found in science or metaphysics. We can think about our context without thinking in terms of grounds and foundations.

What Heidegger is saying descends from the transcendental conditions of possibility discussed in the enquiry Kant initiated and
Hegel continued. But what Heidegger arrives at is not transcendental
in the precise Kantian sense of being a necessary structure of subjectivity, and it is not intended to have the foundational role Kant
sought for his results. I will argue later that Heidegger's enterprise
can legitimately be called transcendental, but his method for establishing his claims is more phenomenological than a traditional transcendental deduction. Our preconceptual inhabitation of the world,
the propriative event, and other conditions Heidegger talks about
can be "seen" if we do not shut ourselves off from the phenomena
by prejudicial presuppositions (see Basic Problems 88f, 225ff/63,
159–60). Though he does not conceive of experience and reflection
in the subject-object manner of Husserl's phenomenology, Heidegger keeps the Husserlian (as opposed to the Kantian) belief that the
conditions making experience possible need not be argued for
indirectly.

Universal imposition appears to be the stable mutual availability
of all things for ordering. But Heidegger also uses words such as
attack and *challenge* to describe it. Under the seeming calm is the
constant shaking urge to enlarge the actual reach of order and availability. In his discussion of subjectivity Heidegger would have attributed this to man's need for self-certainty and then gone on to
ask where this need comes from. In discussing universal imposition
he is more direct: man belongs within universal imposition and is
not its source; man acts within possibilities and a mode of temporality
that solicit and challenge him to further activity.

Precisely because man is challenged more originally than are the energies of nature, that is, challenged into the process of ordering, he is
never transformed into mere standing reserve. Since man drives technology forward, he takes part in ordering as a way of revealing. But the unconcealment itself within which ordering unfolds is never a human
handiwork. . . . It has already claimed man . . . so decisively that he can
only be man at any given time as the one so claimed. (The Question
Concerning Technology 17–18/18–19)

Man has a chance to discover the mutual appropriation of his
own being and the texture of significance that is his world. Universal
imposition is a challenge, a call. Man is the one who receives the
call, who is challenged. He could not be man otherwise, for he can

only be open to the world in some definite way, within some definite understanding of the being of things. But there is no highest being that issues the call. The call addresses him in the fact that he finds himself always already in motion within possibilities that reveal things in a definite way. He cannot exhaust the significance he finds himself within, and he is solicited to respond to it with his own explicit projects.

Avowal and Overcoming

In naming our age the time of universal imposition, Heidegger is asking us to avow that we are challenged in this manner. There is a paradoxical quality to this avowal. We are to name universal imposition as our destiny, the opening of the world within which we are what we are. We name ourselves as those who exist as human insofar as we receive such a call. But this is *not* the meaning of our selfhood in terms of modernity. There are many modern descriptions of our mode of being: we are subjects facing objects, we are manipulated manipulators, ordering and ordered units, the workers and planners, the dominating and the dominated, and so on. These self-definitions all speak in terms of subjects and objects; to say that we exist by receiving the call to universal imposition is to use new terms. To avow that ours is the age of universal imposition is already not to go along completely with our age. We can do this because there is more to us than the definition modernity gives us. In order for modernity to be at all, we have to be more than modernity tells us we are.

Heidegger speaks about the opportunity we have to experience the danger, the challenge, the destiny of universal imposition *as such* and not covered over by yet another metaphysical scheme or highest cause. This experience is already liberating. By realizing that we are under the destiny of universal imposition, we admit our inhabitation on a level that universal imposition does not define. For the everyday technological world there are only things made present. Avowing that we are challenged by the destiny of universal imposition, we avow that we are involved with the granting of presence and not just with the things made present. As this cannot be described with the categories of modern thought, those categories cease to be finally definitive of what it means to be human. As Heidegger says in a magazine interview, they are "to be *aufgehoben* in the Hegelian sense" (*Spiegel* 217/62). That is, they remain but lose their unconditioned power. Nonetheless, the way modernity is to remain yet be over-come, for Heidegger, is quite different from the incorporation of modern categories and institutions into a higher unity, which Hegel had in mind.[1]

Talk of a deeper level of inhabitation carries with it several dangers that Heidegger wants to avoid. One we have already discussed, the danger that we will understand what he is saying in terms of meth-odological individualism. Another danger is that we will imagine some odd cosmology or some atemporal operation going on that results in the various historical epochs characterized by their various ways in which man and things come to presence together. Or we might imagine the various epochs as themselves instances of some more general form that is knowable on its own, as products of some immanent necessity in history, or as limitations on some original fullness of encounter between man and things.

Any of these interpretations would make of Heidegger a meta-physician with a rival account of the basis of the world. He does not want to be that kind of thinker; he wants to give the conditions for whatever way the world may be disclosed, as those conditions are encountered from within the present epoch and the history available to us. He is not writing a countermetaphysics; he wants to discourage any attempt to write either metaphysics or counter-metaphysics by making such attempts face their conditions and lim-its. Heidegger is at times ambiguous about whether he is offering us a new world or the conditions for any world, for he means the two to be connected. We can live in our present world aware of its conditions, and this prepares for a possible new world. Heidegger must tread carefully to avoid having such a life turn into that union of spirit with its own structure and conditions found in Hegel.

Appropriation

If it is not a renewal of metaphysics, then what is this granting of presence that is the context and condition we live within? Behind the everyday effects of modernity that occasion complaint or praise, Heidegger discerns universal imposition as the call for things and man to appear as standing in reserve for ordering and disposition. Universal imposition affects us immediately and overall (*geht uns überall unmittelbar an*) (Identity and Difference 100/35). But universal imposition is not the last word. Heidegger discerns a possibility that our experience of being challenged within universal imposition could

turn us toward something more basic. We have seen the characteristics of universal imposition that make this possible.

Heidegger wants to locate universal imposition in the place where
it is made possible. Universal imposition is not ultimate; something
more primal speaks through it (Identity and Difference 100/36).
There is a place beyond the ground we are assigned in the modern
age (104/39). Heidegger speaks of universal imposition as enclosed
within a wider space (102/38; see also What Is Called Thinking? 57/
33). In *Identity and Difference* he speaks of the journey from our local
region (*Bezirk*) to the larger surrounding realm (*Bereich*) that makes
it possible. This image is misleading in a number of ways, but it
emphasizes that modernity will be "overcome" when it is seen in
its proper context.

Recall that in Hegel civil society loses its absoluteness when it is
located within the movement of the concept expressed in the concrete totality of the state. The mutual mediations of the three moments of the concept provide the context for any historical shape
of spirit. That mutual movement cannot be factored into a pure
form with some contingent content inserted into it. For Hegel there
is a decisive identity between the shapes of spirit and the motion
that makes them possible. The form of the concept is its own content. Modernity is caught up in an activity whose transparency to
itself is the final motion of what it means for anything to be at all.

For Heidegger universal imposition, like any epoch in history, is
complete in itself. There is no dialectical tension to be resolved by
a move to a larger world. Tensions there may be, and Heidegger
will have much to say about the kinds of nonidentity and nonunity
involved, but there is no Hegelian dialectic. Universal imposition
does not need to be inserted into a larger concrete whole in order
to be fully itself. The terror of modernity is the power of this seamless
field within which all things can come to presence, albeit a presence
that enforces a forgetfulness of its own happening. But that happening is not a missing item within the modern world.

What does offer something more than modernity? With Heidegger there is no ultimate realm, no place beyond modernity that we
can investigate purely on its own. He intends to agree with Hegel
that there is no empty form for which the various historical epochs,
ours included, are contingent contents. In contrast with Hegel there
is no final coming together, no logic of an absolute form that is its
own content. For both thinkers, there can be no ultimate separation

of form and content, but what Heidegger means by this and his reasons for it are quite different from Hegel's.

While Heidegger does not appeal to any final concrete totality, there still must be something more to say than just describing universal imposition, or there will be no way of coping with modernity except on its own terms. Heidegger says: "What we experience in universal imposition as the constellation of man and being through the modern world of technology is a prelude to what is called *das Ereignis*. . . . In *Ereignis* the possibility opens for us of overcoming the simple dominance of universal imposition in a more original happening [*Ereignen*]" (Identity and Difference 101/36).

The word *Ereignis* is difficult. Heidegger argues that it cannot be properly translated, since it is as basic to this thinking as was the Greek *logos* or the Chinese *tao* to theirs (Identity and Difference 101/36). Still, we should speak in English, or the term will become something to conjure with rather than to think about. Heidegger has chosen carefully; the German word catches up and unifies many different connotations. The ordinary German usage signifies a happening or an event. The word appears to contain the root *eigen*, "own, proper," which can suggest man coming into his own, finding himself. This also echoes the verb *er-eignen*, "to appropriate," which speaks of man and things being appropriated (ap-propri-iate, brought into their own) together in the current constellation of their encounter. There is also the suggestion of placing before the eyes, showing something new, coming to light (*er-äugnen*; this is the historical root of the current German word).[2]

Because of the concentration of many themes in one German word, it is difficult to find a single English equivalent. Translators generally use neologisms based on "appropriate" or "own." Thus we have "appropriation" (Joan Stambaugh), "disclosure of appropriation" and "enownment" (Albert Hofstadter). The connotation of an event is captured in "e-vent" (William Richardson). Both are present in "event of appropriation" or "appropriating event" (Theodore Kisiel and Joseph Kockelmans), and "propriative event" (David Krell). When I have needed up until now to refer to aspects of *das Ereignis* I have generally used phrases such as "the opening of fields of possibility" or have spoken in terms of a "call," translating Heidegger's *Anspruch*. Now that *Ereignis* is explicitly introduced, I will employ David Krell's translation, "propriative event," which expresses many though not all of the connected themes involved in the German word.

The Open Space

Because of the dominance of universal imposition, which plays out and levels out the metaphysical impulse to search for causes and grounds, we moderns are especially situated to experience the propriative event on its own. Universal imposition can lead us to the propriative event not as an effect leads to its cause nor as a content leads to its form, but more as a sound, or perhaps a silence, leads us to the extending space between ourselves and a nearby mountain.

If we become aware of ourselves as claimed and challenged within universal imposition (for Heidegger it is more a matter of awareness than of an argumentative conclusion), we become aware of a determinate appropriation of things and man to be open to each other in certain definite ways. This is our epoch's constellation of "the realm, vibrating in itself, through which man and being together each attain to their essential happening [in ihrem Wesen erreichen]" (Identity and Difference 102/37).

We can become aware of the opening up of that realm, the extending out of that space, its happening as an "event" that appropriates us and things in a determinate way. We can experience ourselves and things being gathered into a particular constellation of presence and absence. This is not a locatable event. In one sense it is always happening; in another sense it is the always-already-having-happened of the past that is the always-already-in-motion we find ourselves within.

We must be careful how we speak, lest we suggest that there is a pure and prior event of opening before any content, something that might be described in a formal theory. One of Heidegger's basic claims about the propriative event is that we should not think of it as constituting a pure space to be filled by contingent historical modes of being. In the West our understandings of the being of things have been dominated by the Greek understanding of true being as constant presence, and this has led to the modern experience of things as neutral facts available for interpretation and use. This suggests, in turn, that we think of the opening of historical spaces for the encounter with things as the constitution of some formal or neutral space. But this only extends the modern understanding rather than penetrating to its conditions. Insofar as Heidegger can speak about any permanent deep structure to man's historical experience, it will involve temporality, finitude, and self-withdrawal, but these will not constitute a formal description of a pure space that we first inhabit before encountering the definite possibilities open to us.

Mutual Need

We are speaking here of the way things are revealed, the way they take on meaning within the texture of the world, the prior understanding we have of their particular ways of presence and absence and time, what Heidegger calls their being. We are speaking of the mutual belonging together of man and the being of things and the mutual need they have for each other (Identity and Difference 92/ 29).

As we have seen, Heidegger rejects the primacy of self-consciousness. Man does not first have awareness of himself and then move from some inner sphere toward things. Man exists as the openness to things revealing a particular world of significance. To be aware of things, and of himself, man must already have a preconceptual understanding of their mode of being. In *Being and Time* Heidegger spoke in terms of man's receptive projection of the dimensions of lived time, whereby man both receives and projects the possibilities that make the texture of the world. Later, he decided that this language still sounded too subjectivistic. He began to speak of man as standing in the open space of the world. The opening of that space was not due to man's projections. Man did not make this open space; it is not man or man's creation. Heidegger suggests at times that the free space imparts itself to man as a destiny, but this still makes it sound as if there were a relation between two entities. Man does not first exist and then extend an awareness that creates or receives the open space. A receptive standing in that space is what it means to be human and aware. What I said earlier about prepropositional and preconceptual awareness within fields of possibility needs to be carried over into this mode of talking. The way man stands in the open is not by having concepts or theories but by being involved practically in his significant lived world with its characteristic modes of the mutual interpenetration of the dimensions of time.

If this is so, then Heidegger can speak of a need on the part of man for that open space. Otherwise man cannot be what he is. But there is need on the part of the open space as well. It would make little sense to talk of such a space without speaking of its receptive inhabitation by a being such as man. If one tried to speak of the open space without speaking of man, one would reify the space into some superentity prior to things. But the open space cannot "be" without man as its receptive support, its "abode" (*Unterkunft*) (see Nietzsche 2:390/4:244).

This mutual need cannot be conceived as the kind of mutual dependence of two entities that need each other for their full actualization, as with two organisms in symbiosis. Nor can the two be conceived to have a dialectical relation. Heidegger argues that the traditional categories of identity and difference must be rethought. The most sophisticated modern attempt to think through these categories in a new way is Hegel's dialectic, but for Heidegger this still relies on the primacy of self-consciousness as the constant presence of a unifying central ground. Thought of this way, the mutual need and belonging together are reduced to stages within the inner development of spirit, a fundamental being that achieves constant presence to itself.

A being such as human existence is needed for things to be revealed. Notice that we cannot say that the open space requires some conscious being. This would make consciousness prior to the inhabitation of the open, but Heidegger is trying to describe what is prior to consciousness considered as a subject-object relation. What is needed is not a perceptive consciousness but a receptive abode for the open space of possibilities that makes possible ordinary presence and absence.

The discussion of the mutual need of man and the open space for each other does in some ways parallel discussions in the idealistic tradition about the need to have consciousness (or, more recently, language) in order for the world to take on meaning. In these cases consciousness or language is usually taken as a property belonging to man conceived as a being complete in itself, a "subject" in both the ancient and modern senses.

Heidegger would claim that his analysis in terms of man's necessary standing in the open undercuts any talk of consciousness or language as a property whose possession makes us human and gives meaning to the world. Man does not possess the open space as a property; nor does man possess a relational property of standing within it. Man exists as standing within that space; man's being human is that receptive standing there. Man is nothing before this. There is no foundation or substrate in man's being to which this is added.

The questions about the relative priority of subjects over objects that fill modern epistemology are for Heidegger not germane to this thought. According to Eugen Fink, "All the concepts that arise in the dispute over idealism and realism are insufficient to characterize the shining forth, the coming forth to appearance of what is" (Heraclitus Seminar 139/85).

Heidegger did say, in *Being and Time*, that without man there would be beings but no being. There would "be" things but no meaning, no insertion in the texture of the world, no availability or revelation. There are two easy misreadings of this statement. The first is to say, as Sartre is often read to say, that without man and his projections things would be choked with themselves, meaningless, absurd. Yet absurdity is not the absence of encounter but a way things can be encountered, a particular understanding of their being. The second misreading is to say that without man things would be neutral facts waiting for an interpretation. Neutral factuality is also a way of revealing things within a particular understanding of their being. Both misreadings assume that things are first revealed or available in some basic neutral way to which meaning is somehow added. But there is no neutral or prior revelation of things. The unconcealedness of things always comes about within some particular understanding of their being.

Without man there would be things in the dark, as it were. There would be neither meaning nor the absence of meaning. There would be nothing missing or absent, no space with vacancies to be filled by things. With man, things stand revealed, but only in some finite, limited way. [3]

The Silence of the Propriative Event

The most important thing to say about the propriative event, taken on its own, is that there is almost nothing to *report* about it. Heidegger speaks of the propriative event as "withdrawing." It is not available for comments. "What closingly withdraws itself is not at first open, in order then to close itself. It does not close itself, because it is also not open" (Heraclitus Seminar 241/150).

The opening of a free space for the appearance of things is not some event that happens elsewhere. It happens not beyond or behind beings but, as it were, in front of them (Nietzsche 2:382f/4:238). Yet that happening is not obvious. The forgetfulness of the propriative event that Heidegger finds throughout the Western tradition

is not due to inadvertence on man's part. The very nature of that
event is to make beings open and available but not to intrude itself.
Heidegger says the propriative event "refuses itself."

This should not be surprising, since the propriative event has
nothing to show for itself. This is so in several senses. As an opening
of the space for the encounter with beings, the propriative event
allows things to rise out of the darkness we spoke of above. If the
propriative event had qualities of its own, they would need to be
made available, unconcealed. It would be some kind of entity among
other entities, and the event of unconcealment would be missed.
The propriative event cannot itself be an entity or event or relation
among other entities. To think it as an entity is to perform the
metaphysical transposition of the wonder about unconcealedness
into the question about grounds and causes.

If it is not an entity in its own right, the propriative event does
not have a structure, inner necessity, or law, or anything about it
that could come to presence on its own. This means there is nothing
in it or related to it that serves as a foundation for its occurrence.
Therefore there is nothing about it to understand, as the word
understand is commonly used. There is nothing hidden in it to be
ferreted out, nothing to be analyzed, nothing to be used as a first
principle or ground or as basis for an explanation.

The propriative event neither *is* nor is it *there*. . . . What remains to be
said? Only this: the propriative event appropriates [*Ereignis ereignet*]. Saying this, we say the same in terms of the same about the same. (Time
and Being 24/24)

The event of appropriation is just itself and nothing more. It is without a
"why?" which asks about grounds or reasons. "It remains," Heidegger
says at the conclusion of his lecture on *The Principle of Sufficient Reason*,
"just play: the highest and the most profound play. But this 'just' is everything, the one, the only." (Pöggeler 1978a, 107)[4]

It happens; that is all. It is the belonging together of man and
the unconcealedness of beings. We can speak of what belongs together and the ways they are together in different epochs. But there
is nothing further to "understand." It can be named, and the name
can be carefully chosen. We can ponder our need and our belonging
to the propriative event. We can wonder at it and open ourselves
to that belonging, finding more original possibilities, retrieving the
original granting of presence and absence which opens our tradition

but has become covered over by ordinary interpretations and projects. All these things, parallel to the "authenticity" of *Being and Time,*
we can do. But we cannot "understand" or "theorize." Wonder may
be the beginning of philosophy, as Plato and Aristotle said, but in
this case that wonder can never become knowledge, never make
the transition to *episteme* the two Greeks desired. This is not because
there is some deep, ineffable intuition to frustrate our thinking but
because we are touching the condition that is not an entity that
appears within a field or context. It is the context of all contexts,
as it were, but it has nothing to say about itself.

For all this, we should not interpret the propriative event as a
matter of simple fact, as if Heidegger were advocating a phenomenological version of positivism. The propriative event is not just a
fact. For Heidegger "facts" achieve their factuality by being set before a subject; the propriative event is something we are always
already involved within. But if we take "fact" in the sense that the
propriative event is immediate, always prior and simply to be accepted, then the propriative event is the immediate "fact" of the
particular belonging together of ourselves and our world, which
allows both to be what they are.

Before he used the term *Ereignis,* and at times later, Heidegger
used the word *Sein,* "being," to designate the opening into unconcealment, as well as to talk about the meaning or sense that beings
had when unconcealed in a particular way.[5] Speaking in that way,
Heidegger said that "being" refused itself and then kept its refusal
to itself. The refusal, the turning away of being was itself hidden.
It was this double hiddenness and not our careless thinking that
made possible the Western metaphysical transposition of the questioning unconcealment. In the modern age and the domination of
universal imposition and its leveling of all grounds and causes,
that double refusal can become visible. In the nakedness of the
modern world the old metaphysical grounds lose their strength,
and the absence of the propriative event can be experienced as
such. We can experience the withdrawal. In one of those long
sentences that chain nouns together, Heidegger states that "thinking takes a step back from metaphysical representing. Being [the
propriative event] lightens as the advent of the keeping-to-itself of
the refusal of its unconcealment" (Nietzsche 2:389/4:243). The unconcealment that brings things out of darkness has been concealed as such, and that concealment itself has been concealed,

but the propriative event can appear as the coming into presence of that absence.

The technological world banishes all the old absolutes and substitutes nothing in their place, only universal functionality. There is the possibility that we will experience this as the final revelation of the world as the totality of knowable and manipulable fact. But there is the further possibility that we will experience differently the strange combination of total availability and overall meaninglessness that is the technological world. We may experience the mode of being of things within universal imposition and may experience the call to that mode of being. That call, the belonging together of ourselves and the world of universal imposition, comes from nowhere within the world of universal imposition. We can experience that "nowhere" as the withdrawal of the propriative event, experience it as the absence of something that is not one of the old absolutes. The death of God can be experienced as the coming to presence of the hiddenness of the propriative event. At the culmination of the West's drive to understand the being of things in terms of presence and availability, we can experience the withdrawal of the condition that has made that drive possible. "The manner of movement most proper to the propriative event [is] turning toward us in withdrawal" (Time and Being 44/41).

We do not come to experience the propriative event itself, as if the propriative event were some basic entity or mysterious happening that until now had not been noticed. We experience rather its hiddenness, its withdrawal, which is to say its character as not an entity. We experience thus the dependence of our world and ourselves on a condition that has nothing to say for itself. In one way this overcomes the Western "forgetfulness of being," but it does not bring into final luminous transparency the conditions for our history. We experience our dependence on a condition that has nothing we can grasp, that cannot be self-present after the manner of Hegel's absolute knowledge. There is no absolute form to be made present, no motion of the concept in which to share with full self-awareness.

The Finitude of the Propriative Event

Our experience of being already involved within the propriative event is an experience of finitude. The propriative event is not an indeterminate openness waiting to be filled in; it has a particular character in each epoch. It is finite and limited. That limitation does not come about through some restriction placed on a prior full openness. We cannot imagine it as if a spotlight fell on only a selected part of a dark stage. In such a case total illumination would be always conceivable, even if it came only by integrating the partial views. Different partial views would be of a whole accessible to the divine sight or to what approximations of that complete vision we could manage to create.

Heidegger means to recognize the finitude of the propriative event without contrasting it with a possible total revelation. Unconcealedness happens only as finite possibilities. In order to make this change in our thought, Heidegger suggests we avoid images of illumination, which have been since Plato involved in contrasts of part and whole. He takes the German word *Lichtung*, which can mean "illumination, lighting," and uses it in another of its meanings, "a clearing in the woods, a place where light comes through the trees." The propriative event opens up a clearing, makes things less heavy and close, allows light. The "clearing out" can be thought without reference to illumination.

"Clear" implies: to clear, to weigh anchor, to clear out. That does not mean that where the clearing clears, there is brightness. What is cleared is the free, the open. At the same time, what is cleared is what conceals itself. . . . The dark is, to be sure, without light, but cleared. Our concern is to experience unconcealment as clearing. That is what is unthought in the whole history of thought. (Heraclitus Seminar 257f/161f)

This image of clearing offers less temptation to imagine that there is a total clearing to be performed. There is no totality, no total view, no first or last word.[6]

Concerning this limitation built into the propriative event, we need to remember Heidegger's early remarks about death and nothingness. The cleared open space of the propriative event remains as precariously finite as any of the descriptions of *Dasein*'s being-toward-death. In *Being and Time* Heidegger argued that man was not a consciousness with an indefinite receptivity for objects but a definite openness within a finite happening of lived time and possibility. Man needed to give up the illusion that he was an object with a sturdy nature. Man must embrace the intrinsic limitations of his mortality. Death does not close off an indefinitely open field of possibilities; it is the expression of the limitation that opens a finite field. In place of grasping for the infinite and pretending to participate in something that grounded him, man must attain authenticity by accepting the groundless, limited facticity of his birth, tradition, and historical situation.

Man does not possess unlimited possibilities that historical limitations restrain (and that technical progress will restore to him). Man is openness within a limited situation. There are no situations except limited ones. There are no possibilities except within such limited openness, no larger realm from which the present texture of the world is a selection.

Man can be creative because possibilities are not ready-made objects; they exist as supported by our receptive interweaving of the dimensions of lived time. We take up the past as possibilities for the future, and in that act we can retrieve basic possibilities within the destiny we receive and bear forward.

All of this remains within Heidegger's later thought, though it is said differently. The situation we take up through the tasks of our generation and our time includes the culmination of the destiny of the West. The lessons of *Being and Time* are repeated in a new idiom, especially in Heidegger's essays on the pre-Socratic thinkers. We exist receptively supporting a finite openness that is not a selection from a larger set of possibilities.

We saw earlier an analogous Hegelian notion of limited possibilities in the objective content of the concept. For Hegel the finite possibilities open to us are rooted in a kind of infinity, the self-coincidence and self-transparency of spirit to itself which justifies our particular limited possibilities as the only rational ones. For Heidegger the finitude is more pervasive and not rooted in anything further that could provide justification. Both thinkers use their doctrine of limited possibilities to challenge the self-certainty and appeals to infinity implicit in modern subjectivity.

The finitude of the propriative event allows different epochs in history. "The propriative event does contain possibilities of unconcealment which thinking cannot determine" (Time and Being 52/ 50). The cleared space within which we live is different from that in the Chinese tradition. The understanding of the being of things operative in Plato is different from, though ancestral to, that operative in Descartes. Heidegger is never clear about the temporal boundaries of different epochs, and they seem able to overlap. For example Hegel and his college roommate Hölderlin seem to be described as moving in quite different spaces. The problem of individuating epochs of the history Heidegger relates is linked to the very difficult question whether we should think of the propriative event as involving individual humans or as affecting us in some social or presocial mode. Heidegger's essays on language imply that it is wrong to conceive of the open space happening for individuals taken singly, but what is to replace this way of thinking is never taken up in his text with sufficient clarity.[7]

Note that we cannot speak of the propriative event itself as something that changes. Doing so would turn it into an entity that endures throughout history. Furthermore, since it is not something that can be made present as possessing a set of properties, we cannot say that there is some internal law or teleology or necessity at work within it. There is no power behind history that sends the different epochs. In some sense we can speak of the propriative event as more basic than the epochs, but we cannot make it a source as if it were a first cause or a ground.

> How is the sequence of epochs determined? How does this free sequence determine itself? Why is the sequence precisely this sequence? One is tempted to think of Hegel's history of the "idea." . . . For Heidegger, on the other hand, one cannot speak of a "why." Only the "that"—that the history of being is in such a way—can be said. . . . Within the "that" and in the sense of the "that" thinking can also ascertain something like necessity in the sequence, something like an order and a consistency. (Time and Being 55f/52)

Within the overall destiny of the West there is consistency and sequence providing a destiny of thought. On the larger scale, speaking of the West as a whole compared with other traditions, there is no reason or necessity at all, only the play of the propriative event. Here, as is obvious, Heidegger and Hegel will collide head on, since for Hegel the structure of the logical sequence demands that what conditions and gathers all things be a movement whose necessary structure can be grasped within itself. Thought can grasp and know its ultimate conditions in their history and their necessity. For Heidegger, Hegel still thinks in terms of unities and grounds instead of stepping back into the groundless play that allowed Hegel's thought of unity and ground in the first place.

The Priority of the Propriative Event

The propriative event is simply prior to anything we might do or say or think within it. It affects us overall and immediately. It opens the possibility for men to encounter beings and comport themselves toward them, but it itself is not a being to be encountered. This means no act or plan of ours can affect it. Ordinary history that chronicles the acts and plans of men cannot touch the deeper history of the epochs opened by the propriative event. Using terms about "being" rather than "propriative event," Heidegger states:

[We are here dealing with] the realm of being itself which we can no longer explain and judge from any other standpoint. (Nietzsche 2:364/ 4:223)

The basic experiences of a thinker never stem from his disposition or from his educational background. They take place in terms of being's essentially occurring truth [its unconcealedness]. (Nietzsche 2:239/4:181)

Is the essential unfolding of the history of being itself the occurrence on the basis of which all history now takes place? (Nietzsche 2:376/4:231)

The day will come when we will not shun the question whether the opening, the free open, may not be that within which alone pure space and ecstatic time and everything present and absent in them have the place which gathers and protects everything. (The End of Philosophy 72f/385)

To the question how this priority of the propriative event relates to what we know scientifically about consciousness, brain function, and the like, Heidegger would respond that such scientific descriptions and causal explanations are themselves one way things can be revealed, and so depend on the propriative event. Thus they are never in a position to explain the basic unconcealment which makes them possible. To talk about beings is already to be within some cleared region, some understanding of the being of things. Talk of causes avoids the issue; the propriative event is not a causal process, not a process at all. It slips away behind any attempt to explain it. "Because being and time are there only in the propriative event, this has the peculiar property of bringing man into his own as the being who perceives being by standing within true time. . . . Man is admitted to the propriative event. This is why we can never place that event in front of us, neither as something opposite us nor as something all encompassing" (Time and Being 24/23).

It seems at first that Heidegger is saying that the propriative event is unavailable to us. Yet we all manage to talk about the presuppositions of our living and talking. Sometimes this leads towards self-referential paradoxes, but we find ways to avoid or limit them. Just because we are within the field opened by the propriative event should not exclude our talking about it.

Heidegger certainly does talk at length about the propriative event, and he admits that his thinking must go on from within the modern field; there is no Archimedean point beyond the opening of unconcealedness (see Time and Being 9f/9f). But the way Heidegger comes to talk about the propriative event is quite different from the way we talk about our presuppositions. Our problems in talking about the propriative event are not to be solved by finding clever means to avoid self-referential paradoxes. That approach gives answers to the wrong questions. The propriative event is not a presupposition, not something we "hold," not a property of our language or our action. To ask for information about the propriative event, to ask "what is it?" is to presume it is an "it" that has an essential character we could report on. But the propriative event is not an "it," not an entity we can make present within some field. In the usual sense of the word *presence* the propriative event cannot be made present at all.

But we can be aware of living within the propriative event, and we can talk about this. If proper care is taken to shield the word *experience* from interpretations in terms of subjects and objects, Heidegger is willing to say it can be experienced.

The risk in the lecture ["Time and Being"] lies in the fact that it speaks in propositional statements about something essentially incommensurable with this kind of saying. . . . [The lecture] points directly at a matter which in accordance with its very nature is inaccessible to communicative statements. On the other hand it had to prepare the participants for their own experience of what was said in terms of an experience of something which cannot be openly brought to light. It is thus the attempt to speak of something that cannot be mediated cognitively, not even in terms of questions, but must be experienced. (Time and Being 27/25f)

The experience in question involves a new use of language. Both of our thinkers demand this. Hegel complains about the inadequacy of the ordinary interpretation of how language works. There are other things language can do, such as the speculative propositions that express dialectical insights. Speculative propositions are not new—Hegel finds them in the major philosophers and mystics—but Hegel systematizes them and shows how they relate to one another.

Heidegger also complains about the ordinary interpretation of the use and function of language. The usual analyses imply that language's business is to express qualities or relations of entities that have constant presence as their mode of being. This is true both in the older Aristotelian analysis of language in terms of subject-predicate form and in the modern analysis in terms of functions and relations. In his essays on language Heidegger argues that language has other less metaphysically influenced ways of showing what makes itself manifest. These ways of language are not new—Heidegger finds them in early Greek thinking and in poetry and the writings of mystics—but Heidegger concentrates on them and claims that they are more primal than traditional philosophical or scientific ways of using language. Like Hegel, Heidegger is not proposing that we do away with the ordinary and the technical uses of language but that we locate them in terms of other uses of language that are more encompassing.

We can talk about the propriative event without turning our talk into traditional metaphysics or into poetry, though it is not so far from the latter. Our talk of the propriative event is not meant to relay some ineffable intuition. Indeed, our talking is not meant to relay any separate experience at all, since the propriative event is not a separate object but "is experienced in language as that which allows it" (The Way to Language 258/127).

Heidegger as a Transcendental Thinker

We should keep in mind that despite the distance that separates Heidegger from traditional metaphysics and from Kant's critical philosophy, Heidegger's thought of the propriative event remains within the general boundaries of transcendental philosophy. Heidegger did not like to have his thought called transcendental. The word usually refers to Kantian attempts to find within subjectivity the conditions for the experience of objects. Heidegger is clearly opposed to any such attempt. I want to use the label, since I think that Heidegger keeps the general stance of transcendental thought. I will generalize the term and use it in the following way: a transcendental thinker tries to discern conditions that make experience, propositions, and truth *possible* within our ordinary modes of life. The conditions sought for are not causal or other "ontic" conditions of the *actuality* of this or that proposition or thought, nor are they necessarily subjective or formal conditions in the Kantian sense, but they do pertain to the basic involvement of man in what allows ordinary life, experience, propositions, and truth to take place. They can be contrasted with the necessary conditions for ordinary life discovered by common sense and the various sciences, and they are presupposed by those conditions.

I do not include in my stipulation that the goal of transcendental thinking must be the attempt to discover foundations that allow certain and sure knowledge in the Kantian or Hegelian fashion. It is enough that the thinker want us to become aware of these conditions and that this awareness work some transformation in our life.

Since Kant, transcendental philosophy has been the preeminent mode of foundationalist thought on the Continent. In the more general sense I am using here, transcendental philosophy does not have to be foundationalist in its aim, though it has usually been so. But it is important to realize that the search for conditions of possibility that reach beyond "ordinary" conditions may continue even if foundationalism is abandoned. Heidegger is not the only example of a nonfoundationalist thinker who remains within the general transcendental stance. Hermeneutic thinkers and those influenced by recent French thought provide other examples, and some analytic philosophers too are more than empirical but less than foundational.[8]

Heidegger abandons the search for grounds. But emphasizing his distance from foundationalism may obscure how near he remains to the transcendental search for conditions of possibility. Even though what he finds access to is in its own way poverty stricken and finite rather than full and foundational, and even though his access to it is not the certitude of a subject grasping its own structure, he claims to get behind the naiveté of others and encounter conditions that are not those turned up by ordinary investigations.

For example, Heidegger often contrasts his investigations with those of scientists and consistently claims to stand where he can see what the scientist is really doing. The thinker can penetrate a certain narrowness that is perhaps necessary to the scientist but that keeps the scientist from living in the full context of his experiences. Heidegger's disciples often take this stance in their disparaging remarks about other philosophies and other fields of thought as "merely ontic" or as not having penetrated to the level of thought where Heidegger is working. There is a hubris here as strong as any that

Heidegger finds in traditional metaphysics. Although he speaks in a more measured tone than many of his disciples, he says of his own thought and its relation to science: "We need no philosophy of nature. It suffices, rather, if we clarify for ourselves where cybernetics comes from and where it leads to. The general charge, that philosophy understands nothing of natural science and always limps along behind it, we can take without being perturbed. It is important for us to say to natural scientists what they are, in fact, doing" (Heraclitus Seminar 27/14). Heidegger's thought needs no information from the sciences and could not be changed by such information. Quite the reverse, it can tell the scientist what is really going on in his work. (See also What is Called Thinking? 90/131.)

The Heideggerean thinker has access to something that reaches beyond while making possible the ordinary modes of discourse. The resulting attitude toward the sciences is not unusual in Continental philosophy. Many Anglo-Saxon philosophers have also shared it, because they claim to understand various necessary propositions, usually formal, about the nature of science. Heidegger would not talk in terms of necessary propositions, but he claims to reach the opening of the particular space that allows science to appear as what it is. These conditions do not provide a foundation from which certitudes are derived, but the step back that reaches the conditions allows Heidegger to claim a vantage point that is transcendental in the general sense defined above.

Again, discussing how his thought about language relates to current treatments of language in terms of information theory, Heidegger says that between true philosophy and such cybernetic interpretations of language there is no longer any common ground for discussion (Vier Seminare 89). Nor is there any real need for discussion. Heidegger claims to have gotten behind what the other is doing and located the conditions for its mode of thinking so thoroughly as to render conversation unnecessary from his point of view and useless from the other's—unless the other were to learn to make the step back to the position from which Heidegger is speaking. He has located the other kind of thought from a vantage point that the other cannot perceive; there is no symmetrical dialogue. We are used to hearing this from Hegel, but Hegel accompanies it with detailed investigations about why the other's field of discourse moves of its own inner tensions into the wider field he claims to be occupying.

Contrary to Hegel, Heidegger's step back decides nothing about the details of the various regions of beings but only about the conditions that allow the unconcealment of any region. Heidegger does not legislate a priori. While this sounds humble and finite, it still enacts the transcendental move. The thinker need not concern himself in any detail with what is going on in other areas. Hegel, the great universalizing metaphysician, depends more on the details of current science, culture, and politics than does Heidegger, the finite phenomenologist. This should be expected: Hegel has tried to overcome the distinction between empirical and a priori (in his own peculiar way, in terms of the logic of necessary contingency without requiring a rationalist deduction of detail), while Heidegger retains a descendant of the split between a priori and empirical.

In his early writings Heidegger seemed to propose a kind of derivation of the modes of being revealed in science and ordinary life. Much has been made of his abandonment of this foundationalist goal he inherited from the neo-Kantians and Husserl. But in his later thought Heidegger still keeps the neo-Kantian and Husserlian asymmetrical relation and lack of dialogue between the observing thinker and the naive natural consciousness.[9]

One might object that I have still portrayed Heidegger too much as a foundationalist. He is seeking to have us attend to the presencing of things rather than to things themselves, to the event of presence rather than to the thing present. This is not really a condition of possibility in the classic sense. I would reply that Heidegger does make the kind of statements quoted above that claim a superior position beyond the naiveté of the ordinary thinker. He also discusses the history of the various epochs, finding in the understanding of being for a given epoch something that precedes and conditions all that goes on within the epoch and cannot in turn be affected by what goes on. And he sees the destiny of understanding being in terms of presence as a condition for the possibility of the whole history of being in the West (cf. Derrida 1982, 325). All this is stronger than merely looking at the event of presencing of whatever presences. It speaks of specific conditions, specific tunings of the event of presence. To ignore this aspect of Heidegger would be to turn the propriative event into something formal that can be applied indifferently to any individual entity (the presencing of this table, of this cloud, of this epoch) or to make it so differentiated that every entity would have its own special mode of presencing, which is not Heidegger's intent.

A Zenlike awareness of the finite presencing of each entity without any historical discussion of conditions of possibility may be something Heidegger would appreciate, and it resembles some (but not all) of what he wonders might be possible in a nonmetaphysical era to come. But there is much more than that to Heidegger's analysis of the history of the West and its metaphysical epochs, if that analysis is to have the bite he intends it to have.

It is strategically important for Heidegger's dealings with modernity that he be able to claim a vantage point on the modern age that is other and in some sense more basic than that age's picture of itself. Much of the intricacy of his later thought stems from the need to keep this vantage point without turning it into a foundation in the Hegelian self-transparency of spirit to itself.

Heidegger's stance above or behind ordinary ways of talking raises the suggestion that he is trying to renew aspects of the mystical traditions. The text quoted earlier is worth pondering for what it says and what it does not say: the propriative event is "Just play, the highest and most profound play. But this 'just' is everything, the one, the only" (*Satz vom Grund* 188). Texts such as this give some weight to the opinion that Heidegger's thought is in some degree "mystical." This opinion is bolstered by his habit of quoting from mystical texts and finding there his own ideas about the clearing and the coming to presence of the world beyond any grounding that can be conceived in terms of causes and metaphysics. This is a mystery to be guarded and preserved from the profanation of our inadequate traditional ways of thought, a mystery that of its own withdraws from presence. That mystery, the presencing of the world in the propriative event, is not available in ordinary language as ordinarily interpreted. It is not, however, a hidden basic entity or process accessible only to some mystical intuition or insight. Nor is there anything in Heidegger closely equivalent to the spiritual paths and disciplines recommended by mystical teachers, despite his occasional borrowings of such terminology. Much of classic mysticism remains involved in the search for grounds and foundations. If Heidegger's thought is related to mysticism, it will not be to such searching but to the mysticisms of emptiness found in some forms of Buddhism and some minority strains within Christianity, although his thought has a historical side generally lacking in such traditions.

While it is appealing to speak of Heidegger in connection with the mystical traditions, the varieties of writings labeled mystical and the ambiguities of his own transcendental stance should make us hesitant to assert this connection too strongly.[10] But however much we must qualify discussions about Heidegger and mysticism, such discussion points out the question we must now turn to: what is the manner in which he envisioned his thought making a difference for our lives in the modern world?

Life in the Modern World

In his interview with the editors of the magazine *Der Spiegel*, Heidegger talked about the role of thought in the modern world.

I see the situation of man in the world of planetary technology not as an inextricable and inescapable destiny, but I see the task of thought precisely in this, that within its own limits it helps man as such achieve a satisfactory relationship to the essence of technology. (*Spiegel* 214/61)

To the mystery of the planetary domination of the unthought essence of technology there corresponds the tentative, unassuming character of thought that strives to ponder this unthought [essence]. (*Spiegel* 212/60)

In a memorial address to the citizens of his home village, Heidegger asked:

Can man, can man's work in the future still be expected to thrive in the fertile ground of a homeland and mount into the ether, into the far reaches of the heavens and the spirit? Or will everything now fall into the clutches of planning and calculation, of organization and automation? (Memorial Address 17/49)

Even if the old rootedness is being lost in this age, may not a new ground and foundation be granted again to man, a foundation and a ground out of which man's nature and all his works can flourish in a new way even in the atomic age? (Memorial Address 23/53)

The quotations from the magazine interview tell us that thought can encounter the essence of technology, that the destiny of universal imposition can open a way to the propriative event. The memorial address gives the impression that Heidegger hopes this might lead at least to a new way of living within the modern world, understanding it better than it understands itself and touching roots it does not know it has. This fits in with the interpretation offered so far. But there are other themes as well. There is the reference to grounds and foundations, when we thought Heidegger was finished with all that. There is the suggestion—even stronger in other writings—that beyond technology a wholly new era might open in which we could live directly and poetically in harmony with the deepest places of man's being.

Yet Heidegger has very limited expectations about what can be achieved here and now. Nothing will bring us into harmony and reconciliation. We will not step into any new age. If there is to be a new mode of living, it will take place on the margins of our present age. The message is finitude, finitude in a new sense of the word, not fulfillment or reconciliation.

Speaking at Davos in 1929, Heidegger said of his philosophy around the period of *Being and Time*: "The fundamental character of the act of philosophizing consists in setting free the internal transcendence of human existence. . . . This liberation [consists of] getting into the depths of the dereliction of our existence, the conflict which is inscribed in the essence of liberty" (Davos 44). This remains in his later thought and it indicates what difference he thinks his philosophy can make in the time of universal imposition. Speaking at Le Thor in 1968, he said: "*Being and Time* did not attempt to present a new meaning of being, but to open our hearing for the word of being" (*Vier Seminare* 83). That hearing becomes the experience of ourselves and of the world as coming to presence appropriated to each other in the particular mode found in the age of universal imposition. That experience sets us free into our historical finitude in the groundless play of presencing, sets free "the internal transcendence" of our existence. The Western tradition usually speaks of setting man free *from* his finitude. Heidegger wants to set man free *for* and *into* his finitude, from which there is no escape but in which alone is freedom.

Unlike Hegel, Heidegger has little to say in detail about the shape of our lives, beyond using one or another institution as a sign of the overall field that rules us. But he realizes that even the little he does say challenges the conception of man at the basis of modern democratic and economic institutions. "The most important thing, if we want to come to clarity in this matter, is the insight that man is not a being who makes himself—without such an insight one remains within the ostensible political oppositions of civil and industrial society, and one forgets that the concept of society is only another name or a mirror or a broadening of subjectivity" (*Vier Seminare* 97). Man the maker of himself and his world is but another version of dominating modern subjectivity. The opposition so touted today between individual and society is written wholly in the language of subjects and objects. It is not progress to move from atomistic to social subjectivity. There is nothing, neither a decisive individual nor a social group making contracts and conventions, that can shape attitudes and meanings in indefinite openness to a world of neutral objects. Man and society are always already within a space whose contours they did not create and do not control. Insofar as modern economic and political theories and institutions presume the distanced modern subject, individual or social, they are questionable.

In that questioning, Heidegger is less interested than Hegel in preserving as much as possible of the freedom and self-determination of modern man. Many of the economic and political developments Hegel applauded, Heidegger deplores. But Heidegger is not urging a return to traditional society.

In accord with his ideas about the role of the past in constituting the texture of the world, Heidegger does defend the importance of roots in some historical tradition. Modern society tries to reduce this rootedness to a collection of facts to be judged by formal, functional rationality.

Everything is functioning. This is exactly what is so uncanny, that everything functions, that the functioning propels everything more and more to even further functioning, and that technology increasingly dislodges men and uproots them from the earth. . . . All our relationships have become purely technological ones. It is no longer upon an earth that man lives today. . . . According to human experience and history, at least as far as I see it, everything essential and everything great has arisen only from the fact that man had a home and was rooted in a tradition. (*Spiegel* 206–209/56–57)

On the one hand, Heidegger's aim is to renew the sense of tradition and to save it from the objectification it suffers in the face of modern subjectivity. Tradition is not something we can judge from a distanced standpoint according to subjectively chosen goals. On the other hand, we have already seen that for Heidegger, though our roots may go into the soil of a tradition, there is no metaphysical rock beneath. The same awareness that roots us again in the soil of the world from which we spring also tells us that there is no final ground. We rest on the abyss of finite openness. There is no "why" to what we have been granted, and no escape from groundlessness. Except this: we are aware of our participation in the propriative event. This awareness goes beyond the space opened up for us, but it reaches no foundation for self-certainty, only the opening of that space and the history of other ungrounded openings. We remain within our finitude and mortality.

Heidegger does not stay within the standard modern dilemma. He neither affirms modern rootless subjectivity nor sends us back to traditional society. We need to investigate just what impact he believes all this might have on our daily life and on modern institutions.

Thinking

In Heidegger's later writings the term *thinking* (*Denken*) replaces *philosophy* for naming the task of liberating and radicalizing man's fundamental transcendence and his appropriation into the finite opening of the space where man stands with things. This thinking is what must come about if modernity is to be overcome in whatever sense this is possible.

In this thinking, which is neither science nor philosophy as traditionally understood as a search for certitude, foundations, and ultimate unities, we can experience the clearing that lies behind the Western world and our current situation.

Our concern is to experience unconcealment as clearing. That is what is unthought in what is thought in the whole history of thought. In Hegel, the need consisted in the satisfaction of thought. For us, on the contrary, the plight of what is unthought in what is thought reigns. (Heraclitus Seminar 259/162)

Ecstatic inherence in the openness of the locale [*Ortschaft*] of being is the essence of thinking. (Nietzsche 2:358/4:218)

We are being urged to liberate and to be fully what makes us human in the first place. We are to become what we are. How is it that we have a choice about this? The condition that allows us *not* to be fully what we are is, ultimately, the self-withdrawal of the propriative event. It withdraws behind the beings made unconcealed, because it has nothing to say for itself. This withdrawal allows us to define ourselves wholly within the terms of the beings revealed and to miss our own role as the receptive abode for the propriative event. Thus we can fall into something like the inauthenticity spoken about in Heidegger's earlier writings (see Zimmerman 1981). We can live without making our resolved own what is in fact our deepest enabling possibility. As in the earlier writings, though for somewhat more complex reasons, this "falling" is unavoidable. This is particularly true in the universal functionality of the modern world, though our world also provides a unique opportunity to enter into thinking in the proper way.

This thinking can sound quite individualistic, a personal adjustment that has no effects on the modern world itself. And it sounds quite elitist. Heidegger says: "A few people, outside of all publicity, work untiringly to guard the life of a thinking which is attentive to being" (*Vier Seminare* 90). What could be the results of such a thinking? What does it *do*?

The activities this thinking engages in are suggested by what Heidegger spent his time doing. He tried to discern the overall field that made modernity possible, examining various aspects of modernity and their history and finding in them the call to universal imposition and the mutual need and finitude of man and the propriative event. He tried to rethink the origins of the West and discern the destiny granted us with the Greeks, its limits, and the unthought possibilities it might still contain. He tried to rethink the essence of man and the essence of language without using the traditional categories of subjectivity, consciousness, representation, and so on. Much of this thinking involved trying to experience certain basic words more originally, often by pondering real or suggestive etymologies. He tried to think how we could dwell within the finitude and mutual need of our situation without the forgetfulness characteristic of the Western tradition. The products of all this thinking were essays and talks, some poems, and a rather withdrawn way of life.

All of this seems quite ineffectual. There was no effort at social change. Heidegger criticizes much of modern life, and he may say that a given modern way of analyzing our society is flawed, but he makes few positive and no immediately useful suggestions.

Heidegger might reply that before accusing him of powerlessness we should consider the alternatives. We could perhaps set out to plan to master technology and social change, deciding what kind of society we want and evaluating the means to achieve it. This would only replay the will to power and modern subjectivity. We could try to inculcate values or find meaning in the world, but this would be more subjectivity and representation. Heidegger even suggests that someone, accepting his analysis that the root of modernity lies in the self-concealing withdrawal involved in the propriative event, might then decide to "attack" that "problem." Such a person would live as if the unconcealment of beings were something we could make present to ourselves. But this is precisely the modern attitude, leaving us back where we started.

We cannot overcome modernity by our own action. The best we can do is to experience universal imposition as the withdrawal of the propriative event. In thinking we let the propriative event be present as withdrawing, as different from any entity we can make present. We experience it as claiming us, even when the claim is the modern call to deny that such a claim exists.

Such thinking can lead to an experience of modernity in which we transcend the self-definition of man in universal imposition as manipulable manipulating units. Where does this lead? Nowhere else but to dwelling where we are now. "To think the propriative event as appropriation [Ereignis als Er-eignis] means to build on the structure in this realm which resonates within itself. Thinking receives from language the building tool for this structure [Bau] that floats in itself" (Identity and Difference 102/38). We dwell when we take up as our own what is given to us by language as the opening of a cleared space and a call. We dwell caringly and thankfully in the place granted us. We care and build language by fighting the leveling out of its heights and depths. We seek to retrieve possibilities covered over by daily living and daily language but available in the old words of the tradition and in the new words of the poets. Dwelling in our world we will live in touch with the propriative event that is "experienced in the revealing done by language as that which allows it" (The Way to Language 258/127).

Heidegger says that by thinking we may be able to keep our two-thousand-year inheritance from being squandered in ten or twenty years (Vier Seminare 90). There is a significant doubling: we come to experience the Western tradition as closed, completed, played out, but in so doing we are fighting to keep it open, drawing out so-far-unthought possibilities offered in the granting of the Western destiny. This is one connection between Heidegger's efforts and those of Derrida.

None of this will overcome modernity or give us a new world. Nothing will make universal imposition go away. We dwell where we are, in the modern world, but with an experience of the clearing that keeps us from resting in any of the unities or grounds our world offers as if they were the last word.

This mode of living in the modern world I will call (somewhat contentiously) "deconstructive living." The term is not directly Heidegger's, and it has deliberate connotations of later thought. But Heidegger did speak of a de-construction (*Ab-bau*) of the tradition that, in his practice, was close to the way of dwelling (*bauen*) that does not rest in the ultimacy of the grounds or unities or principles offered us in our world.

Preparing for a Far Future

Deconstructive living is one of Heidegger's recommendations about living in the modern world, but there appear to be others. Heidegger also speaks about thinking as a preparation "for a far future." Thinking prepares for the advent of a new mode of dwelling on the earth. Thinking cannot make the new arrive; it can only "begin to prepare in advance the conditions" for such a turn (*Vier Seminare* 128).

In the *Spiegel* interview Heidegger talks about the effect of his thought:

Philosophy will be unable to effect any immediate change in the current state of the world. This is true not only of philosophy but of all purely human reflection and endeavor. Only a god can save us. The only possibility available to us is that by thinking and poetizing we prepare a readiness for the appearance of a god, or for the absence of a god in the time of decline; for in view of the absent god we decline. (*Spiegel* 207/57)

The preparation of a readiness may be the first step. It is not through man that the world can be what it is and how it is—but also not without man. . . . A mediated effectiveness is possible through another thinking, but no direct effect. (*Spiegel* 209/58)

I know nothing about how this thinking "has an effect." It may be that the path of thinking may lead one to remain silent in order to protect this thought from becoming cheapened within a year. It may also be that it needs three hundred years for it "to have an effect." (*Spiegel* 212/60)

Heidegger's talk about preparation, coupled with his remarks about the end of metaphysics and the culmination of the West's history, make it sound as if the preparation is for some advent that will totally transform and begin again man's world. The god that could save us seems to be a new turning of the propriative event (but cf. Kockelmans 1984, chap. 6). This suggests an "eschatological" interpretation of Heidegger's thought: the last age is upon us, and a great change is coming. We must prepare ourselves to receive the new time. The role of John the Baptist is a pleasing one, at least until the final party, because one can feel that one knows more than other people and yet be spared the responsibility of proclaiming the new in detail.

If we interpret Heidegger as telling us to get started on preparations for a new world, however, much of his thought twists out of shape. A fully eschatological reading of Heidegger would be an attempt to escape our fate instead of encountering its essence as Heidegger advised earlier.

There is a passage in one of the Four Seminars that bears on this question. The seminar discusses Marx's definition of man as a producer. Heidegger then asks whether we can manage to relinquish the modern call to exist as either producer or product. He points out that doing so would entail renouncing the ideal of progress and would cause a general shrinkage of production and use. He seems to be discussing possible social changes that we might make, but he continues with "a simple, immediately obvious example: in the perspective of such a renunciation there could be no more 'tourism' possible. Instead one would restrict oneself and stay at home. Is there now in this age still something like 'staying at home'? any dwelling? any tarrying [*Bleibe*]? No, there are 'dwelling machines,' city cluster centers, in short: industrial products, but no homes any more" (*Vier Seminare* 127). Heidegger goes on to talk about a "new realm" in which we could live, a realm freed from definitions in terms of subjects and objects, a realm where man could dwell in relation to that from which he receives his call. But then he says that entry into that realm is not going to be accomplished by the thinking which he has set in action. If we imagine that thinking could accomplish such a change, we are still caught in a model of man as producer. Heidegger's thinking can only begin to prepare the conditions for such a change. He denies that we can move directly into a world where we dwell simply in the nearness of the propriative event. We can only prepare and wait. This means that things will continue to come to presence according to universal imposition.

What does our preparation and waiting consist in? It is ambiguous to say, as Heidegger does in the interview quoted above, that the new world cannot be without man. This is true in terms of the mutual need of man and the propriative event. But does it also mean that certain definite dispositions and receptivities are needed for any given change to occur? This seems unlikely. Did the change in the meaning of being from Greek *eidos* to Roman *actualitas* require preparatory activities on the part of the Romans? If Heidegger were to say this, it seems, he would open the door for whole ranges of ordinary "ontic" activities to influence the history of the understandings of being, which he has said cannot be so influenced.

We exist within and through the cleared space granted to us; our actions are made possible within that space. We cannot by our own actions modify that space. There seem to be no special preparations that we could make for a new age. The propriative event overcomes us, not by force but by changing the horizon within which all our activities have meaning and the call that shapes our self-understanding.

If the propriative event has the primacy Heidegger says it has, then nothing we do will hasten or retard it. We do not have any choice about whether there will be a new age. Plato did not prepare for or choose the new "word of being" addressed to him. New worlds may come, but we cannot make them come or resist their coming.

There is no way an elite of thinkers could speed the coming. Could these thinkers perhaps be more prepared to greet the lord when he comes, while the rest rejected him? It would be wrong to say that some people could be more fit to receive some new revelation of unconcealment than others, because that would detach individuals from the propriative event and suggest that there was something we could do, outside our appropriation, to influence it. This is a subtle replay of modern subjectivity, not a liberation from it.

The eschatological interpretations that proclaim a new age and ask us to be among the privileged few thus contradict too much of what Heidegger has said. The preparations he is speaking of concern our relation to the present epoch and its enduring conditions. They are, in fact, just what we have been speaking of as deconstructive living. Should there be a new era outside of metaphysics, our having done these preparations that let us live more in tune with the presencing of our own time and with its conditions will fit us to be more aware and thoughtful in the new time. If the new time is one no longer dominated by metaphysics, then our attempts to experience the present age as a destiny and calling within the propriative event, that is, nonmetaphysically, will not be so discontinuous with the new age. But the preparations should not be thought of as partial prefigurement of some full experience yet to come. Nor will they hasten its coming.

This interpretation of the exhortations to prepare is supported by Heidegger's remark that "the fact that thinking is in a preparatory stage does not mean that the experience [which is being prepared for] is of a different nature from the preparatory thinking" (Time and Being 57/53). Because we and the clearing need each other and neither is a firm ground, we will always live retrieving possibilities granted in a finite event that we may come to experience in its self-withdrawal. To live in the nearness of the propriative event as far as we can involves seeing through universal imposition and metaphysical attempts at grounding and final unity, yet not seeing through these to any new unity but only to our fragile dwelling in mutual need with the finite event of clearing. This enables us to retrieve our "two-thousand-year inheritance," without being completely defined by the usual force of that inheritance. This is one way we could give meaning to Heidegger's remark about a "mediated effect" of thought.

The Fourfold

There seems to be more to Heidegger's discussion of preparation than I have been allowing him to say so far. For example: "The essence of technology cannot be led into the change of its destiny without the aid of the essence of man. . . . The overcoming of a destiny of being, here and now the overcoming of universal imposition, comes to pass each time through the arrival of another destiny, a destining that does not allow itself to be logically and historiographically predicted" ("The Turning" 38/39). The first part of this quotation refers to our sheltering reception of the cleared

space. The second seems to counsel us to await a new opening of
a new cleared space. Together they suggest that the opening of that
space depends on our making ourselves receptive, though we cannot
cause a new turning of the propriative event.

As I pointed out above, Heidegger never says that previous turnings in history required preparatory receptivity. What could be special about our situation? What is unique to us as opposed to the
Romans or others is that we are at the end; there will not be another
turning in the history of "being." That destiny is played out. What
comes, if it comes, will be of a different quality, lacking a centrally
imposed "meaning of being." When Heidegger talks about possible
future ages free of the banes of our own he seems to expect them
to be nonmetaphysical eras, no longer "epochs" in which the withdrawal of the propriative event is itself withdrawn from us behind
some meaning of being understood as a variety of constant presence.
In such an era without metaphysics our finite appropriation would
be the (still self-withdrawing but not concealed as such) togetherness
of a world without a ruling, unified understanding of being. The
temporalizing togetherness of man and things, known as such, would
include many different modes of presencing of different things, here
meant in the full sense in which Heidegger contrasts things with
objects, as in the lecture "The Thing."[1]

Heidegger's term *the step back* is significant here. Perhaps our
stepping back from universal imposition to the propriative event
prepares for such a new age because it begins a freedom from metaphysical concerns. In one of his seminars Heidegger says: "In the
propriative event the history of being does not so much come to its
end as now appear as the history of being. There are [*es gibt*] no
destined [*geschickliche*] epochs of the propriative event. The destining
sending [*das Schicken*] is out of the propriative event" (*Vier Seminare*
104).

Sometimes it sounds as if we could reach the future age just by
ridding our thought and action of a few traditional Western categories. So some interpreters go about preaching against subjectivity
or substance or presence or representation, as if these were mistakes
we had made. This is surely a misreading of Heidegger's intent.
There are not just a few intellectual or moral errors to overcome.
Still, there are passages in which Heidegger seems to say we could
begin thinking even now in a new way free of metaphysical
temptations.

One will not succeed in thinking the propriative event with the concepts
of being and the history of being. (*Vier Seminare* 104)

At the end of the lecture on identity it is stated what the propriative
event appropriates, that is, brings into its own and retains in mutual appropriation, namely the belonging together of being and man. In this belonging together, what belongs together is no longer being and man but
rather—as appropriated—mortals in the fourfold of world. (Time and
Being 45/42; see Marx 1971, 240f, 228)

Heidegger talks in his later writings of "the fourfold" (*das Geviert*).
He seems to be introducing a new vocabulary to replace the traditional metaphysical way of talking. His discussions often have a
pastoral tone reminiscent of peasant life in the Black Forest, and
Heidegger seems to be talking of the present or future. The vocabulary in question is developed in the lecture "The Thing" and elsewhere to discuss the mutual inherence and mirror play of mortals,
earth, sky, and gods that constitute "the worlding of the world."
Each of these four world "regions" or "neighborhoods" is to be
allowed to "while" or temporalize in its own way involving and
mirroring each of the others. The way Heidegger develops this theme
is too complex for easy summary here, and we are concerned with
its overall place in his thought rather than its details. [2]

Talk about the fourfold fits into his series of attempts to think
about man's dwelling without using traditional metaphysical or subjectivistic categories, but it seems to have special importance. What
is the role of this new vocabulary? If we can think in terms of the
fourfold, are we moving into the new age? Does it finally leave behind
our Western heritage?

I have been opposing what one might call an "eschatological"
interpretation of Heidegger's remarks about preparation for a new
age, arguing that his extreme statements about our role in preparing
for a new age should be interpreted charitably in terms of deconstructive living. His talk of the fourfold poses related problems. Is
he talking about a deep meaning of our present world, or about the
past, or a new age, or in some way about the event of there being
any world?

We might call the first suggestion the "romantic" reading of the
fourfold. The nineteenth-century romantic poets and thinkers faced
a world described by triumphant Newtonian science. Reacting against
what they perceived as a cold and mechanical world and against

other aspects of their age, the romantics said that by some special faculty other than scientific understanding, perhaps by intuition or imagination, we could be in touch with living Nature on a level deeper than that which science describes. We could live in the wider, deeper world of which science gives only an external description.

Could it be that Heidegger's talk of the fourfold functions in this way? He would then be saying that when we learn to perceive we will be aware of the ringing togetherness of the fourfold, a level on which there are even now true "things" instead of "objects," a level prior to and richer than the impoverished world manifested to us in the superficial technological awareness of our everyday life.

Such a romantic interpretation is very tempting, especially with texts like "The Thing," "Building Dwelling Thinking," and "Out of the Experience of Thinking." These suggest some deep awareness still to be found in corners of peasant life almost completely overwhelmed by triumphant technology. The elegiac tone of some of Heidegger's writings sounds like a romantic protest against loss of our roots in a deeper reality. The fourfold then describes a deeper mode of encounter with things that will reveal so much more of their true nature.

It is certainly true that Heidegger thinks we have lost contact with our roots, but are those roots to be found in a different, deeper revelation of the being of things that is somehow "underneath" the technological world? As satisfying as this romantic interpretation might be, it is a mistake. I argued earlier against the modern presumption that neutral factuality is the way things "really" are, that historically varying interpretations of the being of things are subjective overlays on some constant basic meaning of being. A similar argument applies against this romantic interpretation of the fourfold. There can be for Heidegger no historically constant basic revelation of things that is then covered over.

If universal imposition is what truly clears the space for us to be, then it is not covering over some deeper and fuller revelation of things in terms of the fourfold. There is nothing under the technological skin but finitude and the mutual need of man and the propriative event. It is not consistent to claim that things first come to presence as within the fourfold and then universal imposition covers up this original presence.

This is another reason why mystical interpretations of Heidegger's thought need to be approached carefully. Too many of them presuppose that we are getting back to some deeper way things really are all along, but such an idea violates Heidegger's thought about the finitude and historicity of all unconcealedness. If universal imposition is the cleared space where we now dwell, there is no deeper world we can reach now, and the romantic interpretation has to be rejected.

If talk about the fourfold and the descriptions of peasant life are not statements about some historically constant basic revelation of things, then what is Heidegger doing? There seem to be three possibilities left: either the fourfold describes a *previous* world that is now becoming lost to us, or it describes a *future* world that might become open to us, or it describes the "worlding" of *any* world. To my mind the best reading is a combination of the last two. The fourfold describes the "worlding of the world" in any age. It provides not a deeper world but a different way of experiencing the preconceptual and prepropositional inhabitation of our world. It is a kind of formal description of the belonging together that is the propriative event in any of its tunings. Talk of the fourfold has the advantage of bringing in neglected dimensions of the event of the world, and it avoids the metaphysical temptation to interpret man, things, and being in terms of constant presence.

On this reading, even universal imposition could be experienced in terms of the fourfold; this would not be to experience some deeper level of unconcealment in things, but to experience the unconcealment even of technological objects in a less metaphysical way. It does not mean that we would experience again the world of human closeness and tradition found in Heidegger's description of the wine jug or the bridge. Our world would remain universal imposition, but we could experience in a new way the mutual claiming involved in the call to manipulation and order, the earth as standing reserve, the absence of the gods. We would experience in this, enabling it, the finite openness of our mortality within the unrevealed earth that bears up our world. [3]

If the fourfold gives a nonmetaphysical description of the worlding of any world, including our own, then it is especially appropriate to describe the hoped-for future era when the worlding of the world would no longer be covered over by the metaphysical meaning of time and being. Talk of the fourfold does not describe the content of that future era, for such an era would not have "content" in the way the previous epochs in the history of the West were guided by ruling meanings of being. The fourfold describes the experience of the presencing of things in a nonmetaphysical era.

Such a future age is not ours to create. Talk about it throws us back to understanding the happening of our present age. If this is correct and if both the eschatological and the romantic interpretations of Heidegger's texts are questionable, then in the end the impact of his thought on our lives will be focused on the recommendation to find beyond the current mode in which things are revealed to us the finite groundless happening of our appropriation into that open space; this is what I earlier called "deconstructive living."

I have implicitly rejected the interpretation of the fourfold that makes it a description of a past or vanishing world. But that interpretation raises an important issue. Does the destiny of the West contain the seeds of its own overcoming? The descriptions of the fourfold do echo earlier modes of life. The step back that Heidegger urges has been made by thinkers and poets in all ages, though not explicitly as such. We are privileged because in our age, due to the nature of universal imposition, there is the possibility of a less self-concealed nearness of the propriative event. But that nearness has been experienced and spoken of indirectly throughout history. In what sense, then, are the possibilities for overcoming modernity themselves deep within the destiny of the West, and in what sense are they something new?

Heidegger seems to hesitate on this matter. One reason lies in his claim that universal imposition is the culmination of the West. He vacillates on the question of whether technology has absorbed all Western possibilities into itself, as does the final stage of Hegel's history. Is technology the working out of a destiny to its fullness, or its exhaustion, so that a new beginning is required, or are there other possibilities within the Western destiny that technology cannot reach? (See Marx 1971, 116–18.)

In the *Spiegel* interview Heidegger declares that only a god can save us. Universal imposition has leveled out the legacy of the West so that only its technological destiny can be found. We must await a new turning of the propriative event. Yet he also says (*Spiegel* 214/ 62) that only from within the Western tradition can universal imposition be overcome, not by some import from a foreign tradition, such as Zen Buddhism. Here it seems that there are reserves in the West that have not been caught up and exhausted in the dominance of universal imposition. We do not need to wait for a new world.

Heidegger's usual practice is to work at retrieving from past thought or poetry possibilities that the present age is blind to. It remains ambiguous how those possibilities relate to our present world. The alternatives are the same as those we saw concerning the fourfold. Is Heidegger retrieving a deeper world under our everyday world, or fragments of an old world, or portents of one to come? Or is he showing us the move from our world to the happening of our world? Again, I think the last is the only consistent interpretation.

What becomes difficult for Heidegger at this point is to give that awareness of the worlding of the world some effect on our lives without turning it into a second world or a romantic deeper world. I have tried to describe that effect in terms of deconstructive living, and later I will argue that this should involve accepting greater multiplicity in our world(s) than Heidegger is prepared to allow. The deeper issue here is the primacy of the propriative event considered as appropriating us to one ruling meaning of being. Could it be that universal imposition is not the whole story even now, which means there is not one meaning of being in the modern age? I will suggest later that Heidegger thinks of destiny, the opening of possibilities, in still too unified a way.

Political and Social Consequences

I previously raised the question of whether the effects of Heidegger's thought were not wholly private and individualized. The answer to that question is not straightforward, but there are communal and practical consequences to his thought. In this chapter I have canvassed various interpretations of the impact he envisions his thought having on our life in the modern world, and I have emphasized deconstructive living with its awareness of our finite appropriation and consequent seeing through to the groundlessness of our unities and "firsts."

This does not seem to be of much social consequence. How are those who think in Heidegger's special way doing more than saving themselves privately from being totally defined by the world of universal imposition? Heidegger speaks of his elite thinkers as helping to prepare the conditions for a dwelling that surpasses what is possible today, but I have argued that this really means deepening our relationship to what claims us now.

Does this have any social or political impact? A century before, Hegel had little hesitation offering advice about the modern world.

It is true that he said in the preface to the *Philosophy of Right* that it was not the philosopher's business to offer advice about how the world should be in the future. But it was the philosopher's business to discern the movement of spirit in the present, and on that basis he could criticize those aspects of present reality or theory that did not keep pace with what had already been achieved in principle. He could offer such advice because he tried to reach some foundation that could serve as a basis or measure.

Heidegger believes that the traditional advice-giving function of philosophy is finished. Philosophy has run out of metaphysical grounds on which to base advice, and the new thinking with the peculiar kind of transcendental move he propounds does not reach any measure. Science has appropriated the business of finding principles and giving advice, though he is sceptical of the value of advice based on a limited understanding of man's true relation to what claims him. We should be cautious in accepting the advice of the decision theorists and social scientists.

Beyond issuing such cautionary remarks, the Heideggerean thinker does not assume the advisor's role in any detail. The task of the thinker is to ponder and realize man's relation to the propriative event. It is "a liberation of man from what in *Being and Time* I called 'fallenness' among beings" (*Spiegel* 209/58).

Thinking performs this work in a spirit of openness and receptivity. It has no access to norms that could judge what is made unconcealed. To offer advice about how we should live or what form of institutions we should strive to create would be to put thinking within a pragmatic calculative context that would destroy its essence.

Heidegger occasionally does venture one or another opinion about institutions, but he does so in a questioning manner. "For me today it is a decisive question how any political system—and which one—can be adapted to an epoch of technology. I know of no answer to this question. I am not convinced that it is democracy. . . . Behind [political systems today, including democracy] stands the conception that technology in its essence is something that man holds within his own hands. In my opinion this is not possible" (*Spiegel* 206/55). Heidegger's worries about democracy stem from the will to power he sees in the desire to master our problems and from his reflections about public opinion as a manipulable commodity in the world of universal imposition. In any case, pronouncements such as this have no great practical value, nor are they meant to do more than provoke our thought. There is no political theory to be built on such opinions, nor does Heidegger pretend to have the needed political sophistication.

Heidegger does not want to build a political theory. In 1950, after some reflections on Stalin, he wrote that the sphere of politics appeared to be an independent realm of actuality but was in fact only playing out prior relations of being and meaning (*Seinsverhältnisse*; see Pöggeler 1982, 49). The determining relations that make our world and the decisive changes that might overcome it do not happen in the political sphere, though they might be echoed there. We see once again the signs of Heidegger's transcendental stance. The thinker can try to clarify the understanding of being that determines the sphere of possibilities for politics, but the thinker can give no advice on concrete matters except to point out the space within which they move.

At this point the obligatory reference must be made to Heidegger and the Nazis. For a time in the early thirties Heidegger believed that the National Socialists might be facing up to the essence of the technological world in the manner that he saw as necessary. He supported them in a limited way and, during a short period as rector of his university, performed some questionable actions on their behalf. After a while both he and the Nazis became disillusioned with each other, he resigning as rector, they placing him under surveillance.[4]

As Karsten Harries (1976) points out, the key problem is not why Heidegger might have been led into supporting the Nazis. Thinkers often project onto unworthy political movements issues and options that they feel are crucial for their age. Perhaps Heidegger read into the Nazis the ideal he found attractive in the writings of Ernst Jünger (Kockelmans 1984, 267). The real problem is Heidegger's silence on politics thereafter. Was he claiming by his silence that there is no way to discern the signs of the times?

Heidegger does not want to leave us in the hands of experts and their calculative thinking, but he provides no superexpert philosopher to replace them. Yet we have to make decisions. Does the thinker leave us without any help? The *Spiegel* editors who interviewed Heidegger pressed him on this repeatedly, with growing vexation. They received no advice, only a denial that a true thinker could proffer advice (*Spiegel* 212/60).

Still, though we are without firm foundations, we are not without recourse in our decisions. We have all the sense and discernment we have ever had. For example, consider Heidegger's decision about teaching in Berlin, and the "advice" he received.

Recently I received a second invitation to teach at the University of Berlin. On that occasion I left Freiburg and withdrew to the cabin. I listened to what the mountains and the forest and the farmlands were saying, and I went to see an old friend of mine, a seventy-five year old farmer. He had read about the call to Berlin in the newspapers. What would he say? Slowly he fixed the sure gaze of his sure eyes on mine, and keeping his mouth tightly shut, he thoughtfully put his faithful hand on my shoulder. Ever so slightly he shook his head. That meant: absolutely no! (Why Do I Stay in the Provinces 218/30)

Systematic and scientific ways of buttressing this human discernment have always been frail supports. Whatever our theories, when we decide, we are always left lacking sure measures. But we can find fallible help in quiet times and good friends. The themes evoked earlier from Heidegger's discussion of death and authenticity are also appropriate here.

One might object that given the primacy of the propriative event, our human discernment could work within a world which included strange paths. Heidegger would accept this limitation, because anything else would return to the metaphysical attempt to ground and secure a path for our lives, rather than living and deciding in mortal openness without guarantees. That this may lead to conflict and tragedy he would readily admit.

"But," the objector could continue, "you have said that only a god can save us. Only a new opening of presence can change our world; the decision is not up to man. How can man know whether he is being addressed by a god or a demon?" Heidegger might reply that such a distinction cannot finally be made, for there is nothing to serve as a measure for the propriative event. How would such a measure "be" and be made available to us? Our situation is perhaps better described in terms of the Greek tragedy than the Christian tale of clarity and redemption. In this Heidegger makes his own much of the Nietzschean *amor fati*.

There remains a problem even if we accept what Heidegger is implying about our human discernment and its mortal location. The question would remain how such personal, vulnerable living can be translated into communal practices for making decisions and living together. On such issues Heidegger confesses he has no advice to give (*Spiegel* 212/60).

We will not find in Heidegger any specific institutional recommendations such as those Hegel makes for overcoming problems within the modern world. There are nevertheless some broadly political and institutional implications to his thought, although he does not draw them explicitly.

The most often cited practical and political implication is actually the most questionable. Heidegger's discussion of open acceptance and letting-be (*Gelassenheit*) in our relation to things and the propriative event has been interpreted as favoring certain kinds of community and politics. Such interpretations are helped by Heidegger's general suspicion of politics and the big powers, and by his nostalgic references to peasant life, to rootedness and tradition, and to the need for dwelling on an earth that has not been reduced to a manipulable object. Heidegger makes no utopian proposal, but some thinkers have found his assertions and images helpful for their own proposals, which usually move in holistic and ecological directions hostile to the continued expansion of technology and to modern progress.

While Heidegger might be sympathetic to the intentions behind such use of his thought, he would probably worry that such proposals remain within the sway of modern subjectivity. Despite their Heideggerean language, they remain proposals for individual changes of attitude and programs for social reform, as if social priorities and individual psychology were the ultimate conditions of the problems of modernity. And often such proposals embrace a holistic metaphysics that is as foreign to Heidegger's intent as any other metaphysics, even though the terminology might sound appealing.[5]

Among the social and political implications that can be more legitimately drawn from Heidegger's thought, three stand out. First, Heidegger believes that things should be named for what they are. There is a consistent unmasking throughout his account of modernity. Many trends and theories and practices are named as fronts for the will to power and as cures that worsen the disease they purport to heal.

Second, Heidegger's thought discourages planned revolutions. Anything we might plan and carry out will be within the space of universal imposition. We will not found a new realm. No revolu-

tion based on human action can change the space within which
we move.

Third, the deconstructive living I spoke of earlier need not be
purely theoretical. Heidegger finds that the sway of metaphysical
"firsts" has always rested on the groundless mutual play of man
and being within the propriative event. Reiner Schürmann has
shown how political and social consequences can follow from this.
In the modern age the decay of metaphysically firm first principles
into universal functionality has become an increasingly obvious
fact of life. We live in the age after the death of God, providing an
opportunity for entry into the propriative event. But though the
gods are dying, the "firsts" in other spheres remain. In politics and
society we continue to live as if there were well-grounded first
principles that legitimated classifications and dominations of all
sorts. Let the "firsts" die in these spheres too, not by active murder
but by helping along a decay already in progress. We have, in
Schürmann's words, "the task of unlearning the search for one
measure-giving ultimate authority" (1983, 36; cf. Schürmann 1982).[6]
This leads toward an anarchic "life without principle" whose political and institutional effects might be as far reaching as they are
obscure.[7]

Such effects cannot be planned out according to some principle
of unity and order. Though the word *anarchic* suggests disorder and
individualism, the antiprinciple implications of Heidegger's thought
begin to offer a way of thinking about communal unity. It is not a
matter of new institutional forms so much as demands to be put on
whatever mode of communal decision making we can achieve. What
social and institutional relations are in fact to be established is left
to human discernment and creativity. The anarchic consequences
place a check on decision making and planning but do not provide
blueprints. No forms are guaranteed.

The demand to unbuild "firsts" is not normative in the sense that
it appeals to some grounded way in which things ought to be. In
particular, it is not another version of modern individualism. Social
and political "firsts" do not arise on the basis of the beliefs and
attitudes of prior individual selves; their possibilities are found in
the texture of the world in which such modern individuals encounter
themselves. Nor are "firsts" to be unbuilt in the name of individualism. Rather the demand to deconstruct them stems from a per-

ception of the current shape of man's open space and what it means for man to be aware of the groundless opening of that space.

This deconstructive living would not sweep away old political principles and institute a new world. Such living would remain offcenter and found no new center. We cannot on our own bring about the uncentered world Heidegger envisions beyond the darkness of the technological times. But we can see through the technological world. Vattimo speaks of the awareness of the propriative event "suspending the peremptoriness and cogency of the contexts" in which we live our historical life. We "stand in front of the totality of relations of grounding and grounded" in our age and see it as one historical possibility rather than the essence of reality. We "suspend the continuity of the texture-text (*tessuto-testo*)" in which we find ourselves. This does not result in yet another genteel historical relativism. Nor does this awareness lift us above our age to some suprahistorical vantage point. We are left in our present world, but with its grounds removed. Our actions can take account of this. What such a life without principle might mean cannot be planned in advance, but the liberation involved is not the liberation of modern formal subjectivity. To go further along this line demands a closer examination of the relation of desire and selfhood than can be found in Heidegger.[8]

There are, then, obscure but real political implications to be drawn from Heidegger's thought. Heidegger himself has not drawn these implications. This could be a reflection of his personal and social position, but it relates as well to his stance as a thinker. His thought keeps to a distinction which, although it is not identical with the old distinction of theory from practice, has similar effects in this case. He still thinks within the Husserlian dichotomy of the observing phenomenologist and the naive consciousness. The phenomenological thinker understands the context and the conditions of possibility for life, while consciousness in the natural attitude is unaware of the context and conditions in its lived experience. Although officially Heidegger's thought avoids this dichotomy, it remains in his transcendental stance. He almost always yields to the temptation to rank those involved in a life of action as living naively within the Heideggerean equivalent of the natural attitude. The thinker describes the conditions for that natural life of action but does not deal with its details any more than the thinker understanding the nature and conditions for modern science need deal with the details of current science.

Compared with Hegel on modernity, Heidegger is at once more radical and less useful. Heidegger would be proud of both these evaluations. We do not hear from him anything parallel to Hegel's discussion of civil society and state, but we receive an analysis that tries to find the conditions that have made discussions like Hegel's possible. Hegel, of course, has his own version of those conditions. It is to a comparison of the two thinkers that we now turn.

10

Hegel versus Heidegger

We have been exploring approaches to modernity that go beyond the standard ways for describing our situation. Although we have been looking at Hegel and Heidegger separately, we have already made some comparisons. It is time to bring them into explicit confrontation so that we can learn from their differences. I will first outline general parallels and differences between the two thinkers, and then focus on the most important issues. Next I will try to let the two thinkers speak about each other, and I will explore the reasons why each would find the other inadequate. After that it should be apparent which questions need our own further thought.

Similarities and Differences

Both our thinkers resist being treated by the usual method of collecting points of similarity and difference. They do not share the standard conception of philosophy as a collection of theses supported by arguments, with face-to-face confrontations and metaphors of combat. Both of them view philosophy in a more encompassing manner, and both try to get behind possible critics rather than confronting them thesis to thesis. They attempt to arrange discussion so that the critics are forestalled before they speak, because they will speak from within a mode of thought that the comprehensive thinker has already considered, located, and found wanting.

But it is just these inclusive moves, Hegel's dialectic and Heidegger's step back, that must be brought into explicit consideration if we are to come to some resolution about the way the two Germans try to get behind standard descriptions of modernity. So far I have stressed how they try to get behind and beyond the basic modern position typified by Weber. Now we will see how Hegel and Heidegger try to outflank each other. The results should nourish our own thinking.

We have already seen that even though Hegel and Heidegger are separated by a century of wrenching changes, the first descriptions they give of the modern age are similar enough to warrant comparison. For both thinkers "modernity" names the time since the Reformation, an age that reaches a culmination in their own days. The nature of that culmination is envisaged differently. Hegel's picture of modernity is probably closer to what the average person today thinks of as typically modern: increasing rationality in life, the individual freedoms of bourgeois liberalism, new economic systems, progress toward a government that is in principle rational, new developments in science and better standards of living. Heidegger's bleaker picture also includes these features, but he interprets them in terms of universal imposition and the technological mode of living in a way than would be unfamiliar to the ordinary person. It is true, however, that some aspects of Hegel's description of modernity are also outside the common person's idea of our age, such as the "end" of art, the inevitability of war, and the important role assigned to philosophy.

Both Germans agree that the modern age is a unified occurrence, not just a collection of diverse trends in economics, politics, art, and other areas. There is a similarity of tone and structure that allows us to call many different developments modern and mean more than that they are happening together. Hegel speaks of the unified shape of spirit, Heidegger of the one understanding of the being of man and things that makes possible the different aspects of modernity.

The two thinkers also agree that in the modern age we live in a way that fulfills many hopes expressed in the Western tradition. But even in this fulfillment we are not yet living as close as we can to the most fundamental conditions of our existence. For Hegel this was true of the one-sided penultimate form of modernity, much of which endured around him as he wrote, but it would be overcome in the final stage, which in principle had already been accomplished. That final stage would keep the achievements of modern freedom while incorporating some aspects of traditional society that the typically modern consciousness still believed it had left behind. For Heidegger modernity in all its stages continues the Western forgetfulness of man's fundamental involvement with the propriative event. It is true that the last stage of modernity, universal imposition, even as it seems to extend indefinitely, can open a way to the propriative event, but this neither provides a completion of modernity, brings back what modernity has undermined, nor inaugurates a new world.

Hegel and Heidegger would agree that the most obvious phenomenon distinguishing modernity is empty subjectivity. The self affirms itself over against the content of its life, confirming its freedom by transcending any given objects or ways of life. Content is fixed, represented, manipulated, and dominated for whatever goals the subject has chosen. Both thinkers would agree that this search for self-certitude through distance and manipulation ignores the basic conditions that make modern subjectivity possible at all.

Hegel and Heidegger disagree on the extent to which individualism is essential to modern subjectivity. For Hegel history has been moving toward individual freedom. Individualism is essential to modernity, and although it will be tempered in the rational state, it will not be denied, since it is a necessary moment in the mediation of universal, particular, and individual within the motion of spirit. Heidegger, on the other hand, sees bourgeois individualism as only one of the possibilities opened up by the essence of the modern age.

Heidegger would also emphasize more than Hegel the domineering aspects of modernity, the will to power and the leveling of all modes of being to the one realm of presentable objects and standing reserve. There are somewhat similar descriptions in Hegel's *Phenomenology of Spirit*, but when he spoke of the attitudes of modern individuals, Hegel either talked about modern citizenship and freedom or about the inward-turning aspects of modern consciousness such as irony and narcissism. He spoke less about technology and the will to power. Heidegger would say that Hegel fails to understand the importance of will in the modern age because Hegel's own solution for the problems of modernity itself is a hidden form of subjectivity as will.

Nonetheless, it is true that for both thinkers one sign of modern subjectivity is the appetite for *always more*. In opposition to this both

Hegel and Heidegger emphasize that man must give up the dream of endless linear progress and enter a circle. He must recognize the circle within which he already exists, a circle that is qualitatively limited in its possibilities. The two thinkers diverge sharply over the nature of that circle, but they stand together in condemning the conception of the self as existing in a space that is an open neutral background of indefinite possibility.

Neither Heidegger nor Hegel would say that modern subjectivity with its achievements and its agonies is our own accomplishment, or our own fault. It is made possible by something not itself subjective: the development and mediations within spirit, or the propriative event that brings man and things together in a particular way. Heidegger would object that the parallel between a Hegelian shape of spirit and an epoch in his own history of being is only superficial.

Hegel and Heidegger both believe that the modern age fulfills something that started with the Greeks, dividing Greek history in two. For Hegel what started was the movement from substantial community toward the full mediation of all social content through the individual. He sees in the Greek tragedians and in the Sophists the signs of this movement from the substantial life of the Homeric age to the troubled time of Socrates and Plato. This begins a new mediation that has its fulfillment in modern times.

Heidegger would claim that what he has seen happening with the Greeks is deeper than what Hegel has seen. The understanding of being in terms of presence and the consequent search for grounds and foundations begins in Greece. This accounts for the changes in individuality that Hegel investigates. For Heidegger, Hegel's description of Greek life characteristically avoids looking at the deepest changes in the way beings stand revealed.

According to Heidegger's essay "Plato's Doctrine of Truth," there was a change from truth as revelation or unconcealment to truth as correctness or correspondence. This is a change in the understanding of what it means for something to be. Thinking and reality are both encountered as entities whose mode of being is constant presence, and truth is their correspondence. What is lost is the awareness of the movement from the dark and the shadow, the process of unconcealment as a finite mortal opening. The pre-Socratic thinkers had named this process in the word *aletheia*. In Greek this word can be taken apart to mean "non-concealment," or the

coming forth from concealment. It came to mean only "correspondence." This loss of the deep experience of truth, and its replacement
by truth as a relation between entities encountered as simply present, can be found in Plato's belief that the essential reality of things
is something constantly available for intellectual sight.

Later, Heidegger admitted that the earliest Greek documents in
fact show that the meaning of *aletheia* had not changed during the
history of Greece. He abandoned the contention that the pre-Socratic thinkers had used "truth" in his sense, but he still claimed
they had named the dark side of the process of unconcealment in
such words as *physis* and *logos*, although they had not investigated
it explicitly.[1]

With this change in his interpretation of the Greeks, Heidegger
gives up the claim of being able to locate the beginning of the
Western forgetfulness of the self-withdrawal of the propriative event.
He still suggests that a mode of living more aware of this withdrawal
and darkness was followed by a mode of living dominated by clarity
and presence. But he offers no dividing line within the Greek world,
though he continues to insist that the Greeks received a destiny that
the West still lives within.

This change in Heidegger's interpretation of the Greeks decreases
the parallel with Hegel's ideas about a change in Greek history. In
another way Heidegger's later interpretation of the Greeks comes
closer to Hegel. For Hegel the change in Greek life was not a peculiar
destiny of the Greeks; it reflects a human tension and duality present
in human history elsewhere but not explicitly posited as such. In
Heidegger's later interpretation of the Greeks, the experience of the
finite arising of presence from darkness, and the forgetfulness of
that event, are contemporaneous. This reflects the trait of all human
situations called in *Being and Time* "fallenness." It is part of our
finitude that there is no secure possession, no steady apprehension
even of our finitude. We get lost amid the beings that surround us,
and we forget our appropriation to the event of clearing. This is
true everywhere, not just in the West. While the specific destiny of
the West remains for Heidegger an event "without a why," after he
changes his interpretation of Plato, that destiny seems to have more
continuity with the general human situation.

Hegel sees the West remaining faithful to the development that
began with the Greeks. Modernity fulfills the Greek legacy in a one-
sided but crucial way. Balance will be obtained by incorporating

something like the substantial community of the early Greeks with a fully developed version of the individuality of the later Greeks. Heidegger, too, sees in modernity the culmination of what started with the Greeks. In universal imposition, however, what was still present in earlier Greek life is not retrieved but all the more thoroughly forgotten. Nor can modernity be overcome in some synthesis of the different aspects of Greek life. At best we could live a deconstructive relation between them.[2]

Hegel and Heidegger agree that we need to get beyond the modern contentless self. There is something wrong with the basic modern dichotomy that says our values, customs, and other content for our life are either brutely given or arbitrarily chosen. Hegel seeks content in customs and ways of life that can be teased out of the structure of freedom itself and so are not opposed to freedom as object to subject. For Heidegger also the modern dichotomy must be undermined. "The freedom of the open space [*der Freiheit des Freies*] consists neither in unfettered arbitrariness nor in the constraint of mere laws" (The Question Concerning Technology 25/25). We find ourselves called, already in motion on paths that are not values for us to judge but possibilities that are us. We can retrieve and renew those possibilities, but they are not facts placed before our judging subjectivity.

The self-sufficiency of the modern individual is illusory. Modern subjects exist only by inhabiting something deeper than the subject-object relation presupposed in most of modernity's accounts of itself. That something deeper is the process by which things have their being in the gathering of spirit to itself, as Hegel would say, or the process by which things are revealed, as Heidegger would say.

Man is needed in the process by which things stand in their being; for Hegel it is man who provides an essential moment of individuality and self-consciousness in the coming of spirit to itself, while for Heidegger man provides the receptive abode for the propriative event and lets what is revealed come to language. But the two thinkers describe differently that *logos*, the gathering together that is the happening of a meaningful world. Although both believe that man's deeper involvement is marked by difference and negativity, they disagree on what this implies. Heidegger argues that Hegel still thinks about the gathering of man and world in a way marked by the Greek emphasis on presence and availability. For Hegel it is absolutely crucial that the gathering of man and world be rendered self-trans-

parent, while for Heidegger it is equally crucial that no such transparency be possible. On this point each thinker would regard the
other as caught within the basic problems of modernity.

For both Hegel and Heidegger, when we discover how man participates in his full context we can undo the hold of the dichotomies
by which modernity structures itself. The division of formal process
from content and the subject-object relation in all its permutations
are not the last word on our situation. This in turn affects other
basic modern dualities such as individual and society or freedom
and order.

For Hegel when the absolute form of the whole appears, we find
a content for living that is not arbitrary (the content is the structured
motion of spirit itself). Nor is it merely given to us as facts for our
judgment (we are the motion of that structure and content made
self-conscious, an event that is part of that motion). The modern
distanced and formal subject is replaced by a concrete totality; any
assertion of distance or formality is a one-sided abstraction. The
seemingly infinite power of modern individuality to negate objects
and create distance and demand always more turns out to be rooted
in the concretely infinite totality and the limited but transparently
guaranteed contours of its openness.

For Heidegger we know ourselves as called, as thrown projects
already put in motion in a world of possibilities that is not a limitation
on some larger field presented to a distanced subjectivity. While
there is no unique or guaranteed content as in Hegel, there is a
realm of possibilities that is neither our construction nor some ob-
stacle we have to surmount. Our freedom is maintained as a receptive retrieval and letting-be of the possibilities granted to us. We
come to presence within them, not the reverse. Modern subjectivity
is replaced by the finite togetherness of man and things appropriated
together. Any assertion of distance or formality can only be a derived
mode of existing that denies this more basic inhabitation. The seemingly infinite power of modern subjectivity to deny, transcend, and
assert its self-certainty turns out to be located within the finite granting of unconcealment.

Thus both thinkers see the awareness of man's full situation un-
doing modern dichotomies. In Hegel a reconciliation trims the absoluteness of modern divisions while preserving their importance.
In Heidegger there is no reconciliation, only a call back to a root
situation that cannot be described in the divisions characteristic of

modernity, though it has its own divisions and negations of another kind.

For both thinkers there is the possibility of a new kind of life in which the involvement of man in the gathering of the world will not be hidden in the way it was before, though the two disagree on what kind of presence will be involved. Modernity will not disappear. For Hegel it is a necessary stage whose accomplishments will be preserved while its one-sidedness is overcome in a fully achieved union of the modern and the classical worlds. Overcoming abstract subjectivity is the final act that ushers in a completed humanity that can now live in a rational, illuminated way, though not without pain and negation. For Heidegger the rule of technology and universal imposition will be "*aufgehoben* in the Hegelian sense" (*Spiegel* 217/ 62). The claims of modernity will lose their ultimacy; we will be able to live in this world as a destiny we have received. Beyond this we cannot see; we can only hope that a new nonmetaphysical world might be opened. Modernity and the long process of its ending fulfill the long history of the West, but that history is only one turn in the directionless play of man and the propriative event.

Finally, in both Hegel and Heidegger the thinker has a special role to play in the overcoming of modernity. The thinker can comprehend what is going on in his age in a way most others cannot. For Hegel that comprehension puts the thinker in touch with and completes the central movement of his age. For Heidegger the thinker remains at the margin. His insight into our finitude removes him from the kind of role a Plato or a Hegel can enjoy. Nor is it clear that Heidegger would prefer such a role. Hegel accepted the call to teach in Berlin in part because he wanted to have more influence in shaping policy and events. Heidegger declined a call to teach in Berlin and chose to remain "in the provinces." The price of immersion in events was too high; it would hinder the step back, which is the essence of thinking. Marginality provides in its way a deeper location than that of a great legislative thinker like Hegel or Plato. Heidegger affirms the loss of a center as the central happening in our age, a happening that the thinker, much in Hegel's fashion, can discern.

As part of his involvement in the overcoming of modernity, the thinker names things for what they are. For Hegel, the philosopher does not begin the completion of the self-grasp of spirit, but he does participate in its final movement by letting it come to self-conscious conceptual form. In so doing he may judge and name holdovers from earlier shapes of spirit. He uses no external standards, only the structure provided by the movement of the logical sequence itself. This act, like all thinking, is strong enough to contain great tensions yet hold them within the movement of reconciliation. For Heidegger the thinker lets come to language what is revealed, and he speaks our involvement in the self-withdrawing propriative event. In so doing he may name denials of man's true dwelling and covert reassertions of modernity's will to power. He uses no external standards but retrieves the genuine possibilities granted to us. This act, like all thinking, proceeds in the questioning openness of risk and finitude.

Crucial Issues

Our two thinkers do not presuppose the standard dichotomies and the standard options found in Weber and in many other discussions about modernity. They try to locate modernity within a context that cannot be described using the standard descriptions, and they see the possibility of a way of life more attuned to our inhabitation of that fuller context.

Our deepest involvement is not with a way of presenting objects to subjects, whether the subjects be conceived as judging individuals or convention-creating communities. We do not find ourselves within an empty structure or a neutral space that receives whatever content is provided and allows indefinite extension of possibilities. We are within a finite and definite opening of possibilities in which we are involved as their gathering abode and way of motion rather than as their distanced judge and planner.

Heidegger's thought moves from the ordinary level of daily living to the world, the pervasive clearing that makes ordinary life possible. This is the space in which we find ourselves as thrown projects. It is the always presupposed context. Then Heidegger moves to consider the happening of that context, its stretching out, our appropriation within it, which is not a brute fact but the mutual belonging together in some definite way of man and things amid meaningful possibilities. Finally, considering the negation and difference inherent in that event, Heidegger recognizes the withdrawing and hiddenness "from which" the event happens.

Hegel too locates ordinary language and action within shapes or fields that structure our historical existence and are always presupposed. He also considers the happening of these shapes of spirit, the belonging together of man and things within the movement of spirit. That movement is infinite in Hegel's special sense and includes negation and circular mutual belonging. But for Hegel there is no withdrawal. The shapes of spirit are available in a pure form in the systematic logic whose final move is the self-comprehension of the absolute form of spirit's motion.

For neither thinker can the context of modernity be made a focal object within a horizon of interpretation. For neither can it be understood by the usual methods of analysis and derivation. But for Hegel there is a self-giving in the transparency of the motion of spirit. That motion has something to give: itself. The self-giving of spirit to itself is not a different process from the revelation of things; that is why we can use the absolute form of spirit's motion to understand states and economies. For Heidegger there is no such self-giving; the propriative event has nothing of its own, no structure or principle or form to give.

The crucial question, then, is whether what makes modernity possible, the *Sache* for thinking, gives itself or withdraws itself. More precisely, does it give itself as withdrawing and lack of totality or as presence, availability, and self-closure? For Hegel it is the coming to presence of spirit that allows things to be revealed; for Heidegger it is the withdrawal of the propriative event. Without closure and self-presence, Hegel would argue, we cannot overcome the dichotomies we face. With that closure and self-presence, Heidegger would argue, we remain caught within the understanding of the being of things that gave rise to the modern dichotomies.

We need then to think about the context within which modernity happens, the conditions that make it possible but cannot be described in its terms. What needs to be recognized is not a set of ultimate facts or principles but the happening that makes possible facts and principles.[3]

It sounds as if we have to think about some ultimate happening that grounds all the rest. There are many models in the philosophical tradition for thinking about ultimate metaphysical or epistemological happenings. But our two thinkers are not using any of these standard models. What they are trying to think is not the creation of order by an act of will on the part of a divine or human agent. Nor is it an imposition of form on some neutral or chaotic stuff, be that cosmological chaos or epistemological sense-data. Nor is it a limitation of some larger field of ontological or cognitive possibility. Nor, finally, are they referring to a derivation from some first principle of cosmological, personal, or epistemological unity. There is no point source for the happening of the world.

What is happening is the extending, the spacing out, the opening up, the being there of a field of possibilities—not as a fact or as given data but as always already being spread out. We must recognize the belonging together of man and beings, world and man, beings and being, absolute and finite, and the other pairs that the two thinkers use. All these pairs are deployments or extendings that are not the exclusive action of either side of the pair. The pairs depend on and are implicated in each other, so that neither side can be thought of as acting alone. Each needs the other in order to be what it is. In the circle formed by the belonging together of these pairs, there is no third thing behind that is being deployed into the circle. Hegel and Heidegger disagree, however, whether the circle itself should be thought of as constituting a third thing, a new unity.

This happening cannot be thought of as a case of fitting together or mutual dependence in the usual senses. It is not like a jigsaw puzzle, where pieces are complete in themselves but interact passively to make a larger whole. Nor is it an active interaction like ecological dependency in which several species depend on one another in order to exist. For both our thinkers the mutual happening is marked by difference and negation in a deeper sense than the ordinary images suggest.

Hegel and Heidegger agree that there is a difference and negation deeper than anything we can reflectively distinguish by separating out aspects or relations of some unitary entity or group of entities (what Hegel calls "external reflection": distinguishing the table as flat, as brown, as high). The deep negativity does not reduce to that otherness whereby two entities, positive in themselves, are different from each other. Both thinkers affirm that there is a level on which things are what they are because the process that lets them stand revealed in their being contains difference and negation.

In Hegel, as we have seen, there is nothing immediate. Things are revealed for what they are because the movement of spirit has opened them up and gone beyond them. In its movement to self-closure, spirit "overreaches" the finite things it constitutes. Finite things perish because they cannot contain the full negativity and differentiation of that movement; only spirit can contain this negation, and spirit is not a thing. This is true of the self as well. We exist by being involved in the motion of spirit, which is not something we create or will or do on our own. To be a self is to be something overreached within that motion in a particular way yet coming back to oneself out of negation and difference. The self does not "do" negation and difference as if these were products of its action. The self exists by means of difference and negation; this motion and its absolute form constitute the field of possibilities that is the openness of the self to things. There are limits to the possibilities open to us, limits established by the logic of the movement by which spirit overreaches its prior shapes toward its union with itself.

For Heidegger we are involved in negation and difference that we do not make. In the propriative event a togetherness of man and world occurs in which each goes beyond the other. They do not just fit together; each is what it is by transcending the other. The world surrounds and goes beyond what I focally encounter; it is this going beyond that characterizes the world as world. My projects are solicited by a world that goes beyond them yet needs man's projects to be a meaningful world at all. I reveal the world as such by my openness to the no-thing beyond which is the event of its happening. I and the world both "exist" by being stretched out in this difference and mutual transcendence that neither creates. Neither side has inner solidity, and, unlike as in Hegel, their mutual transcendence does not make a whole that comes together. There is a limit to the possibilities open to us, because they occur in the event of mutual belonging, but there is no logic to that limitation.[4]

For both thinkers there is no point outside the negation and difference we are involved within. There could be no platform from which we could view from the outside the process by which things are made available. We must use methods descended from those Kant devised for describing the motion and context of thinking from the inside. Although there is no place from which a distanced modern self could wield analytical tools on the context of modernity, there are ways in which we can make it present to ourselves in the appropriate manner. But Hegel and Heidegger do not agree at all on what manner of presence is possible and appropriate.

Heidegger's Criticisms of Hegel

The similarities we have discerned between the Hegel and Heidegger are encouraging for our exploration of the general strategy toward modernity they share. But the differences between the two thinkers are not incidental; they go to the heart of their thoughts and need to be examined more carefully if we are to find new ways for our own thinking.

Heidegger and Hegel would each say that the other reinforces the principle of modernity while trying to overcome it. In the following two sections I will construct a three-cornered discussion among Hegel, Heidegger, and myself as a not so disinterested referee judging the adequacy of their mutual criticism. Although it is true that each of them possesses insights that the other misses, there is no way to bring their views together to form a harmonious whole. We cannot expect any Hegelian reconciliation of these differences. We can hope the confrontation will raise questions and show us positive clues while indicating some of the pitfalls to avoid.

We will deal first with what Heidegger has to say about Hegel, at least as it affects the issues we are concerned with. We could imagine Heidegger summarizing his opinions about Hegel's dealings with modernity:

"Though Hegel describes many of the symptoms of the root situation of modernity, he fails to penetrate to the essence of modernity. He lived in and helped bring to a climax that aspect of modernity emphasizing subjectivity, but though he shows many signs of the universal imposition that reigns today, he has no name for that essence of technology and modernity.

"Hegel's efforts to think through our situation stem from the demands of the traditional metaphysical understanding of being. He must satisfy the demands of reason by making explicit and unified all that has been thought, all that has happened. He must find an insight that shows the wholeness of history and thought and traces it to its ground. My own attempts to think about our situation stem rather from the need to think what has been unthought, what has been unexpressed in what has been said. I do not mean to find some hidden first principle from which everything flows in grounded unity. What has been unthought is the happening of the world, the finite openness of the clearing in which we move. This breaks the claim to wholeness, grounding, and completion.

"Hegel cannot discern the true enigma of modernity because he remains caught within the destiny of metaphysics. He thinks within the understanding of truth as correspondence and of being as constant available presence. He cannot experience the propriative event and its enabling withdrawal as such. He cannot find the deeper finitude that underlies even the infinity of spirit's return to itself.

"Hegel thinks out of what was granted him to speak, and that is still the traditional understanding of being in its modern form as self-certain subjectivity. Because he was not granted to recognize our deeper finitude as such, his efforts provide only a metaphysical cure for a metaphysical condition. He works for foundations and closure; he seeks to mediate the dichotomies of modernity within the self-certainty of the absolute self. He makes many of the appropriate beginnings, but he makes them as if the process by which things were revealed were itself the grounding activity of some highest entity.

"Hegel fails to overcome modernity because he, like the metaphysical tradition as a whole, is destined to forget our real finitude. He still aspires to a life reconciled in the full presence of rationality. Noble as that goal sounds, it is only another version of the attempt to make things and their coming to presence itself totally present without the core of concealment, withdrawal, and finitude that marks our situation. In trying to overcome the excess subjectivity of modernity as he understands it, Hegel actually exhibits and brings to new heights the very drive for self-coincidence, self-certainty, and total presence that lies at the root of modern subjectivity and its will to power. It is not surprising that the world he describes should now seem to us a direct ancestor of the present reign of technology."

We turn now to Heidegger's criticisms in more detail. These are found in many places throughout his writings. In section 82 of *Being and Time* he accuses Hegel of remaining within the traditional understanding of time rather than penetrating to the dispersed temporality that he describes (see Emad 1983). In *Kant and the Problem of Metaphysics* he often contrasts the intellectualized forgetfulness of our finite roots he finds in German Idealism with the emphasis on imagination and temporality he sees in Kant's first *Critique*. He also criticizes Hegel's notion of dialectical overcoming (*Aufhebung*) as based too thoroughly on the goal of self-coincidence, a criticism he repeats elsewhere. In his 1930–31 lectures on Hegel's *Phenomenology of Spirit* and in his essay "Hegel's Concept of Experience,"

Heidegger sees Hegel as the culmination of the Cartesian phase of metaphysics because Hegel holds that all beings are founded in the self-certainty of an absolute self. In the essays in *Identity and Difference* Heidegger locates Hegel within the tradition that thinks metaphysically in terms of self-identity and the grounding presence of a highest being rather than recognizing our deepest finitude as such. In "Hegel and the Greeks" he repeats the picture of Hegel as a super-Cartesian and claims Hegel remained within the Platonic and Aristotelian definitions of truth and being that forget man's true context. These issues are discussed again in the Heraclitus Seminar with Eugen Fink.

I will concentrate on the claims that Hegel remains within the traditions of Cartesian subjectivity and Western metaphysics. The criticisms about time that Heidegger advances in *Being and Time* are not convincingly developed, and the contrasts he makes in *Kant and the Problem of Metaphysics* are based on a questionable interpretation of Kant, though they have value as anticipations of what Heidegger will say more fully later.[5]

I will argue that the claim that Hegel is a super-Cartesian is mistaken. The contention that Hegel remains within the metaphysical tradition I will for the most part accept. This latter is the more encompassing criticism.

Heidegger's interpretation of Hegel as a thinker of subjectivity is set within the larger claim that Hegel keeps the basic metaphysical orientation to grounds, unities, and constant presence. Hegel thinks of the ground of all beings as an absolute self that achieves total self-presence and self-coincidence in the presentation of itself to itself. All other modes of being are reduced to that of objects proposed within the return-to-self of the absolute ego.

Hegel's thinking speaks first of all in the fundamental scheme of the subject object relationship. . . . The absolute idea of Hegel is then the complete self-knowledge of the absolute subject. (Heraclitus Seminar 184/115, 198/124)

The truly actual infinite . . . is the subject, . . . the absolute subject as spirit. The subject, the ego, is primarily grasped as "I think." . . . Hegel and German Idealism in general . . . grasp the totality of what is in its being in terms of ego-ness as infinity. *Hegels Phänomenologie des Geistes* 111)

Spirit is knowing, *logos*; spirit is I, *ego*; spirit is God, *theos*; spirit is actuality, what absolutely is, *on*. (*Hegels Phänomenologie des Geistes* 183)

Heidegger details this criticism in his essay "Hegel's Concept of Experience," which concerns the Introduction to Hegel's *Phenomenology of Spirit*. Through a careful analysis of key sentences Heidegger tries to show how for Hegel everything is grounded in the absolute being's will to total presence and how this functions as the basic measure for the varying shapes of consciousness Hegel treats in his book.

The reading of Hegel's text is subtle and complex, but it is ultimately misleading. It neglects the role Hegel gives to determinate negation and to the series of shapes of consciousness. For this series with its complex echoes and gradual movements, Heidegger substitutes the single repeated movement from natural consciousness to the awareness of the background conditions for that natural consciousness in the fluidity of the absolute's self-presencing. Each transition in the *Phenomenology of Spirit* is interpreted as one more attempt to perform the same step back.

As a result of his emphasis on one repeated step, Heidegger overvalues the transition to the chapter on self-consciousness in the *Phenomenology of Spirit* as if that were the basic movement of the book. Yet one of the purposes of the latter two-thirds of the *Phenomenology of Spirit* (which Heidegger ignores in all his discussions of the book) is to show that infinity, grounding, self-coincidence, and all the other metaphysical goals Heidegger rightly sees Hegel as seeking are precisely *not* achievable so long as one talks in terms of ego and subjectivity. It is necessary to move from any structure involving egos to the structure of spirit, the logical and intersubjective movement of which the ego is only one moment. It is necessary to include the social mediations and structures of mutual recognition that cannot be interpreted as properties of a single ego, be it human or absolute.

There are no immediately given egos in Hegel, as the early sections of the "Philosophy of Spirit" in the *Encyclopedia* make clear. Subjectivity is an achievement within a larger motion. Nor is the final stage of the system properly described as the achievement of an absolute subjectivity. The logical sequence posits and overcomes the opposition between subject and object in its third section. Hegel conceives of subjectivity and ego through the logical categories, not the reverse (despite what Heidegger claims in "Hegel and the Greeks"). Hegel's logic is not a discussion of categories functioning within or pro-posed before some subjectivity, nor a study of the self-coincidence of some ego, human or divine.[6]

It could be objected that I seem to be ignoring the distinction Heidegger draws in "Zur Seinsfrage" between *Subjektivität* and *Subjektität*. Heidegger realizes that Hegel's spirit is not an ego in the usual sense, and he provides a more general conception of subjectivity that Hegel does not escape from. My reply is that Heidegger, as the above quotes show, does want to interpret Hegel in terms of *Subjektivität*. The more general and basic term, *Subjektität*, can involve the notion of a substratum, which does not apply to Hegel, or the general demand for grounding and self-coincidence, which does apply. This reduces the subjectivity criticism to the other criticism of Hegel, for remaining within metaphysics, which I have already accepted.

It is worth asking why Heidegger is so sure Hegel is a Cartesian. In part this is due to Heidegger's method of reading, which is to take a short bit of text and use it as a nodal point for interpreting a thinker's overall direction and the unsaid understanding of being within which the thinker moves. While this method works well with some authors, it fails with Hegel (as it does with Plato), because Hegel's text tends to analogical and multi-leveled reuse of terms, so that one passage may mislead about other passages that sound similar. An example of this is the emphasis Heidegger puts on Hegel's comment that with Descartes philosophy "sights land." Heidegger claims that this shows how Hegel wants philosophy to attain the firm ground of subjectivity. But Hegel uses this metaphor elsewhere in his history of philosophy, for instance with Heraclitus, where it cannot be cited in favor of subjectivity. Heidegger is caught out by Hegel's habit of taking any closing moment of a particular dialectical transition as a foreshadowing of his ultimate goal. Hegel will praise the current achievement, for example, self-consciousness, as virtually complete, just about all we need, only to turn on it at the beginning of the next chapter and condemn it as poverty stricken, immediate, and far from the goal.

On a deeper level, Heidegger reads Hegel as a Cartesian because he presupposes, in line with his own philosophy, that any thinker must work within one unified interpretation of what it means to be. This is the reason Heidegger feels he can discern the whole basic

horizon of interpretation within which a thinker moves by examining only short bits of text. We will have occasion to question this
presupposition later; the issue has arisen several times already: the
simple priority of the propriative event.[7]

Although Heidegger's reading of Hegel as a Cartesian is mistaken,
his general reading of Hegel as within the metaphysical tradition is
correct. Hegel strives for self-coincidence, self-transparency, and
reconciled presence. Yet he does not perfectly match Heidegger's
standard picture of a metaphysician. He does not appeal to the self-
coincidence of some large entity as the cornerstone of the world.
He tries in the *Science of Logic* to finesse many of the standard metaphysical questions about grounds. There is a coming together into
presence, yes, but it cannot be thought of as the career of one
grounding entity so much as as the motion within which all entities
appear.

While it seems clear that Hegel adheres to the general goals Heidegger attributes to the metaphysical tradition since the Greeks, it
is not so clear that Hegel works within an interpretation of the
meaning of being in terms of simple constant presence. We touch
here on the vexing question of how far negation and otherness are
overcome in Hegel's system. Certainly they are not rendered non-
existent. Nor are they treated as simple privations along the line of
the Scholastic treatment of evil. The reconciliation Hegel attempts
does not do away with the negative to achieve some constant unity.
We have already seen how the negative endures in society in terms
of poverty, class divisions, and war. Hegel offers no magic harmony.

For Hegel there is no static intuitive presence at the goal of his
system. Though he owes much to the neoplatonic tradition, Hegel
does not end his system with an intuition of final unity after the
manner of Schelling. Spirit's self-coincidence is something achieved
in a motion. Time is not raised to eternity; it is made self-transparent
in its movement. Man's awareness of the rationality of the real is
achieved by an awareness of a motion man finds himself within, an
awareness that is known to be a manifestation of the pattern, itself
moving, which that motion follows.

Nevertheless, for all this evidence that Hegel should not be read
in terms of simple presence, it remains true that the emphasis is on
unity-in-difference. As Jacques Taminiaux concludes:

[Hegel's philosophy is centered on the question of negation and difference,] but it is not a matter of indifference that this structure, these

themes, these motifs are envisaged by the word *absolute*. . . . The absolute is by definition that which absolves itself from all reference, that which, in the difference and the game of references which it carries, becomes equal to itself, coincides with itself. The result is that at the very moment when it is recognized as radical, the difference is no more radical but derived or, what comes to the same thing, uprooted. It follows that at the very moment when it seemed to be discredited, the scheme of coincidence is only dilated, and words such as concordance, adequation, equality, invade the whole Hegelian text. (Taminiaux 1977, 141)[8]

There remains the question why Hegel's belonging to the metaphysical tradition is a matter for criticism rather than classification. Heidegger is not in fact criticizing Hegel so much as locating him. But if Heidegger is correct in locating himself and us as at the end of the metaphysical tradition, then locating Hegel firmly within it is a way of saying that we cannot take Hegel's philosophy (or those of his descendants who keep the crucial features) as live options for dealing with modernity today. Heidegger is also saying that there is something more to the human situation than Hegel knows, and this is a damaging criticism of a philosophy that aspires to totality as Hegel does.

That something more is the radical finitude of the propriative event and man's appropriation within it. Heidegger wants to find a condition for the possibility of Hegel's system, a condition that Hegel cannot recognize within that system. In this sense Heidegger's basic objection to Hegel is a sophisticated descendant of Kierkegaard's invocation of "existence" as the condition of possibility for Hegel's system that cannot be caught within the toils of the system. But Heidegger does not much respect Kierkegaard's criticism of Hegel, which he thinks remains within the orbit of the philosophy of subjectivity.[9]

The condition that Hegel cannot grasp is the finite granting of the meaning of being, truth, and time that Hegel presupposes and works within. Another way of putting the same point, used by Heidegger in *Identity and Difference*, is that Hegel's key words (*identity, difference, dialectic,* and so on) have more resonances than Hegel can hear. Some of them can lead in a direction away from or behind the closure of Hegel's system.[10]

Although the claim that Hegel thinks about infinity and closure in terms of selfhood and ego is mistaken, the larger claim about the metaphysical nature of Hegel's thought remains correct. Earlier I pointed out that Hegel depends crucially upon the architectonic expressed in the three large sections of the logical sequence. It is present at the beginning in Hegel's injunctions to heed "the demands of reason" or seek "the satisfaction of thought." It provides the only possible criterion for judging among detailed versions of the logical sequence. It might be said to provide Hegel's understanding of what it means to be, and this involves self-coincidence through negation and otherness. Heidegger is right that we can see in all this Hegel's rootedness within the tradition that makes grounding and self-coincidence central to thought, although Heidegger is mistaken when he takes Hegel as positing an absolute ego as a "first" that serves as a ground. The circular movement is stronger than any "first."

If the metaphysical tradition is viewed as itself a limited epoch rather than the permanent nature of thought, then the purity and necessity of Hegel's logical sequence suddenly seems not pure enough, still determined by some historical background and context. More profoundly, that very purity is itself seen to be a particular historical project. It is because Heidegger criticizes Hegel in this way that Heidegger pays no attention to the question of whether Hegel's enterprise succeeds in its own terms. Even if it does, it will succeed only within the space granted by a historical fate the system neither examines nor includes.

Is it then true that Hegel thinks within one unified understanding of what it means to be, as Heidegger believes he must? It is certainly the case that Hegel works under the sign of closure and self-transparency. But Heidegger's descriptions miss something important to Hegel's thought. In the *Phenomenology of Spirit* and the *Science of Logic* Hegel seems to work within a shifting multiplicity of ways of understanding knowledge and being. Heidegger would argue that these are all variations of the metaphysical understanding. They may be as different from one another as the various epochs Heidegger traces within the history of the West, but like those epochs they stay within the metaphysical tradition. Heidegger's step back is to provide an understanding of the arising of such ways of understanding that is different from Hegel's metaphysical account of the same.

Hegel, according to Heidegger, maintains one overall horizon within which the many smaller unities treated in the dialectic appear. That overall horizon is the understanding of what it means to be in terms of absolute selfhood and its infinity, which includes negation. I have argued that there is no positing of an absolute ego as the first entity for Hegel, but I have agreed with Heidegger that there is a presupposed understanding in terms of grounding and self-coincidence.

Should we then, with Heidegger, think of Hegel's overall understanding as one horizon within which the dialectical moments do their tricks? Or is this to read Hegel too much in terms of Husserl's metaphor of things within perceptual horizons? If Hegel's basic understanding can be found in the architectonic of the large sections of the logical sequence, perhaps it should be thought of as a motion within which things appear. Perhaps there is not one unified horizon of interpretation but many, each treated in the dialectic that is the motion of its appearance. The space for our encounter with things would then be structured by the current horizon and, ultimately, by the motion of having horizons of interpretation at all, which is the motion described in the logical sequence—not itself a final horizon of interpretation so much as the thinking of the event of having interpretations.

I am pressing the analogy between Hegel's absolute idea and Heidegger's propriative event. Heidegger would rather say that Hegel's absolute idea is just one more metaphysical and, in this sense, naive horizon of interpretation for the phenomenologist to step back from. I am saying that Hegel too makes a step back. The self-grasp of the absolute idea is not just another world but the self-grasp of the event of our being appropriated into any world.

It is true that Hegel thinks of that event metaphysically in terms of unity, self-coincidence, and grounding. Heidegger is right when he suggests in *Identity and Difference* that there is a kind of difference and belonging together in the propriative event that is not included in Hegel's system, though it makes the system possible. On the other hand, we encounter here again the question of the relative priority of dialectic and phenomenology. Could we make sense of a multiplicity of understandings of what it means to be that happen by interacting and being together and so hold open the space for the appearance of the world rather than themselves emerging against the background of one unified horizon in one dominant event? I will later urge this direction for our own thought, taking clues from both Heidegger and Hegel.

If we accept the general thrust of Heidegger's criticism of Hegel, we will be wary of attempting to overcome modernity's problems by enfolding the modern world within a larger context that is itself a totality we can become aware of. The difficulties pointed out earlier with the machinery of the Hegelian state are symptoms of a deeper problem: Hegel's need to have all the moments of universal, particular, and individual come together in a smoothly mediated and self-coincident whole. This demands that the dispersed individualism of civil society be brought together into a structure that is at the same time self-coincident and fully articulated. If Heidegger is right that a deeper finitude and obscurity underlie Hegel's self-transparent infinity, there can be no such overcoming of civil society and the problems of modernity within a self-complete structure of mediations. There is no implicit deep rationality waiting to be brought to completion. Are we then modern subjects facing, as Weber would have it, a contingent neutral mass of data waiting for our interpretation and judgment? No, for Heidegger is correct that we find ourselves always already appropriated within the finite event of there being a meaningful world. I am suggesting, however, that something like Hegel's notion of an internally divided motion may be helpful in conceiving of that event in a way that overcomes the standard modern self-definition and its problems while avoiding the difficulties in Heidegger's thought to which we now turn.

Hegel's Criticisms of Heidegger

We come now to what Hegel might say about how well Heidegger meets the challenge of modernity. Naturally, there is a problem of voice here: despite his encyclopedic approach, Hegel did not have a chance to discuss Heidegger at any length in his writings. So who will be now speaking, Hegel or I? In what follows I try first to speak from what I take would have been Hegel's position on Heidegger, with which I only partly agree. Then I will add my own comments and judgments to what "Hegel" has said. So here is "Hegel" speaking:

"Heidegger often treats other thinkers as the Husserlian phenomenologist treats 'natural consciousness.' He assumes the position of someone who can see beyond the naive activities of other thinkers to the conditions that make them possible, conditions that the other thinkers could see for themselves if only they were granted to look at what is nearest to their own thought. Heidegger sees his own thought as inquiring behind the naive consciousness to the horizon presupposed in that consciousness, to the unifying meaning of that horizon, to the event of having horizons at all. But I too inquire into the event of our having a meaningful world at all, and I do not discuss it in terms of beings within that world. I would say that he does not stand to me, as he imagines, as phenomenologist to object of study, but we stand together as two thinkers with rival accounts of what it means to be present to and in the world. We differ on the kind of inner dispersal or inner unity involved in that event of things being revealed within a meaningful world.

"My own phenomenological investigations lead to a joining of the investigating consciousness with that investigated. Heidegger only issues exhortations; there is no path leading from natural consciousness to the goal. His step back may be open to us, but no dialectic brings us out from where we are. My system may seem to him too enclosed, but it provides a real pathway instead of just one step.

"If I were to summarize my disagreements with Heidegger I might say that despite his claims to the contrary, I do *not* disagree with his talk about finitude. But I object to his emphasis on unity and immediacy.

"We agree that the pretensions of extreme modern subjectivity must be curbed. Those pretensions appeal to what I have called 'the bad infinite' and the desire for always more. I have stressed finitude, acceptance of where we are, entering the circle of spirit's motion, as a cure for modern emptiness. We must move away from the feeling of infinite indefinite possibility and accept the finite possibilities granted by *die Sache selbst*, the matter for thought, the movement of spirit. This is the mark of mature thought and action; it allows escape from the infinite pretensions of ironic and romantic subjectivity. It allows us to see the one guaranteed set of overall possibilities for the organization of life that derives from the rational structure of the motion of the logical sequence. The 'good infinite' I describe in my logic contains finitude within it. [11]

"What my theory of finitude and infinity does not contain is immediacy. Nothing is immediate and first, neither the finite nor the infinite. Heidegger, however, thinks that finitude must be immediate. His thought involves too much that is simply given or immediately granted. True, the granting, what he (in a pun I wish I had thought of) calls *das Ereignis*, the propriative event, is shot through with a kind of difference and negativity. But what is granted by that event is immediate and must be just accepted. Heidegger's

talk of conflict, withdrawal, difference concerns the granting and
our appropriation within it, not the content of what is granted. This
empowers us, sets us in motion. There is no tension and dialectic
within the content that shapes a given epoch of the history Heidegger
tells. There cannot be, for if there were, Heidegger would demand
a yet further unified horizon within which the tension or dialectic
could play itself out.

"In my thought, both the granting and what is granted are dia-
lectically tense, and no further horizon is needed. The space in
which we move is constituted by the interplay of the oppositions
within the content and by the further dialectical oppositions between
that content and the overall movement described in the logical
sequence. In order for this to be possible there has to be some
identity between the content and the overall form of the movement,
as I show in my logic.

"Heidegger finds this identity too 'metaphysical.' I admit that my
thought belongs within the metaphysical tradition, that I strive for
grounds and unities, though not of any simple kind. Heidegger
sometimes reads me as if I were expressing opinions like those found
in the early writings of Schelling, with an Absolute just sitting there
in constant comparison with finite things. My way of achieving the
metaphysical goals is more complex than that.

"I would urge Heidegger to look at the price he pays for avoiding
metaphysics. Heidegger's immediate grantings lead to an implausible
retelling of history. It is implausible because the beginning stands
so dominant over what comes later, and each age is too unified in
itself. Notice that for me the Greek beginning, and each subsequent
age, has within itself tensions and problems that lead to later developments and changes. For Heidegger we live within the Western
granting of possibilities, and though we have a receptive co-respon-
dence with it, there are no oppositions and dualities leading to
dialectical progress either within it or in our relation to it. We move
only within the space it grants, and we wait for new spaces to be
opened. While there is, for Heidegger, some mysterious connection
that rules the succession of the epochs within the West, it has to do
with the wanderings of errance [Irre]; we play no part in the deep
changes. We can only retrieve and renew what we have been given
or take a nondialectical step back from it. There is none of the
negation and otherness I find built into the shape of any age in
history.

"This immediacy and unity causes another problem. The particular quality of each different epoch, for instance, the medieval as distinct from the modern, receives no explanation. It is just to be accepted as a destiny. Outside of the West there may be even less connection in the aimless play of the propriative event. Heidegger understandably does not want to 'explain' the various epochs in any ordinary way; but does he not owe us some account of their differences?

"This problem arises because the propriative event is the same in all cases, or at least Heidegger talks about it that way. How does it relate to the different contents? Does it bring them out of itself? Then it would sound neoplatonic or Hegelian. Does it receive them from outside? Then it would sound Aristotelian and, in any case, metaphysical. Heidegger does not want it to sound metaphysical, so he gives no account of the arising of the differences of content in the eras and epochs. He denies that the propriative event can be reified into an 'it' at all. But then by what right does he talk about it in connection with all the various epochs and eras within and outside of the West?

"Heidegger might object that he does not talk in this way. The propriative event can only be 'experienced in the revealing done by language as that which allows it' (The Way to Language 258/127). It cannot be experienced separately. True enough, according to his theory. Yet he does talk about it in connection with the many different epochs of the West, and he speaks of an awareness possessed in pre-Socratic times. In his dialogue with a Japanese he even speaks of what Japanese aesthetics may show of that event that Western aesthetics covers up. Evidently there is some sense in which all of these relate to 'the same' while they contrast with it and with one another. Certainly it is not some one entity behind the various epochs, but rather the being appropriated to each other of world and man. But it can still be spoken of as the happening, *described more or less formally*, of the various epochs and eras.

"Now it may seem that I am making of the propriative event something like a universal structure available in a formal description and instantiated in various ways. Heidegger would claim that his basic concepts are not like this, that they are available only in one or another historical coinage [*geschichtliche Prägung*]. This is certainly his intent, though I doubt whether he successfully keeps to it. In any case it is an important difference from my own thought, for I can write a *Science of Logic*, and Heidegger will not. But is it as different as he thinks? It is true that in the logical sequence the conditions that make our being in a world possible can be grasped purely. Yet no form exists without content. The forms I find exist only through their necessarily historical and contingent coinages; that is demanded by their own internal motion. I avoid the separation of form and content by other means than by denying the pure availability of the form of the concept. The question is whether Heidegger really avoids that separation.

"The fact is that for all his careful attempts he still has too much distinction of form from content. The propriative event is thinkable only in conjunction with different epochs, yet it retains the same general structure. In order to tell the history of understandings of being, in order to make the claims he does about metaphysics, in order to talk about the non-Western world the way he does, Heidegger must collect and differentiate the various eras and epochs in terms of their conditions of possibility. The way in which he does this creates a distinction of form from content. He is giving us 'the nonhistorical a priori of the historical a prioris of the various epochs.'[12]

"In my own thought there is a similar distinction of form from content in talking about history. But I then go on to overcome that distinction by talking about the absolute idea which has itself for content. Heidegger would say this is a metaphysical solution, and so it is. But what does he offer? His step back does not do away with the distinction.

"The given content is immediate; we must just accept the space opened for us in our epoch. We know there could be and have been and may in the future be other such spaces. Our situation is not unlike that I described in the section of my *Phenomenology of Spirit* devoted to 'the Stoic.' The Stoic lives in a world he knows is enveloped in a greater 'beyond,' but that 'beyond' is only the assured granting of the precise content of the world in which he lives. He cannot escape his world, for the 'beyond' sends him back to do his duty in the world granted to him. Or if he escapes, he arrives only at a vapid indetermination. Though Heidegger's propriative event is not a 'beyond' or ground of the world, it functions in our lives in a similar way. All the discussions lead to the same step back, just as Heidegger makes the same gestures in front of all texts. But we cannot rest in this formal place. It serves to send us back resolutely to what we have been granted. We can only accept the content of the epoch and move within its space; there are no dialectical tensions or dynamisms we might cooperate with in our action. All our actions remain caught within the granted circle; only a god can save us.

"The immediacy of the grantings give history a strange look. Because of the careful separation of the propriative event from ordinary historiography, there is no place to discuss the events in ordinary history except as clues to what enables them. Cultural, scientific, and environmental influences can have no effect on the space granted to us and can on their own bring about no new beginnings in thought. This is most implausible history; it makes inexplicable why the sensibility of one age is followed by the particular sensibility of the next, as if the sequence had no explanation. I too speak of an an inner history that is the condition of ordinary historical events. But I also try to show how particular transitions in outer history can be seen as rational. One sometimes has the suspicion that in Heidegger's history all the real work is being done by the 'ontic' outer history, which is, however, carefully excluded from the discussion in favor of formal talk about its conditions.[13]

"Heidegger should either absorb everything into the transcendental conditions, as he rightly sees I do, or he should almost completely dispense with the transcendental move, as the misguided author of this present work suggests. His own position is an uncomfortable halfway house that gets caught on the distinction of formal process from particular content despite his efforts to avoid it.

"Perhaps his finite openness and my infinite closure are not so far apart. Heidegger says he wants to think of our living in the world in terms of a finitude that does not mean limitation but belonging. I also try to think about our life without thinking of it as a limitation on some indefinite sphere of possibility or a drive for the 'bad infinite.' I think of the universal and the good infinite, finally summed up in the absolute idea, and I appeal to closure, transparency, self-coincidence. Although I do not use these in quite the way Heidegger accuses me of doing, he is quite correct that I aim for these metaphysical goals. I achieve them in a way that keeps dualities active while holding them in check.

"I am saying that metaphysics in Heidegger's sense is necessary if we are to avoid the separation of form from content. He pays a price for giving up self-coincidence, closure, and metaphysics generally. He cannot successfully avoid the separations that make modernity what it is. Many of his followers either live the pious life in

a formal or nostalgic refuge or live the ironic distances within the
dance of the signifiers. The Stoic becomes the Sceptic, as I said.
Some of his followers even advance to the Unhappy Consciousness.
These tendencies are all present in Heidegger himself.

"Heidegger fails to overcome modernity because he remains caught
on its principle, the separation of formal process from content.
Despite his intentions he ends by either locking us into a premodern
world or reaffirming the ironic and distanced side of modernity. He
does avoid modernity's overly manipulative side, but at the cost of
denying our efficacy in history. He thinks he has avoided the dichotomy between substantive tradition and formal rootless subjectivity, when in fact he only oscillates rapidly between the two."

So far I have tried to reconstruct what Hegel would have said
about Heidegger's thought, though my "Hegel" speaks more politely
than Hegel was wont to do in controversy. Now we need to examine
the criticisms that have been expressed.

One basic qualification to be made at the outset is that for Heidegger as well as for Hegel there is no ultimate distinction of formal
process from particular content that can be posited as such in our
lives. For both thinkers such a distinction can be made in a tem-
porary or provisional fashion, but it cannot be posited as final. Our
lives may include a distinction of form and content as part of their
motion, but that distinction cannot be used for an overall description
of our situation as is possible with the standard descriptions of modern subjectivity. In Hegel, positing such a distinction does not raise
us above the motion of absolute form but only puts us back at an
earlier stage within that motion. In Heidegger, if we try to posit such
a distinction, we find we are still moving within the space of universal
imposition; we have not achieved a point of view above it but only
made one of its standard moves. Heidegger intends no meta-position
from which we can survey the propriative event from the outside
or from a comprehensive self-grasp. Any position we might take is
enabled by that event; the event itself is present as withdrawing; it
does not offer a form Heidegger could make present.

Some readings of Heidegger try to make of the propriative event
a refuge from our sad world. We must learn to dwell in our relation
to the propriative event, and escape the current painful reality. If
Heidegger were saying this, he would be reifying the propriative
event into a source beyond the world, and our situation would be
exactly that of the Stoic in Hegel's *Phenomenology of Spirit*.

This is not quite Heidegger's thought. We have no project of a pure relation to the propriative event. We are thrown projects, which is not the same thing as a project of receiving whatever is thrown to us. Relating to the propriative event is not something we do or a task we carry out. Being appropriated with things in that event is a condition for whatever projects we find ourselves involved in, not itself one of our projects.

Indeed, to the extent that Heidegger does make a separation of formal process from particular content, this has a positive function in his thought. It enables us to experience the groundlessness of the whole network of grounding and grounded relations within which we live. This provides no larger network, but it helps deconstruct the naturalness that attaches to the current relations of grounding and domination. I discussed earlier the ambiguous effects of Heidegger's overcoming of modernity in our everyday life, urging a reading that led to a deconstructive relation to current principles and practices. Heidegger's thought offers no new world, but it includes the hope of a less forgetful relation to the happening of realms of meaning. Both this hope and the deconstructive attitude are made possible by the distinction of form and content. The crucial feature, as with Hegel, is that this distinction cannot be posited as ultimate.

In constructing the remarks from "Hegel" above I presumed he would try to surpass Heidegger by locating him somewhere within the sequences of the *Phenomenology of Spirit* (as a Stoic) and the *Science of Logic* (as failing to overcome the distinction of form from content). What I have said in the last few paragraphs shows that Heidegger does not quite fit into either position. But there remains something correct in the complaints "Hegel" makes. Although Heidegger does not make an ultimate form-content distinction as such, the distinctions he does make have roughly the same effect as far as overcoming modernity is concerned.

The problems arise because of the immediacy and the unity of what is granted in the propriative event. Both are necessary for Heidegger. The propriative event itself is described, especially when he talks about the fourfold, in terms full of mutual dependence and what could be called mediation, though not of a Hegelian sort. Yet what is granted or opened in the propriative event is not so full of inner mirroring and mediation. If the particular unconcealment of beings ruling our age (or that of any other age within the history of the West) were not immediate and prior, it would begin to have features that could be discussed like those of ordinary beings. It would become involved in inner relation, grounding, and explanation and would lose its primacy. Similarly, if the clearing that makes our age possible were not in some sense unified, a call to men and to all beings to be unconcealed and encounter one another within a particular space, then there would have to be some further more-unified horizon opened up within which the multiplicity would itself be made unconcealed.[14]

Heidegger is caught in the middle. He wants to find conditions for the possibility of the ordinary presence or absence of things, conditions that also speak to the situation in our modern age. He wants those conditions to be prior, not to be entities or processes within the world. But he does not want the conditions to be metaphysical "firsts" or grounds. This demands that the conditions have no content that might serve as a first principle. Yet if they were purely formal, the conditions would again be metaphysical, a grounding structure that can be made simply present by a formal analysis of our situation. Also, as formal they would not have much to add to the discussion of any one particular age as opposed to another and so would not especially illuminate our modern situation.

These demands result in the delicate balance of form and content we find in Heidegger's thought. The understanding of the being of things within any given epoch is not a metaphysical first; it cannot serve as a first principle or ground of what is unconcealed. But neither is it purely formal. Nor is it something amenable to sociology or ordinary history. It is beyond the reach of our ordinary actions in the way a transcendental condition is beyond what it conditions.

As the condition for the multiple happenings in any epoch, what we are granted is unified, not something that can be caught up in a dialectic that exploits inner tensions or inner multiplicity. This unity goes hand in hand with Heidegger's transcendental move. Without the unified content of an age the transcendental move would become formal and metaphysical. Without its transcendental priority the description of the unified understanding of being in an age would become another hypothesis for history and the social sciences.

Relations Between the West and the East

The difficulties caused by this immediacy and unity can be seen more clearly if we consider our granted world in its relations to another world that is not historically distant like that of the Greeks but geographically distant and constituted within another tradition. Heidegger's "Dialogue on Language" indicates that he is willing to think about relations and contrasts between the West and other large traditions. He cautions his Japanese visitor against too much enthusiasm for Western categories of thought, and he urges the Japanese people to retrieve the deeper possibilities in what has been granted to them within their own world. The subjectivist, metaphysical way of thinking about experience is a dangerous Western export. It can distort and pervert what may be a fuller and deeper mode of living near the self-withdrawing propriative event.

Yet Heidegger remarks in the *Spiegel* interview that if the West is to overcome technology, this must happen from within and not by an alien implant such as Zen Buddhism (*Spiegel* 214/62). Apparently the West may endanger the East, but the relation is not reciprocal: the West can pervert Japan but Japan cannot save the West. Why this curious asymmetrical relation?

Indeed, how can Heidegger say that these two worlds can have any relation at all? There is not in Heidegger's account of the propriative event any obvious way for two different grantings of presence to come into conflict within an individual or within the spirit of a nation. There seems no way for either salvation or perversion to come from outside. Heidegger usually compares different epochs separated historically with no possibility of mutual influence. When we turn to a geographical separation, the discontinuity so important to his thought about the different grantings of presence seems much more questionable. Yet the account of the propriative event demands that deeply divergent traditions can coexist, each dominated by a different meaning of being. (Or perhaps one is metaphysical and the other is not so centered in a ruling meaning of being.) The idea of coexisting traditions highlights the discontinuity implicit in the primacy of the propriative event. But if we question that discontinuity, we also question the unity of what is granted in the propriative event and the transcendental move as Heidegger makes it.

Heidegger cannot allow two different traditions to influence each other in any deep way. If they can, then perhaps the unconcealment of the being of things that opens the two worlds is not so discontinuous. But if there is really only one granting of unconcealment for everyone, Heidegger's thought of our finitude becomes dangerously formal, and the account of the different epochs within the history of the West becomes a matter for "ontic" or outer history and not for the history of being.

Another way to allow influence would be to claim that the unconcealment of the being of things in each of the traditions is really different from that in the other but there is an inner multiplicity in what is opened up within each tradition. This would allow aspects of one to influence aspects of the other. But this begins to sound like the usual modes of influence cited by anthropologists and not the simple priority of the propriative event Heidegger is concerned to defend. Or perhaps, if deep influence is possible, it is because individuals can escape the space granted to them, enter another, and then return home bearing gifts, or poisons. But this would undo the priority of our appropriation into what has been granted us, and it sounds too much like modern subjectivity. So Heidegger cannot consistently maintain that traditions such as the Western and the Asian can influence each other so deeply as might bring salvation from the East.

Yet Heidegger does say that the West can endanger the tradition of the East. How can this be? Perhaps we can explain in the following way how for Heidegger the West can threaten the East even though the West cannot be helped by the East. We saw earlier that Heidegger's later interpretation of the Greeks, after he had given up talking of a locatable change in the notion of truth, suggests that "metaphysics" and "technology" should be thought of as possibilities inherent in the human situation as such rather than specifically Western possibilities with their own special history.

This interpretation of the Greeks suggests that while technology and metaphysics are a specific Western destiny, they are also the way the West has lived the "fallenness among beings" that Heidegger refers to in *Being and Time* and in the quotation from the *Spiegel* interview cited in the last chapter. Every world is liable to the fallenness amid beings that levels out what has been granted and forgets the propriative event and its withdrawal. In the West that forgetfulness has received a special emphasis through the dominance of the metaphysical understanding of time and of being with its emphasis on presence and foundations. But fallenness remains a more basic characterization than metaphysics. From Heidegger's "Dialogue on Language" he seems to believe that the metaphysical and subjectivist mode of fallenness may not have been the destiny of

Asia, but that does not mean the Asians are exempt from fallenness amid beings.

If this is the case, it suggests how Heidegger might be thinking that the West's granting of presence could threaten the East without there being any influence for good in the other direction. If the West's granting of presence embodied in a special way the fallenness that all worlds are liable to, it could engage those ever-present tendencies in the Asian world. But that Asian world could have nothing positive to give the West, since the authentic possibilities opened up were different in the two cases. For healing and growth each culture would have to look to its own deeper possibilities.

Thus traditions could influence each other if their fallen modes were similar. For example, the way man and nature stand together differs immensely in paintings by French and Chinese artists, or in Italian and Japanese gardens. But both Europeans and Asians often debase a nature that is encountered as a source of materials to be exploited. The effects of this in Europe and in Japan are not so different. The two traditions could be different in their deep authentic possibilities but similar enough in their fallen debased modes.

Such could be the case whether the Asian world was thought of as dominated by one ruling understanding of being or as more like the postmetaphysical age we in the West might hope for. But in the latter case, which fits better with some of Heidegger's remarks, it is not as clear why Asia cannot be of help to us at least in the general way of helping us take the step back to the propriative event.

Although in the *Spiegel* interview Heidegger states that the West cannot be saved from outside, it has been rumored that he was quite impressed with the writings on Zen by D. T. Suzuki (see Chang 1977). I imagine that when expressing such opinions Heidegger was finding in the Japanese writer something similar to the step back he was trying to expound in a nonmetaphysical way. Notice, though, that this is not strictly an influence opening the West to new possibilities but an encouragement to live our tradition in the way in which all grantings of unconcealment should be lived.

These explanations of the asymmetrical relation between West and East seem plausible, though they are not found in Heidegger's text. Notice that they demand a strong unity within the granting of unconcealment in each tradition. If there were inner multiplicity and division within the granting that empowers each tradition, there would be an easier possibility of mutual influence than Heidegger

seems to allow. Inner multiplicity within the two worlds would furnish many occasions for contact, since it is not clear what it would
mean to claim that every aspect of traditions with inner multiplicity
was completely different. Only a strict unity of what is granted within
each tradition can make sense of Heidegger's views about how the
traditions relate. Each world retrieves its own possibilities. Heidegger
would like to see each tradition keep to itself and cultivate the
possibilities granted within its own garden, while everyone shares
in the overarching awareness of the finitude of the propriative event.
Indeed, given the priority and unity of the propriative event, that
is all we can ever do.[15]

I may seem to be laboriously overinterpreting a few scattered
remarks on topics Heidegger admitted he knew little about. But my
point is not to question his knowledge of Asia. It is rather to show
how, in a case where his formidable historical knowledge does not
come into play, his basic presuppositions become very clear. It becomes obvious that there is some unitary granting of presence and
that it is simply prior to anything that happens in ordinary history
or the ordinary encounters of two cultures. It also becomes apparent
that there is something inadequate and unrealistic in this approach.

What has happened to the diversity of peoples and the influences
and borrowings that happen continuously in history? They have
been subordinated to the history of being. Ordinary talk about as-
similation and influence is not at the right level of discourse. Besides
being "without a why," the propriative event is also "without a how."
The division between the deep history of being and the surface
history of ordinary events seems unbridgeable, and so it must remain
if Heidegger is to be able to perform his step back.

Yet it seems improbable. For example, the Japanese today live in
a difficult multiple world where traditional and Western ways of life
conflict and interpenetrate. This conflict is laid upon them as something they find themselves within and cannot choose not to face.
This did not happen because of some possibility wholly within the
Japanese tradition; it was in large measure due to developments in
the West, which thrust itself upon Japan. There is a rhythm of
openness and closure in Japanese history that makes it easier to take
in Western ways, but these ways can also be forced into the lived
world of peoples who do not have that openness, such as the Chinese.
It seems improbable to demand that in all cases when traditions
encounter each other there is a destiny in each for the encounter.

For both Hegel and Heidegger the history of the West assumes great importance for understanding its culmination in modernity. Both insist that history is not an affair of blind chance; both distinguish an outer from an inner history, though Hegel connects the two in a way Heidegger does not. Both see thought as retrospective, opening a path for the future by gathering from the past. They agree that the gathering together occurring in history is not something we do as individuals, that we are gathered up whether we will or not.

In that gathering the Greek beginning plays a determining role, especially for Heidegger. That beginning opens the possibilities we follow. The immediacy and unity of that appropriation cannot be overcome. For Hegel the Greek beginning is only part of a larger development that makes the West's history continuous with the rest of the world. If the unity of his worldwide teleology seems difficult to accept today, perhaps we should say the same about the opposed kind of unity we find in Heidegger. Heidegger opts for discontinuity between unified destinies, but then he has no way to talk about the interactions that occur. It may be that both thinkers insist too much on unity.[16]

Heidegger would insist that the immediate and unified granting that we experience is not to be thought of as if it were some constantly present entity. Nor is the act of retrieving possibilities some blank acceptance. Certainly the world opened to us is within all the difference and negation of the propriative event so well described in *Identity and Difference* and in the passages about the fourfold. But for all this the world that is opened retains its overall unity and immediate givenness. Heidegger makes and remakes his step back, showing how even in texts from the height of the metaphysical tradition the process of unconcealment and its self-concealing can be found alluded to as the unspoken and the unthought. His readings stay within the opposition between the unified meaning of the world that is opened and the self-concealing opening of that world.

"Hegel" was right that there is something amiss in Heidegger's juxtaposition of a formal description of the opening with the immediate and unified call or meaning found in each epoch or era.

Heidegger does not mean the step back to be a meta-position above the world. It is supposed to bring us closer to the happening of the world around us, open us to the sky and the earth, and let us experience ourselves in our deepest calling. But the immediacy and unity of what is granted, which are crucial to the step back as

Heidegger performs it, have the effect of stopping us halfway and making the step back a move to a vantage point from which the naive ones like scientists and politicians can be told what they are really doing. Heidegger's quietism and the self-indulgent sound of his proclamations of our powerlessness can be traced to this unity and primacy of what is granted. They allow him to behave as an a priori philosopher, assured ahead of time that any phenomenon of modernity brought to his attention is fully under the call of universal imposition.

So it would seem that Heidegger's overcoming of modernity does not succeed even on its own terms. We do not attain the promise of deconstructive living, and we do not escape the modern oscillation between what we must simply accept and a version of the distanced transcendental self. Perhaps there is more to be thought about our situation, other ways to take advantage of the strategy that we have seen in Hegel and Heidegger and have pursued through their mutual criticism.

Could we find a way to avoid the standard self-description of modernity and avoid the Hegelian totality but not end up with Heidegger's emphasis on unity and the protective insulation Heidegger's transcendental method places between his conditions and ordinary events and tales?

Further Explorations

We began by looking at the standard self-description of modernity and its basic dichotomies and divisions. Then we examined Hegel and Heidegger, with their strategy of locating modernity within a larger context that both makes modernity possible and limits its pretensions. In the last chapter I tried to compare and contrast our two thinkers, revealing difficulties in both their projects and suggesting further directions for exploration. In this chapter I will sketch how we might begin to think about our modern world in a way that has learned from Hegel and Heidegger but does not quite agree with either. The following chapter will take up some implications for life in the modern world.

Hegel and Heidegger can each be used as a vantage point to highlight problems with the other. This does not mean some synthetic vision can incorporate all the good points of each thinker. There is no way to synthesize Hegel and Heidegger from a neutral point of view or bring them into some Hegelian totality. The two thinkers stand together in not taking modernity's usual dichotomies as the ultimate conditions for life and thought, but they stand opposed on how to describe our true context.

If we cannot synthesize Hegel and Heidegger, neither can we choose one of them to save us. Hegel fails to achieve his overarching totality. Heidegger is correct that Hegel's system rests within a dispersion and temporal "thrownness" that the system cannot mediate into self-transparency. But Heidegger in his own way remains fixed on the unity and immediacy of what is granted us as a clear space. We should not worry, however, about choosing one thinker over another. It is not our task to adopt neatly labeled points of view. There may be labeled options on some questions in specific areas, say, in the philosophy of science, and these may have larger implications, say, in ethics. But the overall task of thinking does not involve getting the right answer on a multiple-choice test containing the current labels. What we can learn from the confrontation of Hegel and Heidegger is the overall strategy the two thinkers share— its possibilities and pitfalls.

The question for our thought, then, is this: if we agree with both Hegel and Heidegger that the standard self-picture of modernity is inaccurate, that the characteristic dichotomies in the Weberian and other modern accounts of what it is to be a self are not ultimate, that modern selves exist within a larger context that cannot be described in their terms—if we agree to all this, how do we think about the larger context in a way that avoids a Hegelian overarching totality and also avoids Heidegger's unified transcendental conditions?

Deep Conditions and History

Hegel has something to show us here. He takes the transcendental move much further, pulling everything into the transcendental realm. The overarching unity of his system overcomes the distinctions of form and content, thing and appearance. He has some trouble drawing a practical line between necessary systematic structures and necessarily contingent detail in the embodiment of those structures, but this is not Kant's distinction of transcendental from empirical nor Heidegger's of ontological from ontic. Hegel's distinction is wholly within the realm of transcendental thought, which in the end swallows everything into itself.

To annul one side of the dichotomy does not leave us with the other side unchanged. When Hegel pulls everything into the transcendental realm, no longer does that realm face an empirical or external realm that it conditions. No structures based on ultimate opposition survive.

I have agreed with Heidegger that Hegel's totality fails, but we can learn from Hegel that Heidegger despite his best intentions still relies on some oppositions of a kind he is pledged to avoid. Perhaps it should be all or nothing with transcendental analysis. In his attempt to avoid Kantian subjectivism and Hegelian totality, Heidegger remains tied to some key oppositions: between form and content, between essential and unessential, and between unified general condition (the mode of unconcealment in an age) and multiple conditioned (all that goes on in the age made possible by that mode of unconcealment).

If, as Hegel's failure shows, we cannot make the transcendental sphere self-sufficient and complete, perhaps the move we require is not exactly Heidegger's step back, but two steps: one with Hegel, weakening the difference between transcendental and empirical, and a second giving up the unity and totality still present in both our Germans. We need to keep Heidegger's emphasis on dispersion and temporality but not his thought of unity and immediacy. This does not leave us with the ordinary and empirical still thought of as in opposition to some possible deep conditions. We are left with something that is neither side of the old division.

Such a turn has suggested itself often in the course of this study. We have noted that both thinkers have difficulty with the relation between their accounts and the ongoing events of ordinary history. Somehow the details of technology, art, science, politics, economics, and so on should be more relevant to the changes in overall understandings of time and being, not just dependent on them. New politics, new science, new religion do not seem on the surface to be reducible to the workings of the one destiny granted with the Greeks or the one Hegelian logical sequence.

Both Heidegger and Hegel deploy the distinction of the essential from the inessential when they talk about history. Heidegger's account of the West often has a reductionist quality as he struggles to keep everything within what was granted in the beginning rather than seeing new beginnings along the way or multiple understandings of being all along. A contrast between the age and the step back to its conditions is not the same as multiple beginnings. Though Hegel has less trouble talking about new beginnings, he demands that they fit into one necessary, unified final story.

Both men believe that the conditions they discover are simply prior to anything ordinary. Perhaps we need to think about the many different spheres of activity and their different kinds of change in terms where nothing is first, nothing is simply enabling in relation to others, and there are no unitary deep conditions—where history is not the deployment of some initial or final granting of presence.[1]

If we give up the notion of prior unified deep conditions (in either the Hegelian or the Heideggerean sense), ordinary history in all its contingency stays in play. The fields of possibilities we find ourselves within cease to be immediately granted, as with Heidegger, or totally mediated, as with Hegel. They cease to be unified in one granting or shape of spirit, and we can discuss them in a variety of ways that do not have to refer to one deep or totalizing story.

Hegel's attempt to go beyond the multiplicity of contingent history is based on the desire for fuller rationality and unity. Some of Heidegger's motivations are suggested in Pöggeler's remark that "as a born theologian, but one who became homeless, Heidegger turned against the historians and philologists who changed a present and future task (with Hölderlin, the task once more to speak of the divine) into informing us about a cultural and literary history already over and done with" (Pöggeler 1982, 48, n. 6).

What would it mean to think about our situation without any overall teleology or development in the Hegelian mode and without any unified epochs in the Heideggerean mode? Can we make sense of the idea that our world is not a unified totality on any level, preconceptual or conceptual? Imagine multiplicity "all the way down," with many partial and totalizing fields of possibilities contingently together providing that within which we find ourselves always already in motion.

Dialectic and Phenomenology

I have remarked on the persistent question of the relative priority of dialectic and phenomenology. Phenomenology works from Husserl's analysis of perception in terms of profiles of objects against horizons of possible actions and appearances. Heidegger's discussion of the "world" takes up and deepens this analysis. In this mode it makes little sense to speak of our inhabiting many worlds at once. We may speak of living in different worlds, for example, those of science and of common sense, but these are specifications from our more original inhabitation. We may have many explicit theories and conceptualizations derived from the richer context of our lived world. But this does not mean that the world is infinitely rich. All unconcealment of things, even on the preconceptual level, is finite. Our world is not a matrix from which all possible conceptualizations could arise. We could not, for example, start thinking in an ancient

Greek way. Theirs was a different world, though one related to our own; the ancient Japanese lived in a world different in deeper ways.

For Heidegger the unconcealment of things and man appropriated together is always finite. It can change as a whole, as when the Greek understanding of the being of things changed into that of the Romans or the Christians. In saying that the lived world provides a rich beginning from which we specify or retrieve more limited explicit conceptualizations, there is a basis for the misinterpretation of Heidegger holding that there is some permanent basic disclosure of things from which all historical worlds are drawn. But the finitude of unconcealment obtains at every level.

In section 21 of the *Basic Problems of Phenomenology* Heidegger discusses the basic temporality of our existence and points to what he calls a horizonal schema that defines the meaning of each temporal ecstasis. The particular kinds of presence with which he was concerned (the handiness of tools and the neutral presence of objects) are variations of the schema of presence, which provides a general "whereto" for the dimension of present time. It is unclear whether this schema of presence is so general that epochal changes would all be its subspecies, or whether it itself can change. Though Heidegger later alters his terminology, the basic metaphor of a unitary horizon remains to influence his discussions of world and of epochal unities (see Sallis 1983).

Put in Heidegger's early terminology, I suggest the schemas of our temporality are multiple here and now, without any systematic unity or even the neatly individuated unity of a list. There may be a very general event of our appropriation with the world, but the multiple motions and meanings we exist by being among are not in any useful sense subspecies of some general horizon of presence.[2]

The metaphor of horizon, with its connotations of unity and a privileged direction, should be used with great caution. Our horizons are multiple, and that multiplicity is not itself a collection or a system appearing within some last unified horizon. In this sense Hegel's images of mutual constitution and interpenetration are more useful than the phenomenological images Heidegger uses, but when disassociated from systematic closure, the former lose their specific Hegelian character.

In a more dialectical way of thinking there need not be so much prior unity in our inhabitation of the world, though that unity develops as the dialectic continues. Hegel has room for multiplicity

and tension within our finite being in the world. Heidegger's practice, for example, his willingness to discuss different turnings of the
propriative event within the same period (as with Hölderlin and
Hegel), may seem to leave more room for contemporary multiplicity
than his statements about the dominance of universal imposition
allow. Usually, however, what seems a contemporary tension or
multiplicity turns out to be a contrast between those, like Hegel,
wholly within the call of the age and those, like Hölderlin, able to
make the step back and reveal the more original or extreme possibilities of the age as a limited opening of presence.[3]

Hegel's dialectic does not use the model of things appearing against
horizons. Space for the appearance of things is held open by a
multiplicity of levels of tension and interaction—and ultimately by
the self-relation through difference described in the logical sequence. Hegel's shapes of spirit have internal opposition and tension
within their return to themselves. Those multiple moments interact
to make a richer whole. The space, to speak metaphorically, is opened
through the dialectical relations of the moments, not in a granting
that is with them but more primal. What is primal is the motion
that interrelates the moments. In the final stages that motion coincides with itself.

Hegel makes more effort than Heidegger to link the detailed differences between worlds to the event of having a world at all. But
it remains true that the dialectic always works under the sign of
unity and self-coincidence that gives necessity to the sequence.
Hegel's emphasis on inner tension and multiplicity is finally subordinated to the unitary system.

Heidegger often says that Hegel's system needs a space opened
by the granting of an understanding of being in terms of circular
infinity and self-coincidence. In Hegel's intention there is no such
prior space. The motion of spirit that is attained in absolute knowledge is not a final horizon within which things appear. It is a motion
through which the event of having horizons happens. The absolute
form of that motion can be known, but that absolute knowledge
does not involve a final horizon of interpretation so much as the
self-consciousness of the movement of the event of having a world
at all.

Heidegger is right that Hegel is too dependent on a meaning of
time and being that is not adequately included within the circular

system. But that need not be thought of, as Heidegger does, as the meaning of a horizon within which Hegel is working without having sufficiently thematized it. That understanding could have been one within the multiple and tense possibilities among which Hegel found himself already in motion. To say that these possibilities must be opened by a unitary granting begs the question of the relative priority of dialectic and phenomenology.

Can we think about our inherence in the context within which we always already find ourselves in motion in a way that has more the multiplicity of the dialectic than the unitary horizon of phenomenology but still escapes the Hegelian closure and self-coincidence? There is no orthodox Hegelian way to do this; closure and self-coincidence are at the heart of Hegel's logic. So-called "open Hegelianism" is always un-Hegelian, though it may be more true to our situation.

There are several ways to open up the Hegelian closure. Basically, Hegel is rendered open by reintroducing the distinction of form from content. One way is to turn Hegel's goals into regulative ideals in the Kantian manner (Paul Ricoeur refers to this as "post-Hegelian Kantianism"). One thinks in terms of completing a Hegel-style system but is always left with fragments. In such a view there is no final age that arrives, but the end is always present as intended though never achieved.

A second approach (found, for example, in Remo Bodei) makes every age the end of history. The Hegelian system is taken as in principle completable for any given age, but it must be redone when the immediate cultural reality, the in itself (*an sich*) to be rendered rational, changes. Spirit is in one way always coming to unity with itself and in another way always outdistancing its current self-understanding and working underground changes that can be caught up with only later, when such changes will continue.

I suggest we press the attack on unity and self-coincidence even further. The goal of totalization is only one possible strategy for dealing with the multiplicity of our spread-out existence. We find ourselves amid things whose meanings stand within networks of possibility that are multiple without being first neatly separable and then related in the way explicit laws or theories might be. There is no one way to count or tie up the components of this multiplicity; they do not stand to one another like items in a list or members of a system, and their identity conditions vary depending on relations of mutual constitution that are not total, that may not be the same in all directions, and that affect our self-understandings.

The context of our inhabitation is neither unified in the various manners of Hegel and Heidegger nor structured by the subject-object relation and indifferently open in the modern manner. Dialectic can be a helpful model for its interacting dimensions, but without the Hegelian structure of closure dialectic becomes rather vague, so "multiplicity" or "mutual constitution" might do as well (or even *bricolage*, if without the connotation that someone assembled it).

This is not some mishmash from which we extract what we want nor some continuum to be cut up as we choose. We are not speaking as Bergson does of something rich and full prior to any distinctions or differentiations. To define it in this way would be to make of it an entity unto itself, something determinate in its character of flowing richness.

Our context is not something prior to or indifferent to the distinctions and relations we make. But neither is it multiple in some surveyable or systematic way. If either were the case, the self, as one entity already complete in itself, would work on that context that was another entity complete in itself, and the subject-object relation would be reasserted as the structure of our insertion into the world. It is wrong to think of that world or context as an object waiting for us to do something to it. We exist as selves through being appropriated with that context, and it "is" as such through that appropriation. They need each other; the event of their happening is not a relation of two entities each complete in itself.

Thinking Multiplicity

Throughout this study the question has recurred whether we can think about what it is to be in our particular world without taking this as a limitation on a wider field of possibilities. Both Hegel and Heidegger try to do so. The overarching unity of the Hegelian logic opens yet encloses limited possibilities without creating them by restricting a wider field. The Heideggerean propriative event lets things and ourselves stand toward each other in a dispersed belonging together that is not a limitation on or a contrast with some full or total presence. Both Hegel and Heidegger try to deal with the definiteness of our situation by thinking about our relation to time in some special sense. But they disagree over whether the dispersal of our temporalization is deeper than the logical self-coincident unity of the universal. Heidegger summarizes the disagreement: for Hegel the concept is the power of time; for Heidegger time is the power of the concept (*Hegels Phänomenologie des Geistes* 143–45). Leaving aside the question of whether Heidegger is right to oppose time and the Hegelian universal in precisely these terms, I have agreed with him that Hegel's thought is rooted in a temporal dispersal the system does not grasp as such.[4]

Can we think of that dispersal in a more multiple way than Heidegger does? To think of ourselves as accepting and retrieving the finite inhabitation within which we find ourselves always already in motion seems a promising counter to the standard modern pictures of the distanced self. But can we think this way without the presupposition of a unified meaning to structure the space opened to us? It would seem that any attempt to introduce multiplicity into our appropriation into the world would demand that multiple fields of possibility be limitations on a more basic cleared space that is itself unified by some overall meaning. How else could the multiplicity be lived *as* a multiplicity? "Multiple worlds" seems a contradiction.

Because it makes them sound self-enclosed, it is indeed wrong to speak of multiple worlds. Our task is not to think how we might live in several worlds at once, each of them complete in its own way, but to think how the world in which we live might be less unified, more internally multiple and not constituted from some one basic space.

Thinking in terms of multiplicity "all the way down" is difficult. There is always the danger that we will return to the standard modern picture. It would seem that the only place where such a multiplicity could come together and *be* a multiplicity would be arrayed in front of us, where we are defined as formal subjectivities presented with a multiplicity of possibilities to relate and judge. If we do not keep Heidegger's deep grantings with their unified open spaces, where else can the multiplicity be multiple in any real sense?

Perhaps we might adapt from Hegel: could there be some motion that we are, a motion that opens yet encloses the place for the multiplicity but does not involve positing as ultimate a distinction of form from content? This motion would not be Hegel's self-coin-cident totalization. Perhaps it would be like Heidegger's temporal dispersal, still described with the distinction of form from content Heidegger uses but without the emphasis on unity and immediacy that remains in his account. Can we keep the Heideggerean notion that we find ourselves always already in motion within a world of possibilities, yet join to this the idea of multiplicity?

At least on the first level of description, that seems to be our situation: to be thrown projects in a number of different ways at once, ways that have no obvious necessary deep coherence. Properly understood it is correct to say that we are the point of unity for the multiplicity, but this is not because we are distanced subjectivities before whom the multiplicity comes together.

As long as we try to imagine the self as some entity confronted with a set or multiple sets of possibilities, we will be on the road that belongs to modernity. Instead, consider that the multiple fields of possibilities that we find ourselves among are not given *to* the self but are what allow there to be a self in the first place. For there to be a self is for the lived past, present, and future to intersect in and as the presence of things. That intersection does not happen without the self, but the self does not happen as an empty place first and then get filled or fill itself by setting up definite limited possibilities. Nor is a deep unity necessary.

For example, consider our use of our native language. The speak-ers and the language do not exist as separate entities that then come together. The language is not a set of rules and historical facts open to development and drift and also a set of speakers with a past way of speaking and choices to make about the future. Though the language can be treated in these ways, they are abstractions. The concrete reality of the language is a system moving because it exists as speakers open to the future in definite ways. The concrete reality of speakers is as thrown or stretched out within the "alreadys" and the concomitant "possibles" of their language system. Complex his-tories and contingent events of all sorts modify what the language is already and is becoming. There may be many changes in opposed directions. There is no sure way to segment off the changes of language from changes and drifts and pressures in the society, in values, in taste. Speakers exist amid this multiplicity without thereby being distanced subjects to whom the various alreadys and possibles are presented for adjudication.

Another example of multiplicity might be found in the movement of science. Hegel thinks of science as moving toward a cumulative total truth, although natural science can never attain the full rationality of philosophy. Heidegger adopts the other extreme of almost total discontinuity. He claims, for example, that Aristotle's physics cannot be said to be in error, since it existed within a different meaning of "nature" (The Question About the Thing 62–65/80–85). Yet even though it was within that meaning, Aristotle's discussion of projectile motion remained inadequate to explain certain kinds of events. His successors knew this and tried to patch up or extend the theory, and their efforts helped create the tensions that led to the new science. Into this came many diverse influences, theological, practical, military, and political, and personal motives on the part of some leading individuals. Amid this multiplicity of different influences and spheres of life, all in some sense interacting, the scientist does not sit as a distanced judge to whom all these influences are submitted. Instead, the scientist is a human thrown within fields by no means unified or even clearly delineated into different influences and possibilities. One of the effects of the new science was to redefine how certain areas of life were to be divided off from one another and what was to count as scientific or theological. Science does not move within some transcendentally established and delimited sphere but exists strung out, as we are strung out, in a multiplicity within which nothing has unquestioned primacy, neither theological statements nor Aristotle's word nor the results of argument and observation nor how these things are to be distinguished from one another. Nor the overall context, for there is no overall context that exists presented as a whole.

It would seem that there is no essence defined in advance for science, or any other sphere of life, no limits that forever bar it from this or that other equally distinct sphere. I am not suggesting that what we call science could change gradually into something else we now call by another name, say, theology. Nor, on the other hand, do I mean that science could expand by reducing everything to what science does now. I am only saying that the current constellation of spheres and limits on the various kinds of discourse and practice we find ourselves within is neither immutable nor established for our present age by a granting we cannot now go beyond. Nor, however, is the current constellation something we can simply will to change and find changed. It is (in good Hegelian manner) too much involved in the structures by which we recognize one another and are ourselves. These, in turn, help constitute relations of power and institutional solidity within our world.

I am suggesting that we and the multiple possibilities in which we find ourselves allow each other to be as the concrete motion of lived time. If this is so, the multiplicity need not be submitted to a distanced modern subjectivity. There need not be any prior place for the multiplicity to come together. We have asked, "Where is the place where the multiplicity is as multiple?" but the question turns out to be ambiguous. In one sense the multiplicity exists in our preconceptual living without any granting of a unified meaning to the temporality of our lives. In another sense the multiplicity is as such only when we chart or separate in practice or theory different spheres and areas of meaning and possibility. This is done not from the distanced modern viewpoint but from inside, without any one privileged view on the whole.

The Unity of the Self

If we insist that none of this happens through a distanced modern subjectivity, what happens to the unity of the self? If we exist within these various fields, why are we not simply torn into various people, now a scientific person, later an economic consumer, on Sundays a religious person, at other times a transcendental philosopher, with little or no communication between them. Five hundred years ago or in China the roles would be distributed differently. If it is really false that above all my roles and masks there is no formally defined self working to maximize whatever it wants, why am I not torn apart and reduced to a collection of masks?

This question is based on a misunderstanding. It presumes that the fields are each complete worlds. I am suggesting that we reject self-coincidence on every level. If there is no unitary epochal granting, neither are there self-enclosed miniworlds, neatly segregated languages, neatly bounded rule-governed areas of meaning and behavior, each a little bubble of possibility within which we can move. That image demands a prior space in which to locate the bubbles, or else it provides no way to speak of the self parceled out among them. We need to open out each of the multiple totalities. They do not need to be opened in the sense that they are at first closed. But we tend to think of them as closed, which is an error.

Wittgenstein's language games and forms of life are sometimes thought of as each enclosing its own unified sphere. Because each is complete in itself, problems are raised about the unity of language and life, and some thinkers rejoice in the fractioning of the self, while others lament it. Analogous problems arise when "conceptual frameworks" are conceived as self-enclosed. But perhaps we should not take rule-governed formalizations of our activities to be as such the structures within which we live. What is controlled by a set of clear rules exists within a context not regulated by those rules. There is always room to bend the rules, create metaphors, and make forbidden combinations of symbols (see Ricoeur 1977; Caputo 1987). And there is no highest set of rules regulating an ultimate context.

In the matters we are speaking of nothing is self-enclosed and self-coincident. This statement echoes Hegel's claim that nothing is immediate. There is multiplicity, contingency, and context all the way down, and no totality.

This means that the question of the unity of the self becomes less urgent, because there are no enclosed wholes to parcel the self out among. Nor is the self a self-coincident entity. None of this prevents us from trying for various kinds of unity or totalization, as long as we realize that the results will be another element in the multiplicity. We should not confuse efforts at totalization with achieved totality. No one field of our possibilities is a self-coincident whole, nor do they taken together form such a whole. We moderns might even try to create or institutionalize a purified self, as long as we realize that we will not be distanced from or come to dominate "the" overall context. There is no total context, but there is always a context. Purifying the self is not a pure act.

Multiple Methods

All this suggests a way of thinking of ourselves and our context that is not the standard modern picture yet avoids both Hegelian closure and the protective insulation Heidegger puts between transcendental conditions and ordinary events. We have a context that is multiple all the way down. A kind of infinite analysis replaces the Heideggerean retrieve of the call that makes us what we are.[5]

There is no end to what we can say, because the context of significance within which we move offers no final unifying condition or horizon. There is no one privileged direction for our analyses. Anything we find can be compared, contrasted, traced, studied for its history, its structure, its archaeology—since there is no view as a whole, there is no last method or result of analysis. And the results can be redescribed by other ways of analysis; no one way is privileged, and there is no one axis on which to judge their priority. No way of talking is automatically eliminated on principle, though many will be rejected by those who try them and find them unsatisfactory. (In saying this I am without much argument taking a stand on some issues in current philosophy concerning whether one or another kind of discourse can resist reductive translation. What I have just said implies a nonreductive position but not one that makes onto-logical claims either by stressing one ontology or by conjoining the ontologies of the various kinds of discourse.)[6]

Abandoning the idea that our world has a deep unitary meaning does more than just saying there are many meanings instead of one. Because they are not closed and self-sufficient, the various meanings we find ourselves within can interact in a way that is reminiscent of dialectic; that is, their interaction can help constitute them. Think, for example, of the mutual constitutive interactions among science, religion, and mythology in various ages, without assuming that their various constellations are each unified in some deep understanding of the reality of things or are engaged in one necessary dialectical motion.

This means that, instead of the Heideggerean immediate grant-ing, the content of the togetherness of man and world has some dimension of mediation, genesis, even explainability. That we are thrown into this constellation rather than another and that this constellation is what it is remain ultimately contingent, but there is considerably more we can say about it. Indeed there is probably indefinitely much we can say about it if there really is multiplicity all the way down, with each element to some variable extent formed from and in relation with others.

Heidegger never meant his thought to reveal a ground or cause; it reveals the groundlessness of our situation. But that thought is intended to keep a certain primacy. If we admit multiplicity and allow interaction and mutual constitution, there is no one granted call for our age, and we have no room for the primacy we found Heidegger asserting in his comment about being able to tell the scientist what the scientist is really doing. There is always more to be said; there is no one granted space the step back can reveal to us. There is still an overall lack of ground, but there are local grounds to be found in historical, functional, and other kinds of discussion. These take on the burden of explaining the occurrence of the worlds we live amid, as far as explanation is appropriate—and that cannot be decided in advance, since unexpected new ways of talking may be opened to us.

There is no linear ordering of methods of analysis that tells us who is furthest back in the search for conditions. There are many directions and no circle that can enclose them all and justify itself as the unique way to do so. Philosophers of all persuasions like to play the game of "I'm furthest back! My regress gets behind your regress." Hegel has one meta-method that locates all other ways of thinking. Heidegger says we should be where we are, but he then uses the unitary granting he uncovers as a way of getting under or around the details and behind all other thinkers. Analytic philosophy is better at facing the details, but it has its own versions of the "I'm furthest back" game. The space that makes this game possible is not structured so as to provide a winner.[7]

Form and Content Yet Again

What I have just said may sound plausible, but it may also seem to violate itself. Am I not playing the game of standing furthest back? Yes, of course. To never play the game of standing furthest back would be, in effect, to claim that from where I was standing it was clear the game should not be played, thus claiming I was furthest back. There is no way to avoid making or implying such claims; what matters is how they are claimed and lived with. There can be a sidelong awareness that the game itself is located so we don't take it perfectly seriously (which is not to say we are really above it all). Universal claims are themselves local performances.

The position I have been suggesting for exploration does demand yet another distinction of formal process or motion from its (now multiple) content. To describe our existence as involved in multiplicity is to speak quite formally. Talk about lived time and the motion we find ourselves always already within plays the same game as Hegel and Heidegger. It is if anything more formal, since there is no unity or determinate content to be had from furthest back. In different ways Hegel and Heidegger overcome the distinction of form from content by having some specially unified content. If we are to think multiplicity all the way down, there can be no such content.

Hegel and Heidegger each see the other as affirming too much unity, and their mutual criticisms are generally correct. Nonetheless the strategy attempted by Hegel and Heidegger remains promising: show that there is no distinction of formal process from particular content that can be usefully posited as ultimate in our lives, thought, or institutions. I have tried to follow this basic strategy. The movement I have been sketching out, because of its multiplicity and lack of privileged content, cannot be posited in our lives as a foundation on which to define a modern detached subjectivity. By itself it offers no form of life.

This way of thinking does not provide modern distanced subjectivity a place to stand. Modern subjectivity needs the subject-object relation as "the" form of our relation to the world. Modern subjectivity is not just distanced, it is unified and unifying. The contents of its life may be scattered, but it is aware of itself as a formal point of unity with an action to perform that is appropriate to such a point of unity: it is a unified free chooser, or a unified maximizer of satisfactions. Replacing this by the motion involving multiple contents does not provide another form that could be used to define an empty self. To know ourselves as thrown among a multiplicity is to know something about how we are stretched out but not to contact a point of unity that is our prior or final self or an action that is ours to do insofar as we are such selves. Taken formally there is nothing in this to be or do. As I said earlier, to be a thrown project does not mean being a project of receiving what is thrown. Without the multiple content what might be called the formal structure of our being in the world is not there. With the multiple content there are possibilities and therefore selves. There is nothing here on which modern-style formal modes of mutual recognition could find a privileged foundation, no pure action for modern formally defined selves to recognize one another as performing.[8]

Minding the Difference

I have been suggesting that we keep Heidegger's description of us as thrown projects and the difference he describes between things and the presencing of things but that we remove the immediate unified content that allows him to talk of epochs in the history of being. We can in more Hegelian fashion speak of the motion of being thrown projects in the world, but the content is no longer total, self-transparent, deep, or unified. Heidegger would probably regard all this as giving up true thinking and giving in to "psychologism" and the social sciences, abandoning the primacy of the propriative event, or abandoning the ontological difference. This is in some measure accurate, since I do not believe modern subjectivity can be overcome from the kind of transcendental stance implicit in Heidegger's protection of the unconcealment of things from multiple influence and ordinary contingent history.

But there is more to say about this objection. Psychologism usually means the attempt to reduce the presencing of things to the results of psychic acts of attitude and belief within a modern and already determinate subjectivity. That is not what I am suggesting. We should agree with Hegel and Heidegger about the constitutive role of the fields of possibility within which we find ourselves; they are not presented to or manufactured by some distanced subjectivity. We do not assemble by a psychic act the various influences and contexts within which we find ourselves. It is rather the reverse: they in their stretched-out existence are where we find ourselves thrown, though we in our stretched-out existence are the locus that makes them possible as well.

If coming closer to the social sciences means refusing to claim that some transcendental opening of unconcealment or Hegelian absolute form of the concept gives us content that is always inherently and untouchably prior to the kinds of descriptions and explanations we find in the social sciences, then I am guilty. But I am not suggesting that we take social scientific explanations as final, that we accept the implied claims to totality often present in the social sciences, or that we think of the self in terms of Weberian methodological individualism.

There is still a sense in which we take the step back. It remains possible to distinguish the happening of our world from the world. Once all the cautions are stated with more multiplicity than Heidegger would allow, we can step back to our mutual appropriation with things, to the motion that is the being there of the world. We cannot find, as Heidegger can, the destiny behind the whole West or come to see modernity whole when we acknowledge universal imposition as its deep condition. We reach only the happening of the togetherness of man and world in its multiplicity and its contingency. But this still has a humbling effect on the pretensions of modern subjectivity.

Heidegger thought long and hard about the differences between

a thing, a thing's meaning, and a thing's emergence from unconcealment. In what I have been suggesting there is no intention of
abandoning the difference as such. But perhaps we should free it
from a residual Kantianism that it retains even in Heidegger. Kant
insists that empirical categories and principles depend on pure transcendental categories and principles in a way different from whatever logical and explanatory relations there may be on the empirical
level. The categories and principles license one nonhistorical metaphysics of nature. Though Heidegger historicizes Kant in this regard,
he keeps the dependence of the "empirical" (for example, the phenomena of modernity) on an "a priori" (universal imposition). Thus
the modern art business depends on the call of universal imposition
in a unique, deep way that is simply prior to and opens the space
for whatever influences might be discussed in historical, economic,
or anthropological analyses of that art business. And so on for all
entities and actions within the field opened up in a given age. What
I am suggesting might be described as keeping the propriative event
but eliminating the Kantian a priori which is the unified content.
But then, without that content the notion of "the" propriative event
must be used cautiously in talking about our mutual appropriation
to and with our world.[9]

In his own way Hegel has already overcome these oppositions,
but he does so in terms of a totalization that we cannot effect. Still,
we can learn from him that it is better to make everything relevant
to everything else than to remain with untouchable oppositions in
the style of Heidegger.

When we free the difference in this fashion, it ceases to be "deep,"
as it is in Heidegger. There is nothing it can tell us. It becomes the
recognition of the presencing of the world, which is not some one,
deep call but the presencing of this rock, this mood, this piece of
mathematics. Or of the world as such, but not of the world "as a
whole" or "in its unified deep meaning."

In Hegel the motion of the absolute form is known to us but not
as a static object of awareness. The dialectic can be expressed only
in a series of propositions giving our moving awareness of something
itself in motion. Even without Hegel's grand totality we can still
speak of such a moving awareness. But since there is no self-coincidence on any level, that awareness remains a sidelong accompa-
niment rather than a deep achievement. It does not raise us above
the multiplicity of our lives, for we find no new place to stand. The

affirmation of the difference between things and the presencing of things becomes a recognition that penetrates all discourse rather than being itself a deep discourse. Its effects are seen in humility, a bit of irony, and compassion.

Perhaps we should think about our present situation somewhat in the way Heidegger tentatively envisioned a possible nonmetaphysical age, without an overall meaning of being but only the multiple yet related presencing of things and their varied calls to us. Our modern world is distinguished by the strength and spread of some modes of presence and the institutionalization of certain modes of identity, but these are not prior in the way universal imposition is said to be prior. They are within the multiplicity, but they do not dominate it a priori or form its hidden unifying condition. [10]

12

The Modern World Revisited

At the beginning of this study we looked at modernity's beliefs about itself and at social science theories that reflect those beliefs. We asked whether modernity's self-description was the last word on our situation. Hegel and Heidegger said that it is not, that there is something deeper going on that makes possible and limits modernity. The previous chapters have traced Hegel's and Heidegger's discussions of modern subjectivity as it exists within a context that cannot be described in the standard language of modernity. While agreeing with this overall strategy I have made some suggestions about how we might begin to conceive such a context without Hegel's self-coincident totality and without the unified content introduced by Heidegger's version of the step back. In this concluding chapter I look at some general consequences this might have for life and thought in our world.

Modernity and Postmodernity

If the dichotomies by which modernity describes itself really were ultimate, there would be no obvious way for modernity to end. Once subjectivity has been emptied, once form has been separated from content and pure modes of mutual recognition have been institutionalized, how do you put these separations back together? If we accept the standard descriptions, it is hard to see how modernity could have any limits short of our destroying ourselves. Nor is it easy to think how we could regress to a traditional society, since as

I argued earlier a willed return to traditional ways is not a return to traditional society but only an extension of modern self-creation.

There has been much talk lately about "postmodernity." Various trends in art, architecture, sculpture, literature, and culture in general are now vaguely labelled postmodern. Much of this movement only reenacts modern distance and self-assertion in a new style. It often repeats the modern attempt to see through previous tradition and the modernist desire to begin from scratch in a self-referential way. But sometimes amid all this there is a new stance towards multiplicity and form.

Jean-François Lyotard has given the term *postmodern* a more precise meaning and has claimed that the postmodern era has begun. According to Lyotard, modernity was characterized by the drive to seize and systematize the world and so liberate human possibilities by mastering the conditions of life in a cognitive and manipulative system. The drive to total mastery of a transparent world has led not only to liberation but also to terror and enforced consensus. I mentioned in the first chapter that Lyotard depicts only one of the ways in which empty subjectivity can be lived, but his is surely a central modern theme. According to Lyotard, the Enlightenment goals of knowledge and liberation of the distanced subject are being outmoded by new knowledge and technology, which more and more reveal, and create, a world where we must make our way with neither fixed rules nor the comforting feeling of mastery over our tools and our language. In this world the overall modern "meta-narratives" of human liberation and progress toward total knowledge are losing their force. We are left with many small narratives legitimating all sorts of practices (and the nonnarrative legitimacy of the sciences), but we have no general agreement on the rules for settling disputes among the multiple narratives. (See Lyotard 1983, 10, 197–99; Lyotard 1984; Lyotard 1985, 195–236.)[1]

Technical, scientific, and artistic changes are forcing us to regulate our lives in a world where traditional meanings have vanished and even the "natural order" has become fluid. This continues the modern emphasis on self-creation but in a situation where there is no distanced subject to survey it all and plan comprehensively.

We bathe in the immateriality of information, distances, speeds, changes of concepts, displacements and dematerializations of all the signs of the old recognitions: the natural order, the cycles of procreation, sexuality, money. . . . Obliged to navigate by sight, we are men without quality, without a mandate for mastery, with the one obligation of inventing the rules of the game. (Theofilakis 1985, ix)

This regulation will have to be redone every three years. . . . In this regulation man is no longer the measure. (Lyotard, in Theofilakis 1985, 12–13)[2]

Thinking about modernity, Weber claimed that the social and technical changes that institutionalized modern individualism expressed in our lives something about the root human condition, about how individual belief supports social meaning. Thinking about postmodernity, Lyotard claims that the technical and artistic changes that open new ways of life reveal a truth about our basic condition that has been covered over by comforting stories about the cosmos or about history. But that truth denies Weber's methodological individualism. We exist as individuals only through a multiplicity of practices and language games with no metaphysical foundation, center, or unified goal. Borrowing and revising images from Descartes and Wittgenstein, Lyotard says that our language (and our world) is like a city with many districts of differently styled construction, without an overall plan, and in a state of civil war in which there are no uncontested authorities and partisans keep changing the names of streets and landmarks (1985, 236).[3]

The darker side of modernity still threatens us: Weber's spectre of numbing bureaucracy administering a society regulated only by considerations of performance and efficiency, the domination of capital, and the conversion of all human relations and culture into commodities, a world of enforced conformity amid superficial variety. We still must resist attempts to seize reality and create forced unity. Lyotard urges: "Let us wage a war on totality; let us be witnesses to the unpresentable; let us activate the differences and save the honor of the name" (1983, 81–82). To do this we need to be outside the great self-enforcing cultural systems. The founders of modernist art did not look for better ways to achieve the official goals. Joyce, Schönberg, Cézanne, and others changed what was meant by artistic success. They redefined art, they started new language games, and so witnessed to that which goes beyond any language game and manifests itself in desire. We must continue seeking new rules and new forms of life, not innovation within the system (1983, 260). The arts are the primary example of this creativity, but Lyotard thinks science too may form an "open system" that cannot be identified with repressive totalities (1983, 64).

I find Lyotard's overall picture congenial, and the forces that he urges us to resist surely need to be resisted. But like Heidegger, he pictures the modern world as more unified than it is, with the consequence that the postmodern gesture becomes too stereotyped. Also, he attributes too much internal rule-governed unity to language games and modes of discourse. For him, it is the tension between these various unities that must be respected, and new life spaces created. This resembles the picture of multiple worlds or conceptual schemes that I criticized earlier. The unity of the rule-governed spheres makes it necessary for Lyotard to enjoin the constant creation of new rules and new modes of discourse, instead of taking advantage of the multiplicity and tension already constituting the domains we find ourselves within. Except for his suggestive but brief remarks about science, his recommendations have too much of the modernist need to create outside the tradition, in opposition to the system.

If modernity is less unified, if there is internal multiplicity, then it may not be necessary always to work outside. There are fewer clear edges to transgress. There is internal tension and multiplicity even within what threatens us. Lyotard resists what needs resisting but perhaps he expresses too much concern to stay ahead of the language of the tribe and belong to the true avant-garde. If the elements of our multiple inhabitation are themselves internally multiple and tense, then there is room for freedom and creativity without the need always to be out ahead.[4]

Our task is less to create constantly new forms of life than to creatively renew actual forms by taking advantage of their internal multiplicity and tensions and their friction with one another. This task is illuminated by Charles Jencks's discussion of postmodern architecture. For Jencks, leaving modernity means giving up the dream of pure universal form and returning to the multiple languages of the people.

When I first wrote this book in 1975 and 1976 the word and concept of Post-Modernism had only been used, with any frequency, in literary criticism. Most perturbing, as I later realized, it had been used to mean "Ultra-Modern," referring to the extremist novels of William Burroughs and a philosophy of nihilism and anti-convention. While I was aware of these writings, of Ihab Hassan and others, I used the term to mean the opposite of all this: the end of avant-garde extremism, the partial return to tradition and the central role of communicating with the public—and architecture is *the* public art. (Jencks 1984, 6)

Some postmodern architecture, though it often shows a too easy eclecticism, embodies a new approach to the unity of form. The created spaces do not share the assumption of so many "modern" buildings that one dominant pure form will follow a few overriding functions. The new buildings accept a need to interact with the language and culture of the inhabitants rather than to create a clean, new, formally pure world. We cannot escape from the networks of meanings and activities already in operation. Even the purest modern building finds a meaning in the local symbolic network. The formally perfect office building may speak of power and of disdain for the human scale. The language already in use cannot simply be avoided to start a new game; the avant-garde cannot escape its context. Still the artist need not simply repeat to us what we already say to ourselves. The local tradition can be turned and modified, its internal stresses played with, its limits transgressed, and its schemes qualified by being conjoined with others.[5] This may demand multiple levels of structure and meaning, as often in music. Or the artist may employ the local language with irony but not with the irony of the superior self who sees through what the local inhabitant takes as gospel. This would be to reenact the distinction between naive tradition and clear-minded modern. Rather we want the irony and play that lead not to division but to a new community, a joint rueful acknowledgement that we are all in the plurality together, that there is no firm base, that we know our fragility and our strengths.[6]

Even if the beliefs that moderns have held about themselves are mistaken, it is significant that they have held them. Modernity's self-description may be inadequate, but giving that self-description has been much of what modernity has been about. Meta-positions, pure rationality, formal analyses, the attempt to create formally pure institutions—these and their relations of power are all ways of dealing with multiplicity by setting up a pole of unity and trying to view our situation as a whole while defining what is to be allowed and what rejected in terms of "the" form of our life. That way of coping with our situation has never been as completely dominant as it would have us believe, but it has had enormous influence for good and evil. The achievements of modernity in human liberation and culture are obvious even though it is fashionable today to emphasize the bad results of many modern strategies.

If there is to be an end of modernity, it would mean lessening the influence of that self-description. It would involve giving up the modern dichotomies and the assumptions of purified forms, unitary horizons, unified contexts, and secure meta-positions (and therefore giving up some of the kinds of irony often labeled postmodern). It would mean affirming multiplicity where there was no "the" form or "the" approach to posit as ultimate and use as a platform for distanced subjectivity. It would mean that there was not some one task for reason or cognition to do. There are many tasks; we live where there are only local contexts. Because it encourages variety, this can look like modern individualism, but the basic posture is different. It agrees with Heidegger that we should resist the temptation to "metaphysics" in practice and thought while recognizing that metaphysics is always with us and has its local uses while, in Vitiello's striking phrase, no longer treating things as if they were "beings" (*l'onticizzazione dell'essente*) (Vitiello 1978, 70).

Discussions of postmodernity presuppose that our age is unified enough that we can speak of its ending. The kind of multiplicity I have been urging would not allow such definitive breaks. In our world many things are happening, and there is no substitute for examination of the details. But even if we discourage the notion of a unified postmodern age, there may well be differences and changes of immense importance occurring even now.

Modernity and Tradition

We can now see one implication that the view we have been exploring might have for our life: there can be no liberating hope for a brand new world. There can be no change of the world as a whole, since there is no world as a whole constituted by a unitary granting of presence or a single basic shape of spirit. There are too many different rhythms and fields and possibilities for all to come to a climax or completion at once, nor are they totally unified within themselves.

This may seem to imprison us in the modern age, but in fact it questions whether the modern age should be so sharply walled off from what has gone before or might come after. Is the modern age as unique as it has described itself to be? If what I have been suggesting were thought out more fully, one effect would be to change our vision when we look backward. The modern age could no longer be thought of as different in one unified fundamental way, because there would be no one fundamental way for each age to exist. The very division into ages would become questionable. This might eliminate hopes for total change, but it would encourage a sense of belonging and fellowship with those who have struggled in the past within the multiple inhabitation that made them what they were.

If we are questioning the dichotomies by which modernity has defined itself, then we question both sides of those dichotomies. To deny modern distanced subjectivity does not then mean we can live only in substantive traditional societies. Both sides of the dichotomy become doubtful; we must question whether substantive rationality as defined in distinction to formal rationality really exists as such. If the multiplicity of our inhabitation casts doubt on the unity and purity that modernity attributes to itself, so must it question the picture of the traditional way of life drawn by contrast with the modern. Substantive traditional life may be a retrospective construct that never existed as it is envisaged. All modes of human inhabitation may be marked by more distance, negativity, and sidelong irony than theorists of modernity have wanted to admit. Although a medieval European was not a modern person, there was much more distance and playing with beliefs, less seriousness and single-mindedness than moderns, caught up in the division between free individuals and restrictive traditions, might suspect. Just as we today are not purely distanced, people in the past were not simply installed within a tradition.[7]

Part of what encourages the dichotomy of modern versus traditional society may be the wish for a situation in which our inner nature can be completely expressed in our way of life. For some thinkers, that ideal was once realized in the lost paradise of a traditional society that expressed the substantive natural law; for others, the ideal will be realized in the promised coming of a freedom that perfectly matches our nature as individuals. But there may be no possibility, traditional or modern, for total self-coincident expression within the motions and multiples that make us up. In a different sense than Hegel would admit, there must be the travail of the negative and the tearing apart of differences that are never reconciled.

Rethinking the Modern World

It may be that our world is not a totality unified enough to be the culmination of history or to be transcended in a unified postmod-

ernity. Though they deny the ultimacy of modern distanced subjectivity, both Hegel and Heidegger make modernity a culminating
age. But if our time is multiple, then there can be no climax, since
eschatology always rests on the distinction of the essential from the
unessential. If no one call or space is essential to our world as a
whole, no one essential change could dominate everything else. We
cannot hope for a total change, though we may hope and strive for
large changes. Multiplicity as I am suggesting we describe it allows
neither Hegelian cumulation nor Heideggerean discontinuities. Both
cumulation and discontinuity are too holistic to describe our
situation.[8]

According to modernity, the self is unified and unifying. The self
is where everything comes to a point, and it creates unity by its
attitudes, beliefs, and decisions. Such self-sufficient, unified subjectivity is impossible. What makes possible the formal rationality
and individualism expressed in many modern institutions is neither
simple nor unified. There may be many necessary conditions of
different types but no single deep happening giving a unified shape
to the dispersed temporality of our existence. Does that mean that
modernity as the unified and unifying age in which we live is an
illusion? No, modernity exists, but not quite as it describes itself to
be. If we want, we can still name our age "modern" in honor of
dominant features of our multiple inhabitation, but modernity is
not the single, unifying meaning of our world.

Modernity is no illusion, but neither is it unique in one deep way.
There are aspects of current life where structures claiming distanced
individuality or formally pure decision processes are important. But
these are not everything; there is no one key phenomenon. We need
to discourage the desire to find one deep happening or pattern that
lets us understand everything else. Weber, Hegel, and Heidegger all
follow this desire for deep interpretative unity.

While there is a tremendous similarity among developments after
the seventeenth century in art, politics, philosophy, and so on, and
much mutual influence, we do not have to conclude that they are
all responses to some one modern call or express some one modern
shape of spirit. There should be room for more or less, for partial
conformity, for multiple influences and overdetermination. Universal imposition may enlighten many aspects of modernity, and
the same is true of Hegel's analysis of modernity in terms of civil
society, but these do not have to be made absolute. Otherwise some

phenomena are forced into a mold they do not entirely fit, and what potential they may have for change and newness is traded for uniform vision. The ecology movement, for example, is in some ways amenable to analysis in terms of universal imposition, but in other ways it is quite resistant to such analysis. There might be some room for us to encourage one or another aspect of such a movement without merely orbiting within universal imposition or enacting the current shape of spirit. Modern institutions show their disunity, for example, in their built-in conflict between rationalization and emancipation and in the way modernity "was successful against its enemies because the enemies were strong enough to resist its complete victory over them" (Shils 1981, 303, 325).

It sounds prosaic and undramatic to say that civil society or universal imposition should be viewed as heuristic tools rather than as transcendentally guaranteed content. So it is, but this is not a genial relativism that urges us to "say anything you like; it's all more or less true." Weakening the transcendental primacy of such content amounts to a call to find the limits of these ways of speaking. We can use them to see what they illuminate and to help locate what in our world transcends them even now.

Rethinking modernity does not require us to say that it is just the same as other ages. If modernity is not in some one, deep way essentially different from past ages, neither can it be declared essentially the same. If there is not enough unity for the one judgment, neither is there for the other. There is no substitute for looking at the details. We can point out distinctive features of our world, and they will be those familiar from the earlier portions of this study. What we add is that these exist within a multiplicity that qualifies and limits them while making them possible.

In recognizing this we continue one important modern trend: self-awareness. We know the multiplicity as multiple; we recognize traditions as traditions. In one way this is nothing special: the ancients were not so defined by their traditions as not to know them for what they were. In another way this is new: there is a freeing amid a multiplicity that decenters our lives. We do have more room to judge and to rationalize our lives, and to see the limitations of that rationalization. What we do not have is the wide open spaces of the modern self-image.

Questioning the exclusivity of the fundamental dichotomies in terms of which so many facets of modern culture and politics articulate themselves should lead to questioning the stated goals of many modern institutions and practices. Goals that are "pure" or "formal" or "value-free" need to be qualified. Qualifying them weakens their hold, because they are especially attractive to the extent that they promise an escape from the ordinary lot of mortals.

Our world has not described itself correctly. It is not so unified, not so pure. Purifying subjectivity or creating formal structures is not itself a pure act by a formally defined self. Procedural institutions and distanced selfhood exist within a context and for many substantive reasons. We need to look for the substantive side of seemingly formal institutions and practices. Such an investigation already exists in the literature devoted to "the critique of ideology." We have seen an example in Hegel's criticism of civil society. Marx followed Hegel's example in his argument that the presumed formally pure and equal procedures of the modern free market hide an ambiguity in the process of surplus value that can be seen when the seemingly equitable exchange system is inserted into its larger context of our social interaction with nature. Marx learned this strategy from Hegel, though he disagreed about the nature of the larger context. That discussion continues today.

If modernity is not so unified, we can find within our world contrary ways and different spaces. Consider the revival of ethnicity and mininationalism spoken about in the first chapter. I remarked that it was puzzling whether these movements should be interpreted as a desire to return to a traditional society or as a greater achievement of modern freedom of association. They liberate individuals from the demands of cultural uniformity, yet they force them into a naturally given identity. And though a Scot or a Basque may have some choice about whether to associate with such a movement, the American or the Spaniard has no such choice. The mixture of modern ideals and traditional patterns seems strange only if we demand that modernity be one unified achievement. It does not completely resolve the status of such ethnic revivals to say that there is no one, deep essence of modernity they are reacting for or against, but it does open the way to thinking about them without having to declare them on the side either of progress or of regression.

Similarly, if the renewed strength of religious and political fundamentalisms today is interpreted simply as a longing for the certainties of a traditional society, then "modern" thinkers can only oppose them. But if modernity is not a unified, deep happening, the fundamentalist reaction cannot be against the whole age, and there may be more grounds for dialogue than might appear.

At the beginning of this study we looked at modern clichés about rootlessness and empty self-development. We need to reject the idea that we are empty selves facing indefinitely open possibilities. We do have content for our lives, but this also means that our possibilities are finite. Yet if we think of the absence of self-coincidence all the way down, there is room for the creation of new roles and the opening of new possibilities, indeed more room than Hegel or Heidegger would allow though less than the standard modern self-description would affirm. We cannot create possibilities from nothing or select them from an indefinitely open field. The possibilities within which we find ourselves already in motion are not neatly numbered and individuated; there is room for creative combination and mutual influences among them; tension and something like dialectic can produce new ways without our having to construct them.

The first chapter also mentioned the question of whether the American political system should be seen as designed around formal procedures for mediating conflicts or as embodying a set of values substantive enough so that not every group or opinion could be tolerated within the community. The second view seems correct. If there are no pure formal selves or processes, the U. S. Constitution embodies a set of values and not merely a set of procedures for adjudicating among various values chosen by different subjects or groups. The embodied values may concern procedures, but they are not purely procedural; they form a substantive vision of what traits of human character should be fostered: tolerance, freedom, individuality, and so on. Those substantive values are embodied in a system that, as one of its central tenets, enforces a separation of the private sphere from the public sphere. And that separation, which can look like a separation of private content from public formal procedures, actually affirms substantive values on both sides.⁹

Living in Our World

Liberation and freedom are important, but they become perilous when described in a fashion that is unattainable and would be deadly if it could be attained. We still have much to learn from Hegel's discussion of "absolute freedom and terror" (Phenomenology of Spirit 414–22/#582–95). Hegel says that to be free we need customs, ways of life that are not our own arbitrary construction or imposed on us immediately but conform to the nature of our freedom. For Hegel the growth away from extreme subjectivity involves submission to customs that we can know as transparently rational. Lacking Hegelian transparency, we have in abundance customs and ways of life, fields of possibility that shape what we are. They are not our creation. Are they then brutely imposed upon us? No, because we are not there first to be imposed upon. The customs are part of the meaningful structure of possibilities that allows us to be at all. Which is not to say that we cannot criticize or strive for change, but there is no liberation in the abstract or in total. Here Hegel's style of analysis of the details and the tensions within structures of mutual recognition proves valuable still. We do not have the power that is attributed to modern distanced subjectivity, but we are not without power.

One of the great modern claims is that the achievement of freedom depends on institutionalizing a purified notion of individual selfhood. But rejecting the modern idea of a distanced self does not destroy our freedom. Indeed the conception of us as thrown amid a multiple past that comes as opening future possibilities allows more freedom and control than Hegel or Heidegger might think appropriate, for we do not move within one transcendentally established sphere. But this does not turn us into distanced modern selves.

I spoke before about Heidegger's description of human discernment without guarantees. That seems appropriate for our situation, though without the suggestion that there is some deep call we can uncover. There may be many movements, many different calls and spaces open to us and opening us. We have no sovereign freedom to create options by fiat, and we make our way as best we can without guaranteed principles to rely upon.

Hegel says modern subjects claim "the right of insight," the right that nothing be imposed on an individual that the individual has not freely chosen or seen the necessity for accepting. I have agreed with Heidegger that neither we nor our world can achieve the self-coincidence that would allow the right of insight in Hegel's terms. There is too much culture, language, and history we find ourselves always already within, and we do not have the one necessary logical sequence to make things transparent to our gaze. Yet the right of insight might be applied somewhat differently. There is no one ultimate ground for our insight to steer by, but there are many spaces we need to explore, many conditions and histories we need to understand. To be aware of the multiplicity we inhabit increases our freedom.

We looked earlier at the peculiar position of the agricultural class in Hegel's rational state. Though the institutional arrangements Hegel develops are weak, the problem he is addressing is very real. Must there not be somewhere an immediate identification with values and ways of life so that not everything in the community will be a matter of reflective choice and calculation? Hegel thinks that the values and customs that make up the particular spirit of a nation have to have some location in the society where they are immediately accepted, for otherwise the citizens will hold them only as a matter of reflective expediency, and all will be reduced to formal rationality.

Perhaps we have not too little but too much immediate identification with values and ways of life. What we lack is unity; seeking it we may confuse its lack with emptiness. This makes distanced subjectivity enticing but impossible. The search for that unity needs to be questioned. We may question or change this or that aspect of the multiplicity around us and within us, but we cannot change it all. There is no point of view from which it can be seen as a whole; we are strung out within multiple fields of possibility that do not come neatly individuated one by one or as a totality. We can be aware of our rootedness and our identification with ways of thought and life only piecemeal.

An appealing image made famous by Otto Neurath appears as the epigraph to Quine's *Word and Object* (see Stroud 1969). We are voyaging on a ship that we must rebuild on the open sea without ever stripping it down completely. This image is still too modern in its presuppositions: the ship as a whole can be held in view, its boards are individually identifiable and surveyable, and planning can go on for the ship as a whole even if construction cannot. Still the ship image suggests much about our situation. Without the magic distance of modern subjects, we make our choices leaning on one aspect of our world while finding our way in another. Without distanced subjectivity as "the" form of our lives, rationality and criticism cannot be equated with some straightforward rule. But this does not eliminate criticism, whose message turns out to be again the distrust of immediacy and totality and domination.

Our choices will be exercised for goals and according to standards that we already find ourselves among. New goals and standards may become available, but they are not simply our creations. None of these goals and standards have unquestioned primacy. But they do not automatically become questioned just because we would like to assert our freedom. They become questionable in their contrasts and mutual constitution. We cannot distance ourselves from everything at once, because we cannot bring to a totality everything in which we are always already involved.

None of this means that we should accept without challenge what we find we are within. There will be some movements over which we have little control even though we are intimately shaped by them, for example, the ins and outs of taste in art or the drift away from its former system of verb inflections in English. Whether our power is so limited in matters of politics and economics remains to be seen; the record is not encouraging. At least we can see how awareness of the context of our lives encourages the unbuilding of totalities and dominations. Constellations of power and structure that try to enforce uniformity or totality deny the basic condition that makes them possible. It would seem appropriate to make room for many kinds of lives, though not on the basis of some principle of atomistic individuality or formal freedom. This reemphasizes the deconstructive living we spoke of earlier, with its infinite analysis of what we find moving about and in ourselves, and action within and without the institutions that surround us.

So have we, in the end, arrived at one more version of modern pluralism? Pluralism it is, but not quite modern. It is not a plurality presented to us for our judgment or manipulation. It lacks the modern position above it all and the definition in subject-object terms. Neither is it the "traditional" assertion that amid plurality there is one true way. What we arrive at is more like the realism of the practical man in all ages who has to live in a multiple world despite what the pundits say.

Whatever its contours (and they form no system) we are not wholly defined by modernity, by postmodernity, or by any of the content of our lives. Within and around the multiplicity of our lives there still is the event of our being appropriated together with the world(s) we find ourselves within. There still "is" the happening of presence, with its negativity and withdrawal, but this is too multiple (or too formal) to carry a message about our age other than its finitude and groundlessness. There is perhaps more here of compassion than theorists of irony have seen, and the message of finitude already attacks modern pretensions. In any case, we must get on with the possibilities and motions where we find ourselves, dealing as best we can without grounds or guarantees, with the distance and difference built into our situation. We are projections toward the future already under way. We have choice and we have standards, but we have no final standards. Our values are tied into history and to who we are; there are many ways they can be approached and discussed and judged. Modernity offered secure grounding in the unity of the self or the formal total picture. Denying that does not mean the absence of any picture. To avoid these extremes does not eliminate the shaky ground we do walk on in our happening together.

Without the standard modern dichotomies we are left with neither the seriousness attributed to the traditional life nor the superior irony claimed for modernity and some forms of the postmodern. There is no secure meta-position above it all, no pure play of reflection we can join to escape being conditioned by the ordinary movements of life. There is still and has always been irony and separation, but it is more humble, a sidelong awareness of contingency and of being always already out beyond what we can be sure of, distanced from what we are but not parted from it.

Our life can be lived without the possibility of final or formal grounding, but also without the spectre of the lack of such grounding. We can understand our multiple context, our rootedness and our rootlessness, and get on with what and where we are. Modernity has been much in the thrall of the fear of scepticism, moral or epistemological. Perhaps we might live without either scepticism or security.

Notes

Preface

1. Commenting on Heidegger, Manfred Brelage says: "Neither the question about being, nor the question about the essential constitution of man, but the insight into the necessary interrelation of both these questions makes the center of Heidegger's thought. If one isolates either of these questions, one turns Heidegger into an anthropologist or a metaphysician, or both together" (Brelage 1965, 205). Hegel also is concerned with this intersection. Heidegger claims, however, that Hegel thinks the being of things in terms of their being thought in absolute thought, while Heidegger thinks the being of things with respect to its difference from beings. "Put more precisely: for Hegel the matter of thinking is the idea as the absolute concept. For us, formulated in a preliminary fashion, the matter of thinking is the difference *as* difference" (Identity and Difference 113/47). (In general, I have incorporated references into the text. The citations used to refer to works of Hegel and Heidegger, such as the one above, are explained in the bibliographies devoted to each thinker.)

2. A remark on gender pronouns: Although in general I have tried to paraphrase them out, in places I have used the male pronoun in the traditional indefinite sense. For some of the thinkers treated, the use of the male pronoun in this sense is quite appropriate. A more vexing problem has been *man* in such phrases as "man and world." I have been unable to find an adequate substitute. *Consciousness* has the wrong implications for the thinkers treated in this book; *humanity* and *humankind* are too abstract and set up the wrong contrasts; *persons* and other plural nouns (and moving to *we*) affirm Weber's methodological individualism and prematurely settle (in the wrong way) the problem of whether Heidegger's *Dasein* is to be

thought of as individuated one to each person. And I am sworn not to use German words. So in many cases I have reluctantly kept *man* in relation to *world* and fields of possiblity.

Chapter One: The Modern World

1. See Sheed (1978, 146) for some cautionary remarks about ethnicity.

2. Admittedly I am simplifying Weber's views; he is more aware of the pitfalls of the ideal type method than are some of his successors, and for him modernity is a complex combination of adaptations and functions, not just one crucial change. But my simplification is not out of line with his desire for unity and with the way his thought has been appropriated. For a discussion of the tradition of distinguishing modernity from tradition and of how Weber's work fits into this ongoing discussion, see Bendix (1967), especially his recommendations for a move away from the standard dichotomy so that one can talk about "modernization without modernity" (313–29). While contrasts between modern and traditional society have been a topic of discussion at least since the mid-eighteenth century, American functionalist sociology and its detractors caused a vast increase in literature devoted to modernization and to advising other nations. See, for example, Parsons (1971), Blumenberg (1983), Crozier (1982), MacIntyre (1981), Foucault (1979), Bernstein (1983), Lyotard (1983), Habermas (1984), Hartmann (1973b). Lyotard, Habermas, and Hartmann all deal as well with Niklas Luhmann's updated functionalist theory of society as a homeostatic cybernetic system. Extensive references to Weber's critics can be found in the notes to Roth and Schluchter (1979).

3. These dilemmas and others are discussed in Berger (1977, 70ff). In *After Virtue*, Alasdair MacIntyre (1981) paints a similar picture of modernity as involving a purified empty self, but his conclusions are much more pessimistic about whether modern individuality has positive worth. The debate over modern formal individuality has connections with Blumenberg's analysis (1983) of modernity in terms of "self-assertion," but Blumenberg's ideas need not imply a self defined in a purely formal way.

4. By speaking of maximizing I do not mean to take a stand on the controversy over whether a rule of maximizing, a rule of satisficing, or some other rule should be taken as describing our judgments. These disputes are within a family of views all of which accept the general modern description of the self.

5. See, for example, Henrich (1952), Kronman (1972), Roth and Schluchter (1979).

6. "There is a widespread feeling that the promise of the modern era is slipping away from us. A movement of enlightenment and liberation that was to have freed us from superstition and tyranny has led in the twentieth century to a world in which ideological fanaticism and political oppression have reached extremes unknown in previous history. Science, which was

to have unlocked the bounties of nature, has given us the power to destroy all life on the earth. Progress, modernity's master idea, seems less compelling today when it appears that it may be progress into the abyss. And the globe today is divided between a liberal world so incoherent that it seems to be losing the significance of its own ideals, an oppressive and archaic communist statism, and a poor, and often tyrranical, Third World reaching for the first rungs of modernity. In the liberal world, the state, which was supposed to be a neutral night-watchman that would maintain order while individuals pursued their various interests, has become so overgrown and militarized that it threatens to become a universal policeman" (Bellah et al. 1985, 277).

7. One recent discussion that remains within the standard modern alternatives is Gillespie (1984). He eloquently discusses the dilemmas of modernity in his treatment of the conceptions of history in Hegel and Heidegger. He contrasts nihilistic subjectivity with a foundational tradition that gives a measure to subjects. He valorizes the dichotomy differently than "moderns" would, but he remains within the opposition rather than questioning it as do Hegel and Heidegger. See Gillespie (1984, 23, 154, 166, 175). He explicitly presupposes the standard "metaphysical" distinctions of eternity from time, being from becoming, nature from freedom, philosophy from rhetoric. This gives his book its strength, but it makes it difficult for him to deal accurately with Heidegger's attempt to find a position that is neither metaphysical nor nihilistic or to do justice to the ways in which Hegel does not fit the standard alternatives. The problem of modernity can perhaps not be adequately treated in categories derived mainly from the conflict between Plato and the Sophists.

8. See Pippin (1982), for an illuminating discussion of the formal nature of Kant's enterprise and the problems this caused.

9. See MacIntyre (1981) and Putnam (1978, 1981). Similar questions arise concerning Jürgen Habermas's appeal to an ideal communicative situation. In his exposition and critique of Habermas, Raymond Geuss has questioned whether despite Habermas's intentions he can provide anything more than formal norms without any guiding content. See Geuss (1981) and Bernstein (1985).

Chapter Two: Hegel's Criticisms of Civil Society

1. The picture of Hegel as a totalitarian stems from Haym ([1857] 1962); it was emphasized in the English-speaking world by Popper (1963). Krieger (1957) situates Hegel within an antiliberal tradition working with a different notion of freedom. These analyses are shown to be misleading in many ways by writers such as Ritter (1982), Weil (1950), and Marcuse (1955). These writers claim that Hegel's intent of preserving the essence of modern freedom and individuality was not fully realized in the institutions he proposed. I do not mean to disagree with the thesis that Hegel was working

with a different notion of freedom from the standard Enlightenment or liberal view, but he has reasons for his differences.

Recently discovered manuscripts make it likely that Hegel toned down for publication more liberal views expressed in his lectures at Jena and Heidelberg and perhaps at Berlin as well (see Ilting 1984; Avineri 1985). The differences relevant to the present study include more extensive criticism of civil society's ability to deal with poverty and more emphasis on the separation of powers in government.

2. For good recent discussions of Hegel's theory of civil society, see the essays collected by Pelczynski (1984a) and also Gillespie (1984, chap. 2).

3. Hegel studies the preinteraction side of man and the more "natural" sides of the personality in the early paragraphs of the philosophy of subjective spirit in the *Encyclopedia*. For more on interaction and the various kinds of primacies involved, see Winfield (1977); Kronman (1972), who develops this theme into a criticism of Weber; and the discussions in Taylor (1975, parts 2 and 4).

4. See Taylor (1979, chap. 2, sec. 5–8; chap. 3). This material is an expanded version of Taylor (1975, chap. 20).

5. On Hegel's criticisms, see Avineri (1972, especially chap. 7), Taylor (1979, chap. 2; 1975, 437ff), and Plant (1984). For a claim that Hegel did see solutions to these problems within modern society, see Walton (1984).

Chapter Three: Hegel's Logic and Its Movements

1. The interpretation I offer of Hegel's logical enterprise is along the same general lines as those offered by Kenley Dove, Klaus Hartmann, and, most recently, by White (1983) and Pinkard (1985), though as will become clear I differ from them on various issues.

2. For recent large-entity interpretations, see Taylor (1975, 1979), Inwood (1983), and Gillespie (1984). Lauer (1977) makes a strong right-Hegelian case, but because of his emphasis on Christian themes he avoids many of the excesses of the cosmic subject. Findlay (1958) creates a complex neoplatonic interpretation that does not fit easily into these classifications; it has aspects of both the large-entity and the transcendental way of reading Hegel.

3. On this see White (1983, 71–74, 88, 144). White does at times talk about the logical categories as in their entirety describing subjectivity (57, 63, 88).

4. See Findlay (1958), Henrich (1971), Düsing (1976, 317f, 321f), Hartmann (1973a), and Winfield (1977). Some of the differences between these authors stem from their taking different sections of the *Science of Logic* as paradigmatic examples of Hegel's mode of procedure. Hartmann uses the logic of being's section on quality, while Düsing uses the section on the determinations of reflection in the logic of essence.

5. In the essence section of the logic, a further refinement is introduced to the action of positing. In that section the categories come in pairs usually distinguished into ground and grounded. One is taken as fundamental, the other as dependent or posited by the first. For example, the thing is fundamental, and its appearance is posited or dependent. Hegel says that the category of ground involves distinguishing within an entity a posited and a nonposited element. "Ground is the essence posited as the not-posited over against posited being" ("*Grund ist das Wesen gesetzt als das nicht Gesetzte gegen das Gesetztsein*") (Science of Logic 2:67/447). This makes two levels of positing. The category involves positing the distinction of a fundamental and a dependent aspect. In particular, this category involves positing that one of the aspects is posited by the other, and so the other, the ground, is posited as not-posited (by the other pole). This double use of "posited" is more complex, because one of the poles is posited as posited by the other. The mode of this second positing varies; it may be conditioning or causation or grounding or expression or appearing or determining or whatever is called for by the particular pair being discussed. The double use of positing becomes more important as the logic continues. The two uses gradually come together until in the final category they cannot be distinguished. In the first instances of its use, this double level of positing might be interpreted as a meta-language description of a positing described in an object language. By the end of the logical sequence such a distinction of levels will not be tenable.

6. "Essence, which is being coming into mediation with itself through the negativity of itself, is self-relating only insofar as it is in relation to an other—this other however not as something which simply is but as something posited and mediated. Being has not vanished; but . . . as regards its one-sided characteristic of immediacy, being is deposed to something merely negative, to appearance" (Encyclopedia #112).

7. "Essence as such is one with its reflection and inseparable from the movement of reflection itself. Consequently it is not essence through which the reflective movement runs; nor is essence a first from which reflection begins. This circumstance makes the exposition of reflection more difficult; for we cannot really say that essence withdraws into itself, that essence inwardly reflects itself, because it is not before or in its movement, and this has no substrate on which it runs its course" (Science of Logic 2:67/448).

8. The pair form and content changes into what Hegel calls formal ground. This will give way to real ground: "The formal ground relation contains only one content for ground and grounded; in this identity lies their necessity, but at the same time their tautology. Real ground contains a diversified content; but this brings with it the contingency and externality of the ground relation" (Science of Logic 2:84/463).

Chapter Four: Categories for Modernity

1. In working through the third section of the *Science of Logic* I have found helpful Léonard (1974, especially 324ff). Important clues about what Hegel is about can be gathered from Pippin's (1982) treatment of Kant; although there are few references to Hegel, the dilemmas Pippin points to are ones Hegel tried to avoid (see, for example, 188, 231). Though I disagree with some of his conclusions, Düsing (1976) is very helpful on the third section of the *Science of Logic*. The same is true of Burbidge (1982), whose interpretation of the necessity of the logic is less conservative than my own (as can be seen, for example, from his treatment of Encyclopedia #575 on his p. 226). See the review of Burbidge in Di Giovanni (1982).

2. This move is prefigured in the move from bad infinity to good infinity in the first section of the logic. For discussions, see Düsing (1976, 269) and Rotenstreich (1974) though the latter has perhaps too individualistic a view of Hegel's "idealism."

3. See Düsing (1976, 255–56) on the dangers of using examples from ordinary language to illustrate what Hegel means by the three moments of universal, particular, and universal.

4. "The nature of things . . . certainly does not set to work by first framing for itself a major premise giving the relation of a particularity to an enduring universal, and then second picking up a separate relation of an individuality to the particular, out of which third and last a new proposition comes to light. [Hegel is referring to the traditional syllogism all men are mortal; Socrates is a man; so Socrates is mortal]. This syllogistic process that advances by means of separate propositions is nothing but a subjective form. The nature of the thing (*Sache*) is that the differentiated determinations of the concept of the thing are essentially united. . . . Everything is a syllogism, a universal that through particularity is brought together with individuality; but everything is certainly not a whole consisting of three propositions" (Science of Logic 2:314/669).

Chapter Five: Applying Hegel's Logic

1. See Taylor (1972) and the critical discussion in Soll (1985). A subtle reading of a different kind is given in Rosen (1982), disagreeing with Taylor's interpretation of Hegel's transcendental argument and with Taylor's imputation of "expressivism" to Hegel.

2. An excellent recent defense of Hegel's success in establishing the beginning of the system and the necessity of the logical sequence is found in White (1983). See also Dove (1970).

3. Admittedly, my strategy with Hegel's logic is to argue that he is making strong claims and then to criticize him for failing to meet his ambitious goals. Various defenses of Hegel that weaken the claims are possible, but these seem to do violence to the text. An important defense that is relevant here is the claim that the repeated involutions of the basic logical movement

(immediacy, reflective doubling and separation, comprehensive unity: being, essence, concept) into itself produce a sequence defined only in those terms, and different "versions" of the sequence are really different correlations of that unchanging pure sequence with external labels derived from history and current thought. For example, there would be a category whose "proper name" was its place as the posited unity of the posited division of the posited division of the immediacy of the immediacy of pure thought, and it would have a label, in this case "finitude." Only the labels might switch in different versions; the underlying categorial sequence would remain the same. This is an attractive idea; the large architectonic movement and its involutions certainly give Hegel's overall thought its structure. But the suggestion proves too much; if it were the case, then there should be no need at all to revise the logic. Just set up the threefold movement and its involution rules, and everything would follow automatically; there would be no labor of thought required (except that the derivation of the threefold movement itself would seem more mysterious in this case). Hegel's revisions do not seem to be a simple matter of switching labels on a movement already perfectly clear in itself. Reading the different versions, one does not feel that names are being moved within an identical sequence. The depth of the involutions varies in the two versions. The traditional terms and their connotations are woven tightly into the text and its motions, not just moved about on a framework that remains perspicuous and invariable. When "form and matter" is switched from before to after "thing and its properties," a different understanding of things and forms is announced, and the logical sequence seems to move differently.

4. The use of the three-part motion of the logic as an architectonic guide to evaluate details on the finer levels can be seen in the works of Hartmann, White, and Winfield listed in the bibliography.

5. In *Absolute Knowledge*, Alan White (1983) defends an interpretation of Hegel's logic similar to mine, and he qualifies Hartmann's interpretation in terms similar to those I propose. White is, however, more convinced of the success of the Hegelian enterprise. He claims that the logical sequence can be criticized in three ways: that some transitions are arbitrary, that some transitions depend on experience or intuition instead of pure thought, or that the totality is not comprehensive. He feels that he can answer all three objections, which he finds in Schelling's critique of Hegel. I am suggesting a slightly different objection: that the logical transitions are not arbitrary but are polyvalent and multiple, that there is no clear way to have made them "right," and therefore that the notion of the totality is vague. I argue this in the first case from the difficulty of deciding which of the versions of the logical sequence is "better." On this point White contends that "to accept the ahistorical validity of speculative logic is not necessarily to accept a fixed grid of categories: more important than comprehensiveness is circularity. Hegel must show that the conceptual relations present in the Logics

of Being and of Essence are inadequate, and that of the Logic of the Concept is comprehensive, but not all accounts revealing these truths need contain precisely the same categories. (This explains the differences between the *Science of Logic* and the shorter logic included in the *Encyclopedia*.) The refutation of nihilism requires demonstration of the inadequacy of all practical views in nihilism's logical sphere [the logic of essence]" (1983, 177). I do not think this answers the objection. By restricting the necessity of the logical sequence to its upper levels, a difficulty is created in drawing the line between the constant and variable aspects of the logic; this introduces something like a distinction of form from content. It also violates the "linearity" of the categorial sequence, which White has earlier affirmed (167). But White agrees that it is the overall architectonic movement of the logic that counts and serves as a criterion. He speaks of the transitions to essence and the concept as being necessitated when thinking in an earlier sphere reaches an impasse and a new method is needed "if it [the overall project of self-grounding, self-determining thought] is not to be pointless" and "if it is not to fail" (53, 55). For White that project is the only genuine meaning we can give to full rationality, and it is our only bulwark against modern nihilism. My fundamental disagreement rests here, since his views seem to depend on sharp dichotomies (form and content, formal and substantive, foundationalism versus nihilism) that are just those I am suggesting need to be questioned as to their ultimacy.

6. This is why in principle Hegel does not have to deduce Krug's pen. But like any philosopher intent on showing necessity Hegel has the problem of drawing a line between necessary and contingent aspects of the content he finds around him. The difficulty of drawing that line, and the implausibility of drawing it in any particular spot short of a distinction of form and content, which Hegel cannot afford, is one of the chief arguments against the whole endeavor. Hegel tries to avoid this problem by setting no fixed line. He has faith in the power of the concept as shown in its purity in the logical sequence, even if the applications are not yet clear. "One must start from the concept; and even if, perhaps, the concept cannot yet give an adequate account of the 'abundant variety' of nature . . . we must nevertheless have faith in the concept though many details are yet unexplained. The demand that everything be explained is altogether vague; that it has not been fulfilled is no reflection on the concept, whereas in the case of the theories of the empirical physicists the position is quite the reverse: these must explain everything, for their validity rests only on particular cases. The concept however is valid in its own right; the particulars will soon find their explanation" (Encyclopedia #353z). Hegel adds to this the claim that in its otherness in space and time the logical sequence must of necessity be found with contingent detail that is truly contingent, underivable and without any essential intelligibility except what empirical sense can be made of it. (Cf. Henrich 1971, 157–86.) Hegel does not draw any

fixed line beyond which this contingent content exists; *all* the categories of the logical sequence will be found with this contingent embodiment. With his faith in the extension of the concept's intelligibility and his doctrine of necessary contingency, Hegel tries to answer the difficulty faced by other a priori philosophers.

7. See Hartmann (1972, 1976b), Dove (1970), Winfield (1977), and Winfield's introduction to his translation (Ritter 1982); see also the bibliographical references in the foreword and first chapter of Hartmann (1976a).

8. Cf. Bodei (1975a) for a sensitive development of this kind of interpretation in a direction somewhat different from Hartmann's.

9. The fact that the logic is acknowledged from within and not presented to an intuiting subject seems to me to undermine the objections of Rosen (1982). Although I agree with Rosen in doubting that the principle of determinate negation can be made to work as Hegel wants, I would connect that problem with the status of the overall architectonic movement of the logic rather than with some presumed neoplatonic fantasies and intuitions.

Chapter Six: Civil Society and State

1. "The Hegelian theorem that the true is the whole is the dialectical thesis that a part has its whole as a consequence, not however the thesis that a fully developed part is the whole. Rather it is reversed: only the whole is fully developed, and the whole stands to the part in the relation that it is the fulfillment of the part" (Hartmann 1975, 485). Cf. Winfield (1977, 43–82) and the preface to Winfield's translation (Ritter 1982, pp. 17–27). Foster ([1935] 1968, 142–79) criticizes Hegel subtly, but his criticism is at times based on the overly formalistic notion of the moral will that results from Foster's own voluntaristic understanding of the origin of determinations in all spheres. On the distinction between political and civil freedom, see Pelczynski (1984b).

2. On the confusion of civil society with the state, see the enlightening contrast by Berry (1982, 160–65) between Hegel's and Hume's reasons for rejecting the Lockean social contract. For a more radical discussion of Hegel's view on social contract, see Benhabib (1984).

3. Foster's comparison of Plato and Hegel is very helpful on this issue, particularly on the differing roles the self-application of form plays in the two thinkers ([1935] 1968, 25–36, 79ff).

4. The dispute over the relative priority of individual and universal in Hegel is summarized in Ottman (1977). See also Taylor's sensible discussion of *Sittlichkeit* and *Volksgeist* (1975, 376–77; 1979, 84ff, 93ff). Taylor's discussion is unsatisfactory to the degree that it relies on the interpretation of Hegel in terms of cosmic subjectivity, but he dispels many misunderstandings of Hegel's notion of *Sittlichkeit*.

5. On Hegel's relation to the classical political economists and his lack of faith in equilibrium, see Bodei (1975c, 45, 52, 75). It is worth recalling

that the economic situation in Europe during and after the Napoleonic wars—the English blockade, its lifting, demobilization, industrialization, and changes in trade patterns and labor laws—hardly offered examples of equilibrium.

6. Hegel's discussion of corporations has many similarities to current ideas about the need for mediating institutions so that the atomized citizen need not directly face the mega-structures of the modern state and economy. On such mediating institutions see Berger (1977, chap. 11) and Berger, Berger, and Kellner (1974, part 3).

7. The suggested political parties are meant to represent overall views of the social whole from the perspective of different classes, rather than representing the interests of particular ways of life as do Hegel's estates. Such parties seem capable of being infected by the same particularity found objectionable in the estates; there is nothing to keep them from becoming coalitions of single interest groups, as in the United States, rather than European style ideological parties. See Hartmann (1976b) and the references given in the notes to the foreword and first essay in Hartmann (1976a).

8. On the estates see Riedel (1970, 74), Winfield (1977, 140–59), Avineri (1972, chap. 8 and 9), and Hartmann (1973b). The system of the three estates is the most universally criticized feature of the Philosophy of Right. The development of the estates within civil society is unclear, and the composition of the various estates seems somewhat arbitrary. No harmony of the various modes of life is achieved in the citizens individually, only in the state as a whole (Taylor 1975, 434f). Even the logical pedigree of the estates is doubtful; it is not evident why Hegel used the triad substantial, reflective, universal rather than the triad universal, particular, individual. Winfield (1977) argues that according to this latter dialectical pattern, something more like Marx's system of classes should have followed from what Hegel says in the "System of Needs" section of the Philosophy of Right. This is true, but it endangers the function played by the "immediate" or "substantial" group, which is important to the difference between civil society and state.

9. About the "right of insight," see among other places the Philosophy of Right (#132z), and Hegel's essay on the constitution of Württemberg, quoted in Ritter (1982, 56).

10. On public opinion, see Foster ([1935] 1968, 176ff). Taylor (1975, 450, 458; 1979, 125ff) points out that Hegel does not argue in the same fashion as modern writers on "legitimacy." But the right of insight remains important in distinguishing modern states from their earlier counterparts whose Sittlichkeit did not include this demand.

11. See Hegel's worried remarks in the Philosophy of Right (#203) and in the sections from his lectures quoted in Ilting's edition of the Philosophy of Right (3:626, 4:515–17). See also Avineri (1972, 156–58), and Karl Marx (1970, 96–115), for discussions of Hegel's problems in lumping together agricultural

workers and landowners. Perhaps these critiques do not fully appreciate what drove Hegel to this expedient. In addition to his general worries about a society where all is instrumental reflection, he has an additional constraint in that the "content" immediately present in the feelings and identifications of people with their nation or land has to be in the appropriate sense the "same" as that justified in the logical sequence.

12. The modern state that most closely resembles what Hegel described is probably contemporary Japan, if the Hegelian terms can be applied in that non-European context. There the government has some power over civil society, large enterprises act somewhat like his "corporations," the agricultural class has a traditional bent and special force in politics, and the citizens keep a consciousness of their special national way of life.

Chapter Seven: Heidegger and the Modern World

1. On the problems posed to Hegel's system by the enormity of modern evils, see Fackenheim (1967).

2. Heidegger cites Eddington's famous example of the two tables, one scientific and one ordinary (The Question About the Thing chap. 1, sec. 4). If Heidegger's notions of science had been less restrictive, he might have been able to appreciate Eddington's example in terms of the two different worlds that are gathered by the same table, but he does not speak of the scientific object as a "thing" (in his special sense of that word) that could gather a world. While he does allow contemporary multiple ways in which entities can stand revealed, he tends to make one primary, as with handiness (Zuhandenheit) in Being and Time, because it is less involved with turning things into stable objects before a subject. He does not discuss how the wine jug or the bridge could gather the world in different ways that are not derived from some one basic gathering. I will suggest later that it would have been helpful if Heidegger had been able to free his efforts to recognize the play of the presencing of things from an attempt to show that the play has a unified epochal structure.

3. Concept and proposition here refer to explicit language use. There is a looser sense of concept, as when we say of an animal that it "has the concept" of some distinction because we observe it making the distinction in its behavior, although no propositional expression of that concept is possible for that animal. Heidegger would probably not object to this usage but would view its sense as derived from the explicit human use of propositions and concepts.

4. Heidegger claims (Vier Seminare 116ff) that Husserl's sixth Logical Investigation exercised a crucial influence on his thinking because Husserl's doctrine of categorial intuition made it possible to free the notion of "being" from the contentless copula. In the neo-Kantian tradition in which Heidegger was educated, "being" or "existence" was interpreted as a purely formal positing through the copula, as Kant had taught. Husserl's doctrine

of categorial intuition gave Heidegger room to consider that a thing's mode of being might be a content given in experience (this does not say it is a "real predicate"). But Husserl presupposed that the only mode of being so given was the objectivity of objects for the ego. Heidegger claimed that his rereading of Plato and Aristotle opened his eyes to other understandings of the being of things, presumably by showing him how the Greeks did not operate within the modern understanding. At the same time they showed him that the basic meaning of being for the West has been articulated in terms of constant presence.

5. The military reference is probably not accidental, since Heidegger's thought on *das Gestell* was influenced by Ernst Jünger's notion of "total mobilization," as Heidegger discusses in "Zur Seinsfrage." See also the remarks on the "withdrawal configuration" of the West's essence in Werner Marx (1971, part 4, chap. 2) and the discussion of Heidegger and Jünger in Kockelmans (1984, 241, 267, 274).

6. Heidegger maintains that the current technological attack on nature is different from the letting-be by which earlier crafts encouraged nature to come to presence on its own. There is a difference between using clay to produce commodities and making the clay appear in its earthiness and malleability in a finished vessel. This claim is not completely persuasive, since Heidegger selects his examples from crafts such as pottery and sculpture while avoiding the more calculative ancient crafts such as shipbuilding and military technology. In this he follows the precedent of Aristotle, but the question of the way nature was encountered and used by the more calculative ancient craftsmen is begged all the same. Heidegger presupposes the point in contention: whether in the Greek world there was one dominant understanding of the being of things.

Chapter Eight: Putting Modernity in Its Place

1. "For a word [in this case, *das Gestell*] to be heard as a word of Being and for that word to transgress metaphysics are the same, for thereby it is no longer held back in the oblivion which marks the limits of metaphysics. And yet the word, heard or read, does not pass from oblivion into unconcealment in the sense of being brought to presence" (Bernasconi 1983, 16).

2. "*Ereignis* is the term for the movement of crystallization by which things enter into an epochal configuration" (Schürmann 1983, 33). "All the paths of Heidegger's thinking ultimately lead back to the unique simplicity of the occurrence whose appropriation is expressed in many ways: presenting, essencing, commissioning, clearing, empowering, wanting, claiming, behooving" (Kisiel, in the translator's introduction to Marx 1971, xxxi). For a helpful discussion of the connotations of *Ereignis* and the strands of thought behind Heidegger's use of the term, see Hofstadter's introduction to his volume of translations (Hofstadter 1971, xix–xxii). See also the discussion of naming *Ereignis* in Haar (1983, 50), Kisiel's note (Marx 1971,

226), and Kockelmans' discussion of the related words *Austrag, Ankunft,* and *Überkommnis* (1984, 85, 90).

3. Eugen Fink suggests that we have a connatural "dark understanding" of "uncleared being" through our bodily participation in the being of things and our encounter with death. (See Heraclitus Seminar; Fink 1977.)

4. The quote from Heidegger is from *Satz vom Grund* (188), and its tone is worth noting in connection with his transcendental stance.

5. On Heidegger's changes of terminology and the connection between *Sein* and *das Ereignis,* see *Vier Seminare* (103ff), *Time and Being* (5ff/5ff, 40ff/37ff), and Vitiello (1979, 200ff).

6. There are parallels here to the thought of Nelson Goodman and others in the analytic tradition. As I mentioned earlier, there are also difficulties concerning just how Heidegger deals with varying manifestations of the same entity.

7. See the questions raised by Richardson about the individuation of epochs and the relation of the propriative event to individuals (1963, 638ff) and the questions Werner Marx raises about the selectivity involved in Heidegger's history of being (1971, 169).

8. Such thinking can be found in Wittgenstein and in Strawson's attempt to give a descriptive metaphysics. Perhaps Davidson and Putnam might be included as thinkers who give formal conditions for language but no foundational entities. With the probable exception of Wittgenstein, however, the analytic thinkers would be in Heidegger's terms "metaphysical," since they want the conditions of possibility to be some form or principle or rules that can be made clearly present.

9. In his study of Heidegger, Manfred Brelage tries to situate him in relation to the neo-Kantian search for grounds in the structure of thought as such. The attempt is not wholly successful, because Brelage tries to make of him more of a foundationalist than he is and reads him too much in terms of structures of subjectivity. Nonetheless, Brelage assembles convincing evidence of Heidegger's close relation to the neo-Kantian tradition. See Brelage (1965, 188–244, esp. 199–200) and Kockelmans (1984, 76).

10. See Caputo (1978), Schürmann (1983), and the references there.

Chapter Nine: Life in the Modern World

1. In this connection one might begin to make sense of the cryptic remarks about the Japanese word *kotoba* ("word, language" like *logos,* but with connotations of emergence rather of than gathering together) in the "Dialogue on Language." Heidegger imagines the East Asian mode of unconcealment as a way that does not involve one ruling meaning of being. So the gathering together is in virtue only of things emerging from unconcealment and not in terms of a metaphysical totality. Later I will suggest, using the term *multiplicity,* that something rather like this may actually be a better description of where we are even now, and where we have always been.

2. Useful overviews of Heidegger's texts on the fourfold can be found in Kockelmans (1984, chap. 5) and Richardson (1963, chap. 15 and 17).

3. Werner Marx describes the fourfold as "Heidegger's positive answers to the question of what will take the place of substance and subject after these traditional modes are destroyed" (1971, 197). He questions whether this is adequate, remarking that "it is difficult to see how the wholeness of the four world neighborhoods 'enables' a specific jug in its specific content of meaning"; and he raises the question of how these special categories of "world" and "thing" could be adequate to the plurality of things amid which we live (200–201). He concludes that the sense of being found in the fourfold is meant to be valid only for a special "creative" realm, or else Heidegger's thought becomes "downright 'utopian' " (202, cf. 240f).

I have suggested that we read the fourfold as describing the event of the worlding of any world rather than itself offering any specific meaning of being. This makes it relevant today, but it also can describe a future era when there is no one ruling meaning of being. My suggestion relieves the fourfold from having to account for the meaning of this specific jug.

On the marginal yet liberating effect of the fourfold experienced as the worlding of our technological world, see Haar (1983, 43–64). Haar walks a fine line between the romantic overinterpretation and the pessimistic underinterpretation of Heidegger's thought. He leaves us with the enigmatic relation between the technological world and our experience of its conditions, especially of the unexhausted essence of the earth. His description points up the problem of the relation of the transcendental and the ordinary in Heidegger, and it echoes Heidegger's own vacillations about what we could expect.

4. The literature on Heidegger's Nazi connections is extensive and impassioned. See especially Pöggeler (1972), and Harries (1976). See also the accounts in Zimmerman (1981) and Kockelmans (1984) and the new material made accessible in Möhling (1981). A pointed discussion and useful bibliography can be found in Gillespie (1984, 198, n. 38).

5. Cf. Zimmerman (1981), where these issues are discussed and an extensive bibliography is compiled, and my review of Zimmerman's book (Kolb 1985).

6. While the general direction of Schürmann's analysis seems faithful to Heidegger, his subtle arguments would need further discussion. In some ways Schürmann, like Lyotard, approaches political questions too much with categories derived from artistic action. And, faithful to Heidegger, there is little "political" discussion, in the common meaning of the word as concerning the problems of devising ways to live together in conditions of scarcity under varied conceptions of the good life. See Dauenhauer (1978) for a critique of Schürmann along these lines. Schürmann is proposing to overcome the kind of discourse Dauenhauer criticizes him for not providing, and whether or not it can be overcome is just the issue to be decided.

7. The phrase "life without principle" is the title of Thoreau's last essay, where it is used to characterize the superficial life of the masses who consume information and entertainment and duty but never think. I have inverted the sense. Heidegger would agree with Thoreau's criticisms of modern anonymous living (*das Man*, once again), but he would disagree with Thoreau's judgment that thinking and true self-recollection lead to some "principle" of unity and harmony on which life can be based, the firm metaphysical rock at the bottom of the stream in the closing pages of *Walden*. Despite this difference, Thoreau's daily practice is not so dissimilar from what Heidegger recommends.

8. See Vattimo (1980, 136, 139, 141). He realizes that Heidegger's position as he describes it comes close to historicism, and he spends much energy distinguishing the two. He also explores the parallels and differences between the suspension he speaks of and the Marxist idea of a prerevolutionary situation. I am doubtful that his distinction between individual actions and those of classes will allow a theory of revolution to be developed out of Heidegger. The block to a Heideggerean notion of revolution is the primacy of the propriative event and Heidegger's sharp separation of ontic from ontological, which Vattimo generally affirms. Yet in a number of places Vattimo seems to suggest a closer coupling between the ontic and ontological (see 51–2, 58, 61, 63–6, 147–8, 167, 170–1, 177, 190). His intent seems correct, but I cannot reconcile it with his affirmation of the simple dominance of the propriative event. His point that action need not be conceived of only in subject-object terms seems to me a key to thought about political and social changes in our times.

Chapter Ten: Hegel versus Heidegger

1. See "The End of Philosophy and the Task of Thinking" (77–78/390). For an illuminating discussion of the issues involved, which shows that this change was not as radical as it might seem, see the early pages of Vitiello's essay "Aletheia: L'esperienza della verità in Heidegger" (Vitiello 1979, 151ff).

2. "Heidegger's purpose was not to restore ancient Greece but to explicate what it left implicit and to articulate what it left unsaid, i.e., *lethe* ["forgetfulness," the darkness from which unconcealment rises in its finitude] and man's transcendence" (Sheehan 1983, 311).

3. On this "happening," see Pöggeler (1970a, 375).

4. For discussions of the complex differences in the senses of negation and difference in the two thinkers, see Vitiello (1978, chap. 1 and 2) and Taminiaux (1977, chap. 6 and 7).

5. On Heidegger and the problem of time in Hegel, see Vitiello (1978, chap. 1).

6. For analyses of Hegel as a subjectivist, see Van der Meulen (1953), Smith (1968), and Bröcker (1965). For critical treatments of Heidegger's analysis in "Hegel's Concept of Experience" and the claim that Hegel is a

super-Cartesian, see Pöggeler (1982), Ricci-Garotti's "Leggendo Heidegger che legge Hegel" and "Heidegger contra Hegel?" (1968), Gadamer (1976, 11–12, 35–36, 77–79, 107), Dove (1970), Kolb (1982). Derrida (1982, 313f) expounds a subtle sense in which subjectivity remains in its being-tran-scended, though this chiefly results in the reaffirmation of Hegel's categories as ontotheological.

7. There is also a historical reason for Heidegger's reading of Hegel as a Cartesian. In his early years one of Hegel's preoccupations was to integrate persons into an ontology involving an absolute conceived in a way remi-niscent of Spinoza and neoplatonism. At that time this program provided Hegel and his friends with weapons to overcome what they took as weak-nesses in Kant's philosophy. When Hegel found a way to conceive the absolute in terms of life that returns to itself through otherness, his language often made it sound as if this was intended as an absolute ego, and in the early Jena years it may have been so. The *Phenomenology of Spirit* itself shows strains of Hegel's changing conceptions of the absolute, which is one reason I have preferred the later writings, which are clearer on the place they assign to subjectivity and ego.

8. Taminiaux's chapters 7 and 8 (1977) are devoted to careful discussion of Hegel and Heidegger. Cf. also Vitiello (1978, chap. 1 and 2) and the similar conclusion he draws (42). There are more "open" readings of Hegel in which his foundationalist goals are subdued. In my opinion such inter-pretations read more recent ideas into Hegel. I have tried to support this opinion by my reading of Hegel's logic on the importance of overarching unity and self-coincidence. If I am correct, when "open Hegelianism" moves away from his emphasis on closure, it follows the right direction for our thought, but does not give an accurate reading of Hegel himself. Our prob-lem is to keep something like Hegel's motion and mutual relation while forgoing his closure and self-transparency. He worked hard, however, to make these inseparable, and we cannot just accept part of his system. Its basic ideas have to be rethought.

9. On Heidegger and Kierkegaard in relation to Hegel, see Heidegger's remarks in *Hegels Phänomenologie des Geistes* (197). See also Vattimo (1980, 59–60) and Schmitt (1977, 88).

10. In the lectures that make up *Identity and Difference* Heidegger at-tempts to turn many of Hegel's key words against Hegel's own text. We can see what will later be called a deconstructive analysis at work. For a different attempt to show that Hegel's language leads beyond him, see Gadamer (1976, 101, 113).

11. On the question of finitude in Hegel's absolute knowledge, see Vi-tiello (1978, 95–101) and Pöggeler (1982, 44).

12. The phrase is from Vitiello (1978, 61).

13. A similar difficulty in relating the two histories is discussed by Gil-lespie (1984, 171ff).

14. Throughout this study I have avoided the term *ontological difference*, preferring other terms from the later Heidegger. We could rephrase the current questions in terms of that difference: to what degree does the ontological difference involve a distinction of form from content, and to what degree must it involve immediacy and unity in the meaning of being granted to us? These questions become interesting when one goes beyond the reflex response that Heidegger must be avoiding all such metaphysics and looks instead at Heidegger's actual practice. We can see that there is room for less unity within our world than Heidegger urges upon us.

15. J. L. Mehta discusses various suggestions in Heidegger's thought for dialogue between East and West (1971, 246ff; slightly expanded in 1976, 464ff). Mehta argues that Heidegger discusses structures of human existence overall, not structures of the local Western tradition, though the West has carried fallenness amid beings to an extreme degree. (Along with Heidegger he has no explanation for this Western extremity except the special dispensation granted to the West; ordinary historical explanations cannot help him in this matter.) Mehta reads in Heidegger the injunction for each tradition to go back to its own roots to recover the impetus and possibilities in its primal words while confronting and going beyond the forced Europeanization of the world. However, the problems I indicated reappear in Mehta's discussion. According to Heidegger, the shared relation of various traditions to the propriative event has no shared content. The space opened to each tradition is too different to allow straightforward mutual assistance. What is shared is the possibility of each making the move from its own granted space to the propriative event itself. Mehta sees this move prefigured in the non-Western traditions' various indigenous critiques of representative thought. Yet the move to the propriative event is deconstructive; it will not bring the spaces of the various traditions into alignment, nor will it allow the unification that Mehta claims is Heidegger's goal: the "planetary construction" of a "universal basic language of Truth from which the languages of the different philosophical and religious traditions can be derived." There is in Heidegger's move no basis for a new shared tradition, only the shared awareness of finitude. Mehta's remarks make even more puzzling why Heidegger says the West cannot be helped by the East. After all, in Mehta's version the West (in the person of Heidegger) is helping the East move to the propriative event within its own traditions. Why does this relation remain asymmetrical? Mehta's discussion provides no answer.

16. On the peculiar dominance of beginnings in Heidegger's historical thought, see Haar (1980).

Chapter Eleven: Further Explorations

1. In this respect we can generalize Pöggeler's remarks about Heidegger's failure to recognize the independence of the political sphere and the importance of new beginnings in history (Pöggeler 1982, 49).

2. The philosophy of Merleau-Ponty (1962, 1964, 1968) expresses similar ideas in a different idiom without the strong emphasis on horizons and unity. For him our context and finitude, described in the preconceptual experience of the lived body, and related notions in his later thought, are not necessarily constituted by a single unified epochal unconcealment of beings in the Heideggerean manner.

3. It is profitable to compare Heidegger's insistence on unitary horizons with Gadamer's remarks (1976, 112) about the richness of the preconceptual world of natural language. There seems to be in such a hermeneutics more possibility that our situation might be complexly related internally than Heidegger admits when he talks of epochs in the history of being. But, as Vattimo shows (1980, chap. 1), hermeneutic thought still works within a schema of unity and a goal of self-coincidence that reminds one of Hegel. Vattimo goes on to claim that we must hold on to the insight that whole worlds can change and so break the continuity of tradition presupposed by hermeneutic philosophers, who are too much under the sway of a model of continuity (although Vattimo tends to confuse continuity with cumu-lation in the Hegelian sense). But Vattimo himself is tied to unity in a different way. In order to have the total changes of world he speaks of and the hopes for radical renewal this offers, he must with Heidegger have worlds with enough overall unity that they can change completely in their meaning of being. This weakens the parallel which Vattimo is eager to show between Heidegger and the correct (that is, Vattimo's, not Heidegger's) interpretation of the philosophy of Nietzsche. I am suggesting that we think in terms of contemporary multiplicity such that there can be no changes of the world as a whole because there is no unified world as a whole (which is not to say that there could not be very large scale changes in our world). The multiplicity we inhabit has no single deep sense to be retrieved by her-meneutic methods, but need hermeneutic approaches be tied to the goal of one unified sense? See Ricoeur (1977, 1984, 1985) and the letter from Gadamer reproduced by Bernstein (1983, 261–65).

4. On the relation of the Hegelian concept and Heideggerean tempor-alization, see Vitiello (1978, chap. 1).

5. The phrase "infinite analysis" comes from Vattimo (1980, 14). What I have been suggesting does not emphasize discontinuity as does Vattimo's picture of epochs that can undergo revolutionary change as a whole, so there are even fewer limits to such analysis.

6. There are connections between this and the kind of conversation urged in Rorty (1979, 1982).

7. I have been stressing multiplicity and mutual constitution in order to counteract the excess unity in the analyses offered by Hegel and Heidegger. One might object that I have not paid sufficient attention to the involvement of darkness and finitude on every level and that stress on multiple mutual constitution rather than finite concealing-revealing is still too much in the

grip of the schema of self-coincidence. I do not mean the stress on multiplicity to preclude other kinds of finitude and disparateness. We must think without appealing to self-coincidence in any dimension. There are no simples and no wholes, whether these be epochs of history, formally defined selves, or basic signifiers. There is nothing to have self-coincident unified consciousness *of*. In his essay "Sending: On Representation," Derrida (1982) questions the unity of Heideggerean epochs and the notion that there is a deep phenomenon called modernity. The multiple "dissemination" he speaks about does not seem precluded by the analysis I am offering, though his language at times sounds quite transcendental. Some followers of deconstruction, however, in their eagerness to show how texts transgress their own limits, attribute too much unity to the texts, to begin with. (In a roundabout way, these considerations are relevant to the questions Werner Marx raises in his concluding chapter about truth and error in Heidegger's world [1971, 248–51].)

8. The direction I have been suggesting for our thought is an attempt to state necessary conditions, but when we search for necessary conditions, there is no privileged method, and we know our results may be overturned by later experience and new examples. One might argue, as do Davidson and Rorty, that the structure we discern is necessary in the stronger sense that we would only recognize as conscious or experiencing beings, beings who "had a world," those who shared with us that structure (Davidson 1984; Rorty 1982, 3–18). The history of claims about "necessary" conditions for language or thought that proved too narrowly conceived should be a caution to us. Also, the arguments advanced by Davidson and Rorty deal with the translation of belief statements and conditions for ascribing linguistic behavior, and they might or might not be extendable to the structures of time and understanding in question here. There have been attempts to imagine kinds of "experience" without these structures, as in the interesting attempts by medieval students of angels to describe a nontemporal consciousness or the descriptions of mystical experience in many traditions. Rather than deciding such issues a priori, it seems well to say that the conditions we find have the provisional status of any statement of necessary conditions: that is, they are limited by the field of examples we have surveyed or been able to imagine.

9. In articles and in a forthcoming book Mark Okrent argues that transcendental philosophers have often confused two distinct tasks. These tasks are a "transcendental" inquiry into the necessary formal conditions for the cognitive capacities which we possess and an "ontological" inquiry into what the necessary conditions for exercising our capacities imply about the nature of the objects intended by those capacities. He tries to show that while the first inquiry yields positive results, these have no ontological implications about objects and no substantive methodological contributions to the positive sciences. The second inquiry thus fails. Okrent severely qualifies Kant's

dictum that the conditions of the possibility of experience are also the conditions of possibility for the objects of experience. (See Okrent 1984a, 1984b.) Okrent's arguments seem to me persuasive. I have always mistrusted claims for transcendentally guaranteed ontology (see Kolb 1975, and the debate concerning transcendental arguments: Strawson 1959, 1966; Stroud 1968, Körner 1966, 1971; Rorty 1970, 1971). The multiplicity I have been discussing is not directly Okrent's multiple languages and ontologies. I have been concerned with whether our prereflective (if that word is still appropriate) inhabitation is within the indefinitely open field of possibilities characterized by theories of modernity or within a deeply unified field of possibilities along the lines suggested in different ways by Hegel and Heidegger. I have argued that neither of these alternatives is acceptable. Along the way I have suggested some formal descriptions of our inhabitation, but these descriptions are not constitutive principles, since there is no "it," no defined capacity, to be made present and interrogated about its constitution. Our appropriation into and with the world may well yield formal conditions that are transcendental in Okrent's sense concerning our more precisely defined cognitive or linguistic capacities. But that appropriation itself, the event of our being stretched out within the fields of possibility, is not a faculty or capacity we possess or exercise or a thing with its own form. While it is a condition for experience and knowledge and propositions, it is not a principle useful in deciding specific questions about language or cognitive systems.

10. See Pippin's discussion of essential and unessential in Kant (Pippin 1982, 86, 115). His characterization of Kant on this matter applies in part to Heidegger as well.

Chapter Twelve: The Modern World Revisited

1. Such a dispute with no shared rules Lyotard calls *"un différend."* To have universally shared rules in the modern manner would demand that one language game and practice be accepted as authoritative, but the narratives that could legitimate such authority are no longer viable because of their demands for a unified teleology and a unified agent of history. Lyotard deals (1983, 197) with the obvious objection that he is telling the meta-narrative of the death of meta-narratives. Insofar as he is telling a story, it has no teleology and so more resembles Heidegger's directionless play of the propriative event (see his remarks on *Ereignis*, 1983, 236). Lyotard has entered into an acerbic controversy with Habermas over the possibility of a universalistic critical discourse in today's society. See Lyotard (1984, especially the essay "What Is Postmodernity?") and Bernstein (1985, particularly the essay by Rorty, "Habermas and Lyotard on Postmodernity," 161–76). It is worth noting that Lyotard's criticisms of the two large modern meta-narratives, those of human liberation and of totalizing knowledge, seem somewhat restricted to the European context. I doubt whether the narrative

of human liberation has in the American context the same assumption of a unified agent of history. Often the American narrative of human liberation less resembles the French story of liberating the people into the state that speaks their unified will than it does what Lyotard approves of when he says that the people are not the sovereign but rather defend *le différend* from the sovereign power (1983, 209).

2. Notice the echo of Weber's instrumental rationality. Théofilakis was Lyotard's principal collaborator in designing the exhibit *"Les Immatériaux"* at the Centre Georges-Pompidou in Paris in the spring of 1985. The exhibit sought to evoke a latent postmodern sensibility through samples of modern technology, information exchange, and works of art, and the creation of contexts within which the viewer could experience the dissolution of the solid modern self and its manipulable material world into a web of relations and matrices of meaning over which we have no sovereign control.

3. Lyotard doubles Wittgenstein's discussion of language games in a suggestive way involving different modes of presentation and rules governing single sentences, as well as different modes of discourse governing the enchainment of sentences and the stakes (*enjeux*) constituted within these different discursive strategies. To this Lyotard adds a complex doctrine about the role of proper names within and among language games. There are some doubts to be resolved concerning his appropriation of Kripke's notion of a rigid designator. And questions must be asked concerning his making the chief locus of uncertainty and plurality the contingent connection at every instance of enchainment, which is described in ways resembling a Sartrean void yawning at every step. See Lyotard (1983, 82–83, 121; 1985, 228).

4. On Lyotard's avant-gardism, see Rorty's essay in Bernstein (1985, 161–76), and the discussion in Jameson's perceptive foreword to the translation of Lyotard's book on postmodernity (Lyotard 1984, vi–xxi). It is significant that Théofilakis celebrates the opening of an infinity of possibilities in the postmodern world (1985, 9). Such appeals to infinite possibility have been typically modern, and they suggest that the empty self still lurks in the background ready to move beyond any current barriers. Théofilakis and Lyotard are surely right about the problem of self-regulation in an age when the natural order has become malleable and the old stories enfeebled, yet even so we do not strike out into empty space; our present position does not leave us without resources.

5. Jencks's discussions of the primacy of symbolic meaning, dual coding for different audiences, and participatory design and his opposition to pure form could be spoken of in the terms I have used about moving away from distanced subjectivity and a unified world (see Jencks 1984, 8, 78, 88). His first example of dual coding is from a sixth century Greek temple (5); the postmodern retrieves the traditional in a new mode. Though he wants architecture to speak with the multiple meanings of our world, he does

have a nostalgia for a unified realm of meaning (112–17, 124, 127, 138–39). In terms of the Jencks quotation in the text, Lyotard sometimes seems closer to the "ultramodern" rather than to the "postmodern." See Jencks (1984, 6) for a discussion of modern, late-modern, ultramodern, and postmodern. These distinctions soon become muddy, since intermediate cases can be interpolated. Only if one holds modern dichotomies of form and content as ultimate can one confidently make such classifications.

6. See Jencks (1984, 93) on this possible function for irony in postmodern architecture (but cf. Eco 1985). In an insightful discussion about Lyotard's views, Philippe Lacoue-Labarthe describes Jencks as a "soft and doubtful" theorist of postmodernity (Lyotard 1985, 168), and Lyotard himself sees Jencks as sponsoring an easily commercialized eclecticism (Lyotard 1983, 76). Soft eclecticism is surely a danger we run, but if a more hard-edged theory demands that we deemphasize our rootedness as multiple thrown projects, then perhaps the softer is better.

7. See, for example, the deviations from Weber's pattern of analysis discussed in Shils (1981, chap. 8–10). Even though Shils' analysis may still owe too much to methodological individualism, his attempt to see modern society as itself a locus of new traditions is very helpful in discerning "what is living and what is dead in the tradition of the Enlightenment" (Shils 1981, 330). See also the discussion of secondary languages in Bellah et al. (1985, especially chap. 11 and 281–82).

8. This might allow more room for the Heideggerean fourfold than does Heidegger's official story of the West. There the fourfold hovers uneasily among being a world behind all worlds, a hope for the future, a formal analysis of our dwelling in any world, and an aspect of the West that is still one among multiple worlds we dwell within. But Heidegger's imposition of unitary epochs restricts the fourfold's role in our present world to that of a formal description of the worlding of any world. If we do not demand one final interpretative horizon for all modernity, then the fourfold can also be used to describe aspects of our present world, without the result being a romantic misinterpretation about a deeper level of unconcealment.

9. Questioning the ultimacy of modern distanced subjectivity also questions the often held assumption of the natural superiority of American institutions as somehow typically modern. The American way of living is thought to be more natural because it corresponds to the pure individuality that is the true reality of every person, whereas traditional ways encrust that individuality with substantive restrictions. See Kolb (1984) for a discussion of this belief in connection with intercultural dialogue.

Bibliography

Works of Hegel Cited in the Text

The titles used in the citations are given first, then the German and English editions.

Encyclopedia
(References by paragraph number in German and English.)
> *Enzyklopädie der philosophischen Wissenschaften im Grundrisse.* 1830. Edited by Friedhelm Nicolin and Otto Pöggeler. Hamburg: Meiner, 1959.

Translated as three separate books:
> *Hegel's Logic.* Translated by William Wallace and John Findlay. Oxford: Oxford University Press, 1975.
> *Hegel's Philosophy of Nature.* Translated by Arnold Miller. Oxford: Oxford University Press, 1970.
> *Hegel's Philosophy of Mind.* Translated by William Wallace and Arnold Miller. Oxford: Oxford University Press, 1971.

Lectures on the Philosophy of Art
> *Vorlesungen über die Ästhetik.* Edited by Eva Moldenhauer and Karl Markus Michel. 3 vols. Frankfurt am Main: Suhrkamp, 1970.
> *Hegel's Aesthetics.* Translated by Thomas Malcolm Knox. 2 vols. Oxford: Oxford Unversity Press, 1975.

Lectures on the Philosophy of History
> *Vorlesungen über die Philosophie der Geschichte.* Edited by Eva Moldenhauer and Karl Markus Michel. Frankfurt: Suhrkamp, 1971.
> *The Philosophy of History.* Translated by J. Sibree, 1899. New York: Dover, 1956.

Lectures on the Philosophy of Religion
  Vorlesungen über die Philosophie der Religion. Edited by Georg Lasson and
    Johannes Hoffmeister. 3 vols. Hamburg: Meiner, 1966.
  Lectures on the Philosophy of Religion. Translated by E. B. Speirs and
    J. B. Sanderson, 1895. 3 vols. London: Routledge and Kegan Paul,
    1962.
Phenomenology of Spirit
(References by page in German and by paragraph number in English.)
  Phänomenologie des Geistes. Edited by Georg Lasson and Johannes Hoff-
    meister. Hamburg: Meiner, 1952.
  Hegel's Phenomenology of Spirit. Translated by Arnold Miller. Oxford: Ox-
    ford University Press, 1977.
Philosophy of Right
(References by paragraph number in German and English.)
  Grundlinien der Philosophie des Rechts. Edited by Johannes Hoffmeister.
    Hamburg: Meiner, 1955. (See also the edition edited by Karl-Heinz
    Ilting, which includes material from Hegel's lectures. Stuttgart: Fro-
    mann, 1973 et sqq.)
  Hegel's Philosophy of Right. Translated by Thomas Malcolm Knox. Oxford:
    Oxford University Press, 1967.
Reason in History
(References by chapter and section in German and English.)
  Das Vernunft in der Geschichte. Edited by Georg Lasson and Johannes
    Hoffmeister. Hamburg: Meiner, 1955.
  Reason in History. Translated by Robert Hartmann. New York: Bobbs
    Merrill, 1953.
Science of Logic
(References by volume number and page in German and page in English.)
  Wissenschaft der Logik. Edited by Georg Lasson. 2 vols. Hamburg: Meiner,
    1963
  Hegel's Science of Logic. Translated by Arnold Miller. London: Allen and
    Unwin, 1969.

  Works of Heidegger Cited in the Text:

The titles used in the citations are given first, then the German and English
  editions. The references are to page number in German and English
  unless otherwise noted.
The Age of the World Picture
  "Die Zeit des Weltbildes." 1950. In *Holzwege*, 69–104. Frankfurt am Main:
    Klostermann, 1963.
  "The Age of the World Picture." Translated by William Lovitt. In *The
    Question Concerning Technology and Other Essays*, 115–54. New York:
    Harper and Row, 1977.

Basic Problems
  Die Grundprobleme der Phänomenologie. 1927. Frankfurt am Main: Klostermann, 1975.
  The Basic Problems of Phenomenology. Translated by Albert Hofstadter. Bloomington: Indiana University Press, 1982.
Being and Time
  Sein und Zeit. 1927. Tübingen, Germany: Niemeyer, 1963.
  Being and Time. Translated by John Macquarrie and Edward Robinson. Oxford: Blackwell, 1967.
Building Dwelling Thinking
  "Bauen Wohnen Denken." 1954. In *Vorträge und Aufsätze,* vol. 2, 19–36. Pfullingen, Germany: Neske, 1967.
  "Building Dwelling Thinking." Translated by Albert Hofstadter. In *Basic Writings,* 323–39. New York: Harper and Row, 1977.
Davos
(References by page number in the French edition.)
  Débat sur le Kantisme, Davos 1929. Paris: Beauchesne, 1932. This is a record of a discussion between Cassirer and Heidegger held at Davos, Switzerland, in March 1929.
  "Arbeitsgemeinschaft Cassirer-Heidegger." In *Ergänzungen zu einer Heidegger-Bibliographie,* edited by Guido Schneeberger, 17–27. A special volume issued by the *Zeitschrift für philosophischer Forschung,* Bern: 1960.
  "A Discussion between Ernst Cassirer and Martin Heidegger." In *The Existentialist Tradition,* edited by Nino Langiulli, 192–203. Atlantic Highlands, N. J.: Humanities Press, 1971.
Dialogue on Language
  "Aus einem Gespräch von der Sprache. Zwischen einem Japanen und einem Fragenden." 1959. In *Unterwegs zur Sprache,* 83–155. Pfullingen, Germany: Neske, 1971.
  "A Dialogue on Language." Translated by Peter Hertz. In *On the Way to Language,* 1–54. New York: Harper and Row, 1971.
The End of Philosophy
  "Das Ende der Philosophie und die Aufgabe des Denkens." 1966. In *Zur Sache des Denkens,* 61–81. Tübingen, Germany: Niemeyer, 1969.
  "The End of Philosophy and the Task of Thinking." Translated by Joan Stambaugh. In *Basic Writings,* 373–392. New York: Harper and Row, 1977.
Hegel and the Greeks
(References by page number in German.)
  "Hegel und die Griechen." 1958. In *Wegmarken,* 255–273. Frankfurt am Main: Klostermann, 1967.
Hegel's Concept of Experience
  "Hegel's Begriff der Erfahrung." 1950. In *Holzwege,* 103–92. Frankfurt am Main: Klostermann, 1963.

Hegel's Concept of Experience. Translated by J. Glenn Gray. New York: Harper and Row, 1972.

Hegels Phänomenologie des Geistes

(References by page number in German.)

    Hegels Phänomenologie des Geistes. 1930–31. Frankfurt am Main: Klostermann, 1980.

Heraclitus Seminar

    Heraclit. Frankfurt am Main: Klostermann, 1970. (Not the volume in the *Gesamtausgabe* series with this title.)

    Heraclitus Seminar 1966/67. Translated by Charles Seibert. University, Ala.: University of Alabama Press, 1979.

Identity and Difference

    Identität und Differenz. Pfullingen, Germany: Neske, 1957.

    Identity and Difference. Translated by Joan Stambaugh. New York: Harper and Row, 1969.

Kant and the Problem of Metaphysics

    Kant und das Problem der Metaphysik. 1929. Frankfurt am Main: Klostermann, 1973.

    Kant and the Problem of Metaphysics. Translated by James Churchill. Bloomington: Indiana University Press, 1962.

Memorial Address

    "Gelassenheit." 1959. In *Gelassenheit*, 11–28. Pfullingen, Germany: Neske, 1960.

    "Memorial Address." Translated by John Anderson and E. Hans Freund. In *Discourse on Thinking*, 43–57. New York: Harper and Row, 1966.

Nietzsche

(References by volume number and page in German and English.)

    Nietzsche. 2 vols. Pfullingen, Germany: Neske, 1961.

    Translated in four volumes.

    Nietzsche: Volume 1, The Will to Power as Art. Translated and edited by David Krell. San Francisco: Harper and Row, 1979.

    Nietzsche: Volume 2, The Eternal Return of the Same. Translated and edited by David Krell. San Francisco: Harper and Row, 1984.

    Nietzsche: Volume 3, The Will to Power as Knowledge and as Metaphysics. Translated by Joan Stambaugh, David Krell, and Frank Capuzzi, edited by David Krell. San Francisco: Harper and Row, 1986.

    Nietzsche: Volume 4, Nihilism. Translated by Frank Capuzzi, edited by David Krell. San Francisco: Harper and Row, 1982.

Nietzsche's Word

    "Nietzsches Wort 'Gott ist tot.'" 1950. In *Holzwege*, 193–247. Frankfurt am Main: Klostermann, 1963.

    "The Word of Nietzsche: 'God Is Dead.'" Translated by William Lovitt. In *The Question Concerning Technology and Other Essays*, 53–112. New York: Harper and Row, 1977.

Origin of the Work of Art
  Der Ursprung des Kunstwerks. Stuttgart: Reclam-Ausgabe, 1960.
  "The Origin of the Work of Art." Translated by Albert Hofstadter. In
    Poetry, Language, Thought, 15–88. New York: Harper and Row, 1971.
Out of the Experience of Thinking
  Aus der Erfahrung des Denkens. Pfullingen, Germany: Neske, 1954.
  "The Thinker as Poet." Translated by Albert Hofstadter. In *Poetry, Lan-
    guage, Thought*, 3–14. New York: Harper and Row, 1971.
Plato's Doctrine of Truth
  "Platons Lehre von der Wahrheit." 1942. In *Wegmarken*, 109–44. Frankfurt
    am Main: Klostermann, 1967.
  "Plato's Doctrine of Truth." Translated by John Barlow. In *Philosophy in
    the Twentieth Century*, vol. 2, 251–70. New York: Random House, 1962.
The Question About the Thing
  Die Frage nach dem Ding. Tübingen, Germany: Niemeyer, 1962.
  What Is a Thing? Translated W. Barton and Vera Deutsch. Chicago:
    Regnery, 1969.
The Question Concerning Technology
  "Die Frage nach der Technik." 1954. In *Vorträge und Aufsätze*, vol. 1,
    5–36. Pfullingen, Germany: Neske, 1967.
  "The Question Concerning Technology". Translated by William Lovitt.
    In *The Question Concerning Technology and Other Essays*, 3–35. New York:
    Harper and Row, 1977.
Satz vom Grund
(References by page number in German.)
  Der Satz vom Grund. Pfullingen, Germany: Neske, 1957.
Spiegel
  "Nur noch ein Gott kann uns retten." 1976. *Der Spiegel*, May 1976, 193–219.
  "Only a God Can Save Us." Translated by William Richardson. In *Hei-
    degger: The Man and His Thought*, 45–72. Chicago: Precedent, 1981.
The Thing
  "Das Ding." 1951. In *Vorträge und Aufsätze*, vol. 2, 37–59. Pfullingen,
    Germany: Neske, 1967.
  "The Thing." Translated by Albert Hofstadter. In *Poetry, Language, Thought*,
    165–86. New York: Harper and Row, 1971.
Time and Being
  "Zeit und Sein," 1968, and "Protokoll zu einem Seminar über den Vor-
    trag 'Zeit und Sein,'" 1969. In *Zur Sache des Denkens*, 1–25, 27–60.
    Tübingen, Germany: Niemeyer, 1969.
  On Time and Being. Translated by Joan Stambaugh. New York: Harper
    and Row, 1972.
The Turning
  "Die Kehre." In *Die Technik und die Kehre*, 37–47. Pfullingen, Germany:
    Neske, 1962.

"The Turning." Translated by William Lovitt. In *The Question Concerning Technology and Other Essays*, 36–49. New York: Harper and Row, 1977.
Vier Seminare
(References by page number in German.)
  Vier Seminare. 1968. Frankfurt am Main: Klostermann, 1977.
The Way to Language
  "Der Weg zur Sprache." 1959. In *Unterwegs zur Sprache*, 259–68. Pfullingen, Germany: Neske, 1965.
  "The Way to Language." Translated by Peter Hertz. In *On the Way to Language*, 111–38. New York: Harper and Row, 1971.
What Is Called Thinking
  Was Heisst Denken? Tübingen, Germany: Niemeyer, 1971.
  What Is Called Thinking? Translated by Fred Wieck and J. Glen Gray. New York: Harper and Row, 1968.
Why Do I Stay in the Provinces?
  "Warum bleiben wir in der Provinz?" 1934. In *Nachlese zu Heidegger*, edited by Guido Schneeberger, 216–18. Bern: Francke, 1962.
  "Why Do I Stay in the Provinces?" Translated by Thomas Sheehan. In *Heidegger: the Man and his Thought*, 27–30. Chicago: Precedent, 1981.
Zur Seinsfrage
  "Zur Seinsfrage." 1955. In *Wegmarken*, 213–54. Frankfurt am Main: Klostermann, 1967.

General Bibliography

This list includes works by authors other than Hegel and Heidegger that are cited in the text, as well other works relevant to the comparison of Hegel and Heidegger with regard to modernity.
Albricht, Reinhard. 1978. *Hegel und die Demokratie*. Bonn: Bouvier.
Alderman, Harold. 1969. "Heidegger's Critique of Science." *The Personalist* 50:549–58.
———. 1970. "Heidegger: Technology as Phenomenon." *The Personalist* 51:535–45.
Allemann, Beda. 1970. "Martin Heidegger und die Politik." In *Durchblicke: Martin Heidegger zum 80st Geburtstag*, edited by Vittorio Klostermann, 246–60. Frankfurt am Main: Klostermann.
Avineri, Shlomo. 1972. *Hegel's Theory of the Modern State*. Cambridge: Cambridge University Press.
———. 1985. "The Discovery of Hegel's Early Lectures on the Philosophy of Right." *Owl of Minerva* 16:199–208.
Bellah, Robert, et al. 1985. *Habits of the Heart: Individualism and Commitment in American Life*. Berkeley: University of California Press.
Bendix, Reinhard. 1967. "Tradition and Modernity Reconsidered." *Comparative Studies in Society and History* 9:292–346.

Benhabib, Seyla. 1984. "Obligation, Contract, and Exchange: On the Significance of Hegel's Abstract Right." In *The State and Civil Society: Studies in Hegel's Political Philosophy*, edited by Z. A. Pelczynski, 159–77. Cambridge: Cambridge University Press.

Berger, Peter. 1977. *Facing Up to Modernity*. New York: Basic Books.

Berger, Peter, Brigitte Berger, and Hansfried Kellner. 1974. *The Homeless Mind*. New York: Vintage Books.

Bernasconi, Robert. 1983. "The Transformation of Language at Another Beginning." *Research in Phenomenology* 13:1–23.

Bernstein, Richard. 1983. *Beyond Objectivity and Relativism*. Oxford: Blackwell.

———, ed. 1985. *Habermas and Modernity*. Oxford: Blackwell.

Berry, Christopher. 1982. *Hume, Hegel, and Human Nature*. The Hague: Nijhoff.

Bitsch, Brigitte. 1977. *Sollensbegriff und Moralitätsbegriff bei G. W. F. Hegel*. Bonn: Bouvier.

Blumenberg, Hans. 1983. *The Legitimacy of the Modern Age*. Translated by Robert Wallace. Cambridge: MIT Press.

Bodei, Remo. 1975a. *Sistema ed epoca in Hegel*. Bologna: Il Mulino.

———. 1975b. "System und Geschichte in Hegels Denken." In *Hegel-Studien*, Beiheft 17, 113–15.

———. 1975c. "Hegel e l'economia politica." In *Hegel e l'economia politica*, edited by Salvatore Veca. Milan: Mazzotta.

———, et al. 1977. "Differenza nel concetto hegeliano di società civile." In *Società Politica e Stato in Hegel, Marx e Gramsci*. Padua: CLEUP.

———. 1980. "Introduzione." In *Hegel: la politica e la storia*, edited by Giulio Pavanini. Bari: de Donato.

Brelage, Manfred. 1965. *Studien zur Transzendentalphilosophie*. Berlin: de Gruyter.

Bröcker, Walter. 1965. "Hegel zwischen Kant und Heidegger." In *Auseinandersetzungen mit Hegel*, 7–32. Frankfurt am Main: Klostermann.

Burbidge, John. 1982. *On Hegel's Logic*. Atlantic Highlands, N. J.: Humanities Press.

Butler, Clark, ed. and trans., and Christiane Seiler, trans. 1984. *Hegel: the Letters*. Bloomington: University of Indiana Press.

Caputo, John. 1978. *The Mystical Element in Heidegger's Thought*. Athens: Ohio University Press.

———. 1987. "The Emancipation of Signs: Derrida on Husserl." In *Deconstruction and Philosophy*, edited by John Sallis. Chicago: University of Chicago Press.

Cassirer, Ernst and Martin Heidegger. 1932. *Débat sur le Kantisme, Davos 1929*. Paris: Beauchesne.

Chang, Chung-ying. 1977. "Reflections." In *Erinnerungen an Martin Heidegger*, edited by Gunther Neske, 65–70. Pfullingen, Germany: Neske.

Crescini, Angelo. 1977. *Tramonto del Pensiero Occidentale*. Udine, Italy: la Nuova Base.

Crozier, Michel. 1982. *Strategies for Change.* Translated by William R. Beer. Cambridge: MIT Press.

Dauenhauer, Bernard. 1978. "Does Anarchy Make Political Sense? A Response to Schürmann." *Human Studies* 1:369–75.

Davidson, Donald. 1984. "On the Very Idea of a Conceptual Scheme." In *Inquiries into Truth and Interpretation,* 183–98. Oxford: Oxford University Press.

Derrida, Jacques. 1982. "Sending: On Representation." Translated by Peter and Mary Ann Caws. *Social Research,* 49:294–326. The French title is *Envoi.*

Descartes, René. 1972. *The Philosophical Works of Descartes.* Translated by E. B. Haldane and G. V. T. Ross. 2 vols. Cambridge: Cambridge University Press.

Di Giovanni, Georgio. 1982. "Burbidge and Hegel on the Logic." *Owl of Minerva* 14(September):1–6.

Dove, Kenley. 1970. "Hegel's Phenomenological Method." *Review of Metaphysics* 23:615–41.

———. 1973. "Hegel and the Secularization Hypothesis." In *The Legacy of Hegel,* edited by J. J. O'Malley, et al., 144–55. The Hague: Nijhoff.

Düsing, Klaus. 1976. *Das Problem der Subjektivität in Hegels Logik.* Bonn: Bouvier.

Eco, Umberto. 1985. "Innovation and Repetition: Between Modern and Postmodern Aesthetics." *Daedalus,* Fall, 161–84.

Emad, Parvis. 1983. "The Place of Hegel in Heidegger's *Being and Time.*" *Research in Phenomenology* 13:159–73.

Fackenheim, Emil. 1967. *The Religious Element in Hegel's Thought.* Boston: Beacon Press.

Findlay, John. 1958. *Hegel: A Reexamination.* Oxford: Oxford University Press.

Fink, Eugen. 1977. *Sein und Mensch.* Freiburg, Germany: Alber.

Floistad, Guttorn. 1983. *Contemporary Philosophy: A New Survey.* Vol. 4, *Philosophy of Mind.* The Hague: Nijhoff.

Foster, Michael. [1935] 1968. *The Political Philosophies of Plato and Hegel.* Oxford: Oxford University Press.

Foucault, Michel. 1979. *Discipline and Punish.* Translated by Alan Sheridan. New York: Random House.

Gadamer, Hans-Georg. 1976. *Hegel's Dialectic.* Translated by P. Christopher Smith. New Haven, Conn.: Yale University Press.

———, Max Müller, and Emil Staiger. 1971. *Hegel, Hölderlin, Heidegger.* Karlsruhe, Germany: Badenia.

Galgan, Michael. 1982. *The Logic of Modernity.* New York: New York University Press.

Gerth, H. H. and C. Wright Mills. 1975. *From Max Weber.* New York: Oxford University Press.

Geuss, Raymond. 1981. *The Idea of a Critical Theory.* New York: Cambridge University Press.

Gillespie, Michael Allen. 1984. *Hegel, Heidegger, and the Ground of History.* Chicago: University of Chicago Press.

Guzzoni, Ute, ed. 1980. *Nachdenken über Heidegger.* Hildesheim, Germany: Gerstenberg.

————, et al. 1976. *Der Idealismus und seine Gegenwart.* Hamburg: Meiner.

Haar, Michel. 1980. "Structures hégéliennes dans la pensée heideggérienne de l'histoire." *Revue de metaphysique et morale* 85:48–59.

————. 1983. "The End of Distress: the End of Technology." *Research in Phenomenology* 13:43–63.

Habermas, Jürgen. 1970. *Toward a Rational Society.* Translated by Jeremy Shapiro. Boston: Beacon Press.

————. 1975. *Legitimation Crisis.* Translated by Thomas McCarthy. Boston: Beacon Press.

————. 1984. *The Theory of Communicative Action.* Vol. 1, *Reason and the Rationalization of Society.* Translated by Thomas McCarthy. Boston: Beacon Press.

Harries, Karsten. 1964. "The Gnoseo-Ontological Circle and the End of Ontology." *Review of Metaphysics* 18:577–85.

————. 1976. "Heidegger as a Political Thinker." *Review of Metaphysics* 29:642–69.

Hartmann, Klaus. 1966. "On Taking the Transcendental Turn." *Review of Metaphysics* 20:223–49.

————. 1971. "What Is a Social Category?" *Idealistic Studies* 1:65–72.

————. 1972. "Hegel: A Non-Metaphysical View." In *Hegel*, edited by Alasdair MacIntyre, 101–24. Garden City, N. Y.: Anchor Books.

————. 1973a. "Zur Diskussion: Zur neuesten Dialektik-Kritik." *Archiv für Geschichte der Philosophie* 55:220–42.

————. 1973b. "Systemtheoretische Soziologie und kategoriale Sozialphilosophie." *Philosophische Perspectiven* 5:130–61.

————. 1975. "Gesellschaft und Staat." *Hegel-Studien*, Beiheft 17, 465–86. Bonn: Bouvier.

————, ed. 1976a. *Die ontologische Option.* Berlin: de Gruyter.

————. 1976b. "Ideen zu einem systematischen Verständnis der Hegelschen Rechtsphilosophie." *Perspectiven der Philosophie* 2:167–200. English translation in Pelczynski 1984a, 114–36.

Haym, Rudolph. [1857] 1962. *Hegel und seine Zeit.* Hildesheim, Germany: Olms.

Henrich, Dieter. 1952. *Die Einheit der Wissenschaftslehre Max Webers.* Tübingen, Germany: Mohr.

————. 1971. *Hegel im Kontext.* Frankfurt am Main: Suhrkamp.

————, ed. 1983. *Kant oder Hegel?* Stuttgart: Cotta.

————, et al. 1982. *Hegels Philosophie des Rechts: Die Rechtsformungen und ihre Logik.* Stuttgart: Klott-Cotta.

Hofstadter, Albert. 1971. *Poetry, Language, Thought.* New York: Harper and Row.

———. 1975. "Ownness and Identity: Rethinking Hegel." *Review of Meta-physics* 28:688–97.

———. "Enownment." In *Martin Heidegger and the Question of Literature*, edited by William Spanos, 17–37. Bloomington: Indiana University Press.

Hoy, David. 1979. "The Owl and the Poet: Heidegger's Critique of Hegel." In *Martin Heidegger and the Question of Literature*, edited by William Spanos, 53–70. Bloomington: Indiana University Press.

Ilting, Karl-Heinz. 1984. "Hegel's Concept of the State and Marx's Early Critique." In *The State and Civil Society: Studies in Hegel's Political Philosophy*, edited by Z. A. Pelczynski, 93–113. Cambridge: Cambridge University Press.

Inwood, Michael. 1983. *Hegel.* London: Routledge and Kegan Paul.

———, ed. 1985. *Hegel.* London: Oxford University Press.

Jencks, Charles. 1984. *The Language of Post-Modern Architecture*, 4th ed. New York: Rizzoli.

Klostermann, Vittorio, ed. 1970. *Durchblicke: Martin Heidegger zum 80st Geburtstag.* Frankfurt am Main: Klostermann.

Kockelmans, Joseph. 1984. *On the Truth of Being: Reflections on Heidegger's Later Philosophy.* Bloomington: Indiana University Press.

Kolb, David. 1975. "Ontological Priorities." *Metaphilosophy* 6:238–58.

———. 1981. "Hegel and Heidegger as Critics." *The Monist* 64:481–99.

———. 1982. Review of *Hegels Phänomenologie des Geistes*, by Martin Heidegger. *The Owl of Minerva* 13(March):3–6.

———. 1983. "Heidegger on the Limits of Science." *Journal of the British Society for Phenomenology* 14:50–64.

———. 1984. "American Individualism: Does it Exist?" *Nanzan Review of American Studies* 6(Spring):21–45.

———. 1985. Review of *The Eclipse of the Self*, by Michael Zimmerman. *Canadian Philosophical Reviews* 5:43–46.

Körner, Stephan. 1966. "Transcendental Tendencies in Recent Philosophy." *Journal of Philosophy* 63:551–65.

———. 1970. *Categorical Frameworks.* Oxford: Blackwell.

———. 1971. "The Impossibility of a Transcendental Deduction." *The Monist* 51:313–31.

Krell, David. 1975. *Early Greek Thinking.* New York: Harper and Row.

———. 1979. "Art and Truth in Raging Discord: Heidegger and Nietzsche on the Will to Power." In *Martin Heidegger and the Question of Literature*, edited by William Spanos, 39–52. Bloomington: Indiana University Press.

———. 1980. "From Fundamental Ontology to Frontalontologie: A Discussion of Heidegger's Marburg Lectures of 1925-1926, 1927, and 1928." *Research in Phenomenology* 10:208–34.

———. 1981a. "Memory as Malady and Therapy in Freud and Hegel." *Journal of Phenomenological Psychology* 12:33–49.

———. 1981b. "Results." *The Monist* 64:467–80.

————. 1982a. "Work Sessions with Martin Heidegger." *Philosophy Today*, 26:126–38.

————. 1982b. "Analysis." In *Nietzsche, Volume 4, Nihilism*, edited by David Krell, 253–394. New York: Harper and Row.

Kremer-Marietti, Angèle. 1957. *La Pensée de Hegel: Suivi d'une étude de Jean Wahl sur Hegel et Heidegger*. Paris: Bordou.

Krieger, Leonard. 1957. *The German Idea of Freedom*. Chicago: University of Chicago Press.

Kronman, Anthony. 1972. *Individual and Interaction in the Social Thought of Max Weber*. Ann Arbor, Mich.: University Microfilms.

Lacoue-Labarthe, Philippe. 1985. "Où en étions-nous?" In *La Faculté de juger*, edited by Jean-François Lyotard, 165–94. Paris: Editions de Minuit.

Lauer, Quentin. 1977. *Essays in Hegelian Dialectic*. New York: Fordham University Press.

Léonard, André. 1974. *Commentaire litterale de la logique de Hegel*. Paris: Vrin.

Lewis, Charles. 1981. "Recent Literature on Hegel's Logic." *Philosophische Rundschau* 28:115–30.

Lyotard, Jean-François. 1983. *Le Différend*. Paris: Editions de Minuit.

————. 1984. *The Postmodern Condition: a Report on Knowledge*. Translated by Geoff Bennington and Brian Massumi. Minneapolis: University of Minnesota Press. The French edition was published by Editions de Minuit in 1979.

————, ed. 1985. *La Faculté de juger*. Paris: Editions de Minuit. Lyotard's own essay in the volume is entitled "Judicieux dans le différend."

MacIntyre, Alasdair, ed. 1972. *Hegel: A Collection of Critical Essays*. Garden City, N. Y.: Anchor Books.

————. 1981. *After Virtue*. Notre Dame, Ind.: University of Notre Dame Press.

Marcuse, Herbert. 1955. *Reason and Revolution*. London: Oxford University Press.

Marquand, Odo. 1964–65. "Hegel und das Sollen." *Philosophisches Jahrbuch* 72:103–19.

Marx, Karl. 1970. *Critique of Hegel's Philosophy of Right*. Translated by Joseph O'Malley. Cambridge: Cambridge University Press.

Marx, Werner. 1971. *Heidegger and the Tradition*. Translated by Theodore Kisiel and Murray Greene. Evanston, Ill.: Northwestern University Press.

Mehta, Jaraval L. 1971. *The Philosophy of Martin Heidegger*. New York: Harper.

————. 1976. *Martin Heidegger: the Way and the Vision*. Honolulu: University Press of Hawaii. (An expanded version of Mehta, 1971.)

Merleau-Ponty, Maurice. 1962. *Phenomenology of Perception*. Translated by Colin Smith. London: Routledge and Kegan Paul.

————. 1964. *Signs*. Translated by Richard McCleary. Evanston, Ill.: Northwestern University Press.

————. 1968. *The Visible and the Invisible*. Translated by Alfonso Lingis. Evanston, Ill.: Northwestern University Press.

Möhling, Karl. 1981. "Heidegger and the Nazis." In *Heidegger: The Man and the Thinker*, edited by Thomas Sheehan, 31–44. Chicago: Precedent.

Murray, Michael, ed. 1978. *Heidegger and Modern Philosophy*. New Haven, Conn.: Yale University Press.

Neske, Gunther, ed. 1959. *Martin Heidegger zum siebzigsten Geburtstag*. Pfullingen, Germany: Neske.

————, ed. 1977. *Erinnerungen an Martin Heidegger*. Pfullingen, Germany: Neske.

Nozick, Robert. 1974. *Anarchy, State, and Utopia*. New York: Basic Books.

Okrent, Mark. 1984a. "Hermeneutics, Transcendental Philosophy, and Social Science." *Inquiry* 27:23–49.

————. 1984b. "Relativism, Context, and Truth." *The Monist* 67:341–58.

O'Malley, J. J., et al., eds. 1973. *The Legacy of Hegel*. The Hague: Nijhoff.

Ottmann, Henning. 1977. *Individuum und Gemeinschaft bei Hegel*. Berlin: de Gruyter.

Palmer, Richard. 1979. "The Postmodernity of Heidegger." In *Martin Heidegger and the Question of Literature*, edited by William Spanos, 71–92. Bloomington: Indiana University Press.

Parsons, Talcott. 1971. *The System of Modern Societies*. Englewood Cliffs, N. J.: Prentice-Hall.

Paz, Octavio. 1973. *Alternating Current*. Translated by Helen Lane. New York: Viking Press.

Pelczynski, Z. A., ed. 1984a. *The State and Civil Society: Studies in Hegel's Political Philosophy*. Cambridge: Cambridge University Press.

————. 1984b. "Political Community and Individual Freedom in Hegel's Philosophy of State." In *The State and Civil Society: Studies in Hegel's Political Philosophy*, edited by Z. A. Pelczynski, 55–76. Cambridge: Cambridge University Press.

Pinkard, Terry. 1985. "The Logic of Hegel's *Logic*." In *Hegel*, edited by Michael Inwood, 85–109. London: Oxford University Press.

Pippin, Robert. 1982. *Kant's Theory of Form*. New Haven, Conn.: Yale University Press.

Plant, Raymond. 1984. "Hegel on Identity and Legitimation." In *The State and Civil Society: Studies in Hegel's Political Philosophy*, edited by Z. A. Pelczynski, 227–43. Cambridge: Cambridge University Press.

Pöggeler, Otto. 1956. *Hegels Kritik der Romantik*. Bonn: Bouvier.

————, ed. 1970a. *Heidegger: Perspektiven zur Deutung seines Werks*. Cologne: Kiepenheuer und Witsch.

————. 1970b. "Hegel und die Anfänge der Nihilismus-Diskussion." *Man and World* 3:162–99.

————. 1972. *Philosophie und Politik bei Heidegger*. Freiburg, Germany: Alber.

————. 1976. "Philosophie im Schatten Holderlins." In *Der Idealismus und seine Gegenwart*, edited by Ute Guzzoni, et al., 361–77. Hamburg: Meiner.

―――. 1978a. "Being as Appropriation." In *Heidegger and Modern Philosophy*, edited by Michael Murray, 84–115. New Haven, Conn.: Yale University Press.

―――. 1978b. Review of *Vier Seminare*, by Martin Heidegger. *Hegel-Studien* 13:333ff.

―――. 1981. "Selbstbewusstsein und Identität." *Hegel-Studien* 16:189–217.

―――. 1982. "Neue Wege mit Heidegger?" *Philosophische Rundschau* 29:39–71.

Popper, Karl. 1963. *The Open Society and Its Enemies*. Princeton, N. J.: Princeton University Press.

Puntel, L. Bruno. 1973. *Darstellung, Methode, und Struktur*. Bonn: Bouvier.

Putnam, Hilary. 1978. *Meaning and the Moral Sciences*. London: Routledge and Kegan Paul.

―――. 1981. *Reason, Truth, and History*. Cambridge: Cambridge University Press.

Quinton, Anthony. 1975. "Spreading Hegel's Wings." *The New York Review of Books*, May 25, 34–37; June 12, 39–42.

Ricci-Garotti, Loris. 1968. *Heidegger contra Hegel*. Urbino, Italy: Argalia.

Richardson, William. 1963. *Heidegger, from Phenomenology to Thought*. The Hague: Nijhoff.

―――. 1981. "Heidegger's Way Through Phenomenology to the Thinking of Being." In *Heidegger: The Man and the Thinker*, edited by Thomas Sheehan, 79–94. Chicago: Precedent.

Ricoeur, Paul. 1977. *The Rule of Metaphor*. Toronto: University of Toronto Press.

―――. 1984. *Time and Narrative*, Vol. 1. Chicago: University of Chicago Press.

―――. 1985. *Time and Narrative*, Vol. 2. Chicago: University of Chicago Press.

Riedel, Manfred. 1965. *Theorie und Praxis im Denken Hegels*. Stuttgart: Kohlhammer.

―――. 1970. *Bürgerliche Gesellschaft und Staat*. Berlin: Luchterhand.

―――. 1973. *System und Geschichte: Studien zum historischen Standort von Hegels Philosophie*. Frankfurt am Main: Suhrkamp.

Ritter, Joachim. 1982. *Hegel and the French Revolution*. Translated by Richard Dien Winfield. Cambridge: MIT Press.

Rohs, Peter. 1969. *Form und Grund*. Bonn: Bouvier.

Rorty, Richard. 1970. "Strawson's Objectivity Argument." *Review of Metaphysics* 24:207–44.

―――. 1971. "Verificationism and Transcendental Arguments." *Nous* 5:3–14.

―――. 1979. *Philosophy and the Mirror of Nature*. Princeton, N.J.: Princeton University Press.

―――. 1982. *The Consequences of Pragmatism*. Minneapolis: University of Minnesota Press.

―――. 1985. "Habermas and Lyotard on Postmodernity." In *Habermas and Modernity*, edited by Richard Bernstein, 161–76. Oxford: Blackwell.

————, J. B. Schneewind, and Quentin Skinner, eds. 1984. *Philosophy in History*. Cambridge: Cambridge University Press.

Rosen, Michael. 1982. *Hegel's Dialectic and Its Critics*. Cambridge: Cambridge University Press.

Rotenstreich, Nathan. 1974. *From Substance to Subject*. The Hague: Nijhoff.

Roth, Gunther, and Wolfgang Schluchter. 1979. *Max Weber's Vision of History: Ethics and Methods*. Berkeley: University of California Press.

Sallis, John. 1983. "End(s)." *Research in Phenomenology* 13:85–96.

Schmitt, Gerhard. 1977. *The Concept of Being in Hegel and Heidegger*. Bonn: Bouvier.

Schmitz, Hermann. 1957. *Hegel als Denker der Individualität*. Meisenheim/ Glan, Germany: Hain.

Schneider, Friedhelm. 1976. "Hegels Propädeutik und Kants Sittenlehre." In *Die ontologische Option*, edited by Klaus Hartmann, 31–116. Berlin: de Gruyter.

Schulz, Walter. 1953–54. "Über den philosophiegeschichtlichen Ort Martin Heideggers." *Philosophische Rundschau* 1:65–93, 211–32. Reprinted in Klostermann 1970, 95–137.

————. 1959. "Hegel und das Problem der Aufhebung der Metaphysik." In *Martin Heidegger zum siebzigsten Geburtstag*, edited by Gunther Neske, 67–92. Pfullingen, Germany: Neske.

Schürmann, Reiner. 1978a. *Meister Eckhart: Mystic and Philosopher*. Bloomington: Indiana University Press.

————. 1978b. "Political Thinking in Heidegger." *Social Research* 45:191–221.

————. 1982. *Le principe d'anarchie: Heidegger et la question de l'agir*. Paris: Seuil.

————. 1983. "Neoplatonic Henology as an Overcoming of Metaphysics." *Research in Phenomenology* 13:25–42.

Sheed, Wilfrid. 1978. *The Good Word*. New York: Dutton.

Sheehan, Thomas, ed. 1981. *Heidegger: the Man and the Thinker*. Chicago: Precedent.

————. 1983. "Heidegger's Philosophy of Mind." In *Contemporary Philosophy: A New Survey*, edited by Guttorm Floistad, 287–318. The Hague: Nijhoff.

Shils, Edward. 1981. *Tradition*. Chicago: University of Chicago Press.

Silverman, Hugh. 1977. "Heidegger and Merleau-Ponty: Interpreting Hegel." *Research in Phenomenology* 7:209–24.

Smith, P. Christopher. 1968. "Heidegger, Hegel, and the Problem of *das Nichts*." *International Philosophical Quarterly* 8:379–405.

Soll, Ivan. 1969. *An Introduction to Hegel's Metaphysics*. Chicago: University of Chicago Press.

————. 1985. "Charles Taylor's Hegel." In *Hegel*, edited by Michael Inwood, 54–66. London: Oxford University Press.

Spanos, William, ed. 1979. *Martin Heidegger and the Question of Literature*. Bloomington: Indiana University Press.

Stace, Walter. [1924] 1955. *The Philosophy of Hegel*. New York: Dover.

Stillman, Peter. 1980. "Person, Property and Civil Society in the *Philosophy of Right*." In *Hegel's Social and Political Thought*, edited by Donald Verene, 103–17. Atlantic Highlands, N. J.: Humanities Press.

Strawson, Peter. 1959. *Individuals*. Garden City, N. Y.: Doubleday.

———. 1966. *The Bounds of Sense*. London: Methuen.

Stroud, Barry. 1968. "Transcendental Arguments." *Journal of Philosophy* 65:241–56.

———. 1969. "Conventionalism and Translation." In *Words and Objections*, edited by Donald Davidson and Jaako Hintikka, 82–96. Dordrecht, Netherlands: Reidel.

Taminiaux, Jacques. 1977. *Le Regard et l'excédent*. The Hague: Nijhoff.

———. 1981. "Finitude and the Absolute: Remarks on Hegel and Heidegger." In *Heidegger: The Man and the Thinker*, edited by Thomas Sheehan, 187–208. Chicago: Precedent.

———. 1985. *Dialectic and Difference: Finitude in Modern Thought*. Edited and translated by Robert Crease and James Decker. Atlantic Highlands, N. J.: Humanities Press, 1985. This contains the essay mentioned in the previous entry, and translations of parts of the prior entry.

Tanabe, Hajime. 1959. "Todesdialektik." In *Martin Heidegger zum siebzigsten Geburtstag*, edited by Gunther Neske, 93–133. Pfullingen, Germany: Neske.

Tauxe, Henri-Charles. 1973. *La Notion de finitude dans la philosophie de Martin Heidegger*. Paris: Editions de l'âge de l'homme.

Taylor, Charles. 1972. "The Opening Arguments of Hegel's Phenomenology." In *Hegel: A Collection of Critical Essays*, edited by Alasdair MacIntyre, 157–88. Garden City, N. Y.: Anchor Books.

———. 1975. *Hegel*. Cambridge: Cambridge University Press.

———. 1979. *Hegel and Modern Society*. Cambridge: Cambridge University Press.

Théofilakis, Élie. 1985. *Modernes, et après?: "Les Immatériaux."* Paris: Editions Autrement.

Tsujimura, Koichi. 1970. Untitled essay. In *Martin Heidegger im Gespräch*, edited by Richard Wisser, 27–30. Freiburg, Germany: Alber.

———. 1983. "Das Hegelsche 'für uns.' " In *Kant oder Hegel*, edited by Dieter Henrich, 374–87. Stuttgart: Cotta.

Van der Meulen, Jan. 1953. *Heidegger und Hegel, oder Widerstreit und Widerspruch*. Messenheim, Germany: West Kulturverlag.

Vattimo, Gianni. 1980. *Le avventure della differenza*. Milan: Garzanti.

Veca, Salvatore. 1975. *Hegel e l'economia politica*. Milan: Mazzotta.

Verene, Donald, ed. 1980. *Hegel's Social and Political Thought*. Atlantic Highlands, N. J.: Humanities Press.

Vitiello, Vincenzo. 1978. *Heidegger: Il nulla e la fondazione della storicità*. Urbino, Italy: Argalia.

————. 1979. *Dialettica ed ermeneutica: Hegel e Heidegger*. Naples: Giuda.

Wahl, Jean. 1957. "Heidegger et Hegel." In *La Pensée de Hegel*, edited by Angèle Kremer-Marietti, 185–95. Paris: Bordou.

Walton, A. S. 1984. "Economy, Utility and Community in Hegel's Theory of Civil Society." In *The State and Civil Society: Studies in Hegel's Political Philosophy*, edited by Z. A. Pelczynski, 244–61. Cambridge: Cambridge University Press.

Weber, Max. [1905] 1958. *The Protestant Ethic and the Spirit of Capitalism*. New York: Scribner.

Weil, Eric. 1950. *Hegel et l'État*. Paris: Vrin.

White, Alan. 1983. *Absolute Knowledge*. Athens: Ohio University Press.

Will, George F. 1982. *The Pursuit of Virtue and Other Tory Notions*. New York: Simon and Schuster.

Winfield, Richard Dien. 1977. *The Social Determination of Production*. Ann Arbor, Mich.: University Microfilms.

Wisser, Richard. 1970. *Martin Heidegger im Gespräch*. Freiburg, Germany: Alber. English translation: *Martin Heidegger in Conversation*. New Delhi: Arnold-Heinemann, 1977.

Zimmerman, Michael. 1981. *The Eclipse of the Self*. Athens: Ohio University Press.

Index

Absolute, 219; form, 69–76, 99, 111–12, 207; form of freedom, 37, 96–105; idea, 75, 81, 85–86; knowledge, 87–88, 242

Agricultural class, its special position in Hegel's state, 115–16, 268, 280 n. 11

Aletheia, Heidegger on the Greek meaning of, 204–5

American individualism, 3–5, 266, 292 n. 9

Amor fati, in Heidegger, 196

Anarchy, 198

Antifoundationalism, 94, 154, 175, 196

Antimodern groups, 5–6, 265–66

Aquinas, Thomas, 80

Architecture, postmodern, 1, 257–60, 291 n. 5, 292 n. 6

Aristotle: Hegel's use of, 37, 42, 61, 80, 101; Heidegger and metaphysics in, 126–28, 139, 165; Heidegger on the truth of his physics, 247–49

Art, modern, 18–19; as business, 121

Asia. *See* East and West; Japan

Authenticity, 165, 182, 196

Avineri, Shlomo, 33, 273 n. 1, 274 n. 5, 280 n. 8, 280 n. 11

Bacon, Francis, 126

Begriff, translation of, xvi

Being, understandings of, 127–33, 157–63, 222–36, 240–44, 252–55. *See also* History of being; Propriative event

Bellah, Robert, 3, 273 n. 6, 292 n. 7

Bendix, Reinhard, 272 n. 2

Berger, Peter, 7–9, 272 n. 3, 280 n. 6

Bergson, Henri, 244

Berkeley, George, 127

Berlin, different motives of Hegel and Heidegger concerning, 208

Bernasconi, Robert, xvii, 282 n. 1

Bernstein, Richard, 273 n. 9, 288 n. 3, 290 n. 1, 291 n. 4

Berry, Christopher, 279 n. 2

Blumenberg, Hans, 140, 272 nn. 2–3

Bodei, Remo, 243, 279 n. 5

Brelage, Manfred, 271 n. 1, 283 n. 9

Bröcker, Walter, 285 n. 6

Burbidge, John, 60, 276 n. 1 (chap. 4)

Bureaucracy, Weber's fears of, 12

Caputo, John, 249, 283 n. 10

Cassirer, Ernst, 139

Categories, 40–49; and thinkers, 48–49. *See also* Logic; Universal, the

Cézanne, Paul, 258

Chang, Chung-ying, 233

Civil society, 20–38, 68–69, 96–118, 180, 263–64; arguments against the ultimacy of, 31–40, 69–72, 74, 84, 96–109; defined and described, 22–28; economic and cultural